THE STRANGE SHORT FICTION
OF JOSEPH CONRAD

The Strange
Short Fiction of
Joseph Conrad

Writing, Culture, and Subjectivity

DAPHNA ERDINAST-VULCAN

OXFORD
UNIVERSITY PRESS

OXFORD
UNIVERSITY PRESS

Great Clarendon Street, Oxford OX2 6DP

Oxford University Press is a department of the University of Oxford.
It furthers the University's objective of excellence in research, scholarship,
and education by publishing worldwide in

Oxford New York

Athens Auckland Bangkok Bogotá Buenos Aires Calcutta
Cape Town Chennai Dar es Salaam Delhi Florence Hong Kong Istanbul
Karachi Kuala Lumpur Madrid Melbourne Mexico City Mumbai
Nairobi Paris São Paulo Singapore Taipei Tokyo Toronto Warsaw

and associated companies in Berlin Ibadan

Oxford in a registered trade mark of Oxford University Press
in the UK and certain other countries

Published in the United States
by Oxford University Press Inc., New York

© Daphna Erdinast-Vulcan 1999

The moral rights of the author have been asserted

Database right Oxford University Press (maker)

First published 1999

British Library Cataloguing in Publication Data

Data available

Library of Congress Cataloging in Publication Data

Erdinast-Vulcan, Daphna.
The strange short fiction of Joseph Conrad: writing, culture, and
subjectivity/Daphna Erdinast-Vulcan.
p. cm.
Includes index.
1. Conrad, Joseph, 1857–1924–Criticism and interpretation.
2. Modernism (Literature)–England. 3. Subjectivity in literature.
4. Ethics in literature. 5. Short story. I. Title.
PR6005.04Z675 1999
823'.912–dc21

ISBN 0–19–818499–9

1 3 5 7 9 10 8 6 4 2

Typeset by J&L Composition Ltd, Filey, North Yorkshire
Printed in Great Britain
on acid-free paper by
Biddles Ltd, Guildford and Kings Lynn

In memory of
ZE'EV ERDINAST
my beloved father

Acknowledgements

EARLIER VERSIONS AND parts of some of the following chapters were previously published in academic journals. 'A Smile of Fortune and the Romantic Paradox' appeared in *The Conradian*, 15 no. 1 (Spring 1990), pp. 1–11; 'Voyageur, Voyeur, Narrateur: Anti-Romance in Freya of the Seven Isles' appeared in *L'Epoque Conradienne*, vol. 17 (1991), pp. 23–33; 'Where Does the Joke Come In? Ethics and Aesthetics in Conrad's *The Informer*, appeared in *L'Epoque Conradienne*, vol. 19 (1993), pp. 37–46; 'The Planter of Malata: A Case of Creative Pathology' appeared in *Conradiana*, vol. 26, nos 2 and 3 (1994), pp. 187–200; 'On the Edge of the Subject: The Heterobiography of Joseph K. Conrad', appeared in *Genre*, vol. 28 (Fall 1995), pp. 301–20; 'Signifying Nothing: Conrad's Idiots and the Anxiety of Modernism' appeared in *Studies in Short Fiction*, vol. 33, no. 2 (1996), pp. 185–96. I am grateful to the editors for their permission to include the revised versions of these articles in this study.

As the chronology of this list indicates, this study has taken a long time to mature. I would like to thank the Yad-Ha'Nadiv Foundation and the President and Fellows of Wolfson College, Oxford, who enabled me to take some productive time out as a Visiting Fellow in Oxford.

I am indebted beyond formal acknowledgement to friends and fellow aficionados who have read this study or parts of it in the process of maturation, shared my moments of doubt and exhilaration, and kept the conversation going. I would like to mention in particular Jon Stallworthy of Wolfson College, Oxford, Jeremy Hawthorn of the University of Trondheim, Norway, Sarah Gilead of Haifa University, Israel, and two anonymous and very kind readers on behalf of Oxford University Press.

Most of all, I am deeply grateful to the various members of my family, who have been invariably generous, supportive, and tolerant of what must have seemed an unreasonable preoccupation at times. It is in them that my own homesickness comes to rest.

Contents

Note

All quotations from Conrad's work are from the Dent Uniform Edition, 1923–4, and are cited by page numbers in the text. Conrad's author's notes were written for the Doubleday Sun Dial Edition (New York: 1920). The Dent Edition was reprinted from the same plates.

Introduction

SHORTLY BEFORE THE completion of the first draft of this study, I received a strange and wonderful gift. It was a little note sent by Conrad to an anonymous recipient; 'Dear Sir, thanks for the papers which have reached me today. Yours faithfully, J. Conrad.' The casual, undated little message, scribbled on a page torn out of a notebook, and signed with a flourish at the other end of the century, was given to me by John Crompton, a fellow reader of Conrad's work. The intensity of my own response, both to the generous gesture and to the letter itself, took me by surprise. Having been academically brought up to believe in the death of the author, I had never suspected myself of what may well be described as an intellectualized form of idolatry. But the yellowing page with its frayed edges has become very precious to me. It has served, somehow, to ratify the motives which had prompted me to engage once again with Conrad's work. In *Joseph Conrad and the Modern Temper* (Oxford University Press, 1991), I dealt with Conrad's major novels, clustered into modes of response to the cultural crisis of the turn of the century. With one exception, I have kept the authorial subject well out of it. The present study, concerned with questions of writing, culture, and subjectivity in Conrad's short fiction, is in one obvious sense a sequel to the previous effort, an extension of the corpus under discussion. In another less obvious but more important sense, it is the return of the repressed subject, or—to keep to the initial trope—a return to where the corpus/body is buried.

The qualifying adjective 'strange' in the title of the volume requires some sort of gloss. Not all of Conrad's short fiction deserves this tag. Some of it was clearly written with an eye to the popular market, with surprisingly little anxiety (by a writer whose epistolary agonizing over his novels often bordered on pathology), and is often trivial, banal, or disappointingly formulaic. There are, however, a number of short stories which are indeed strange; which do not seem to lend themselves to readerly consumption; which generate the same sense of aesthetic discomfort induced by Conrad's undisputedly great novels. If the well-wrought text is marked by its fidelity to generic rules, by neatness of closure and solidity of structure, these strange stories are decidedly lopsided: there is no sense of an ending or significant closure; layers of narrative are left suspended when the frame narrator is discarded somewhere along the line; generic markers are often inconsistent or confused; and the authorial position is impossibly fluid or ambiguous.

But Conrad's best works are never well-wrought. It is, in fact, their very defiance of the aesthetics of closure, solidity of structure and generic containment—their 'strangeness', as it were—which makes them so powerful and compelling. This sense of aesthetic discomfort is the correlative of another, more significant kind of strangeness. Any imagined terrain may indeed be conceived as 'a strange or alien place by definition—strange in the sense of its cognates, extraneous (meaning 'outside') and extra (meaning 'supplemental')', as Michael Seidel writes, but what we have in Conrad's work goes rather deeper than the definitional exilic tropology of post-Romantic literature.[1] Being particularly vulnerable to this sense of homelessness, which was not only a cultural malaise but a very real historical and psychological state of being for him, Conrad went further than any of his contemporaries in his abdication of the putative sovereignty traditionally associated with the authorial position. It is this kind of strangeness, of not being at home in the world or in the work, which accounts for the unique interaction of culture and subjectivity in the best of his fiction.

The Romantic connection is unavoidable. Almost axiomatic by now, the relationship between Romanticism and Modernism is often predicated, albeit in various guises, on precisely this nexus of subjectivity and homelessness.[2] Whether concerned with the question of origin or the question of destination, Modernism has come to be identified with an ontology of ungroundedness, an

---

[1] Michael Seidel, *Exile and the Narrative Imagination* (New Haven and London: Yale University Press, 1986), p. vii.

[2] The most succinct formulation of this view is probably that of Perry Meisel in *The Myth of the Modern* (New Haven: Yale University Press, 1987), 4: 'Modernism is, in all its historical manifestations, the recurrent desire to find origins or ground despite the impossibility of ever doing so for sure'.

intensely self-reflexive Romantic sensibility, which probes the boundary lines between subject and object, consciousness and world, self and text.

A difficult, ambivalent attitude toward the self's autonomy is . . . not only characteristic of romantic literature but central to the romantic conception of what the self is and does. . . . For a consciousness of the romantic sort, self-making and text-making imply and implicate each other. They play off against each other and do much to determine each other's modes of being. . . . it follows, of course, that self and text-unmaking may well have the same kind of relationship.[3]

When the philosophical question turns into a psychological wound, when we cannot tell the dancer from the dance, writing becomes a refraction rather than a reflection of subjectivity. To use the Conradian trope, it can no longer be perceived as the shell to the kernel, but as the haze to the glow, demarcating the outline of an absent centre.

The capitalized Author is indeed dead and buried. There is no way back to the sanctuary of authorial sovereignty or the cosy assurance of narratives 'the whole meaning of which lies within the shell of a cracked nut'. But the ghostly figure of the departed Author has given way to another, far more demanding authorial being in the text.

No vital 'respect' is due to the Text . . . it can be read without the guarantee of its father, the restitution of the inter-text paradoxically abolishing any legacy. It is not that the Author may not 'come back' in the Text, in his text, but he then does so as a 'guest'. If he is a novelist, he is inscribed in the novel like one of his characters, figured in the carpet; no longer privileged, paternal, aletheological, his inscription is ludic. He becomes, as it were, a paper-author: his life is no longer the origin of his fictions but a fiction contributing to his work; there is a reversion of the work on to the life (and no longer the contrary). . . . The word 'bio-graphy' re-acquires a strong etymological sense, at the same time as the sincerity of the enunciation—veritable 'cross' borne by literary morality —becomes a false problem: The I which writes the text, it too, is never more than a paper-I.[4]

---

[3] Frederick Garber, *Self, Text, and Romantic Irony: The Example of Byron* (Princeton, NJ: Princeton University Press, 1988), p. ix.

[4] Roland Barthes, 'From Work to Text', in *Image-Music-Text*, ed. Stephen Heath (New York: Hill and Wang, 1971), 161.

The 'paper-I' will not be exorcized. Its presence in the text is paradoxically more insistent and more problematic than that of its capitalized predecessor. It operates as mode of subjectivity which spills over the edges of the narrative and refuses to recognize any textual boundary lines.

I believe that the news of the 'death of the Author', ostensibly diagnosed and articulated by Postmodernism, was—to invert Twain's *witz*—belated rather than premature. It was actually more of an authorial abdication, or a suicide, which took place about half a century earlier. What we have in Conrad's work is not the all-centring, coherent, sovereign, omnipotent, and authoritative figure of the traditional author (if such a figure ever really existed) which has served Barthes and Foucault as a straw figure to be theorized away, but another kind of authorial subjectivity at work. It is the much more elusive figure, described by Derrida as the 'subject of writing': a system of relations between strata; 'the Mystic pad, the psyche, society, the world'.[5] But while obviously indebted to 'Postmodernist' insights regarding the nature of textuality and authorial subjectivity (insights which, it is arguable, are actually hindsights if we take Conrad's work as a point of departure), my reading of Conrad's work does not endorse a view of the author as a 'vast absence', nor of writing as 'defacement'.[6] What I offer instead is an attempt to negotiate the rift between the textual and the historical subject, to diagnose the irreducible psycho-cultural specificity of the author's presence, though not his sovereign status, in the text.

Part I of the study, entitled 'On the Edge of the Subject', is inspired by the early writings of M. M. Bakhtin, and offers a conceptual matrix for my reading of Conrad's work through the dynamics of what I have called 'heterobiography' in *Under Western Eyes* and in 'The Secret Sharer'. This detour through the novel in a study devoted to the short fiction is designed to provide us with a broad conceptual matrix, not only for the study of authorial subjectivity but for Conrad's position at the cultural-historical junction of Modernism, linking the present investigation to the previous study. Heterobiography, as I would use the

---

[5] 'Freud and the Scene of Writing', in *Writing and Difference*, trans. Alan Bass (London: Routledge and Kegan Paul, 1981), 198.

[6] Paul de Man, 'Autobiography as Defacement,' *Modern Language Notes*, 94 (1979), 919–30.

term, is not the obverse of 'autobiography', but an alternative mode of interaction between the textual and the biographical subject, an isomorphic relationship —a dynamics of permeation rather than an empirical correspondence of 'fiction' and 'biography'—which energizes and boils over the borderlines of the written corpus. The kind of authorial presence which emerges in these two related works is a thoroughly permeable and precarious mode of being. It is a signature of subjectivity under erasure, as it were, the inscription of an authorial subject who is never securely present or adequate to itself. We will follow the isomorphic relationship spiralling across or running over the edges of both text and subject: between Conrad's *Under Western Eyes* and Dostoevsky's *Crime and Punishment*; between Razumov and Haldin; between the narrator of *Under Western Eyes* and Razumov; between Conrad the Modernist and Dostoevsky, his designated 'other' in the writing of the novel, who, according to Bakhtin, had made the first step towards that authorial abdication which concerns us here.

'The Secret Sharer' enacts the return of autobiographical desire. Against the breach of sovereign subjectivity in *Under Western Eyes,* Conrad deploys a strategy of aestheticization in the short story, setting up an imaginary relationship of identification, which enables the subject—both the textual and the biographical subject—to bolster up an artificial sense of selfhood against the threat of psychic dissolution. Against the transgression of boundary lines or the dynamics of heterobiography which operate as a structuring principle in the novel, the narrator of 'The Secret Sharer' tries—with a degree of *méconnaissance* which applies to the author himself—to aestheticize and frame himself; to reclaim the ground lost in the writing of the novel; to return to an autonomous, imaginary enclosure of subjectivity.

In Part II of the study, entitled 'The Strange Short Fiction', the focus shifts from the relationship between the biographical and the textual subject towards the relationship between culture, authorship, and subjectivity. This part of the study deals with specific problems of authorial subjectivity grouped into five sections, and offers close readings of several short stories in a rough chronological order, following Conrad's conversion of his Romantic legacy into the currency of Modernism. Chapter 1, entitled 'Writing and Fratricide', offers a reading of 'The Lagoon' and 'Karain', two apparent literary 'clones', against each other. The near-identity of settings, plot lines, and narrative strategies makes for a particularly interesting case of literary fratricide: 'Karain', I would suggest, can be read as a deconstruction of its own literary prototype. The attempted containment of the native Other within a frame of glossy exoticism or a sphere of illusion and superstition is thoroughly deconstructed in 'Karain', as the two perceptual spheres—that of the superstitious natives and that of the rational Westerners—prove to be more permeable than the narrator would like. Here again the osmotic relationship echoes in the workings of authorial subjectivity. For Conrad, too, the aesthetic containment of the other is a safe method of self-constitution, but the strategy of self-cloning through the production of 'second-hand Conradese' and the quasi-ethnographic narrative stance gives way to a different, relativized inscription of subjectivity in the text. It is a willed deposition of the authorial subject as well, a departure from the secure enclave of exoticism and imperial adventure stories, and the beginning of the road which will eventually take Conrad into the heart of darkness.

Chapter 2, entitled 'The Pathos of Authenticity', deals with the problem of origins and destinations in two of Conrad's early stories, 'The Idiots' and 'Falk'. In my discussion of 'The Idiots' I focus on the conception of the narrativized self, and on the Modernist failure of closure, which applies both to the retrospective coherence of narratives and to the apparently incurable human need for some structuring master-narrative of subjectivity. The story, I would argue, is both a symptom and a diagnosis of the simultaneous collapse of both senses of the ending, which is closely related to the failure of both biographical and authorial paternity. What makes this short piece interesting is the isomorphic relationship between the narrative and the narration: the failure of paternity within the text is ultimately a failure of authorship and the metaphysical and psychic anxiety of paternity is echoed in the author's own anguished sense of orphanhood. The discussion of 'Falk' centres on the concept of 'authenticity'—a nostalgia for grounding, for plenitude, for a solid kernel of subjectivity—carried over and translated from Rousseau's Romantic legacy into the discourse of Modernism. Looking at two alternative readings of this story—'vertical' and 'lateral', as I have labelled them—I would suggest that the story evidences an intersection of incompatible sensibilities, symptomatic of Conrad's ambivalent and rather uncomfortable cultural position at the very edge of modernity.

In Chapter 3, entitled 'The Poetics of Cultural Despair', I examine Conrad's discursive strategy as a mode of anarchist practice enabled, once again, by the Romantic context. Against the familiar reading of Conrad's irony as a distancing strategy or as a corrosive tactic which does not allow for an authorial ethical stance, the chapter offers a reading of Conrad's ironic mode of writing in 'The Informer' and in related stories like 'An Anarchist' and 'An Outpost of Progress' as a cognitive structure of subject-ivity, related to questions of complicity and agency and motivated by a sense of moral outrage. It is the Romantic sense of an 'explanatory collapse', to use Morse Peckham's expression, which triggers the use of irony not as a rhetorical device, but as an intensely self-reflective mode of subjectivity which constantly undermines and transcends itself.

Chapter 4, entitled 'The Romantic Paradox', relates the troubled dynamics of subjectivity in Conrad's work to his ambiva-lent relationship with Romanticism as a mode of being and with the genre of romance as a mode of writing. The chapter focuses on two short stories: 'A Smile of Fortune' and 'Freya of the Seven Isles', two stories which seem to follow the generic conventions of romance only to subvert or parody them. In 'A Smile of Fortune' the narrator himself seems to be constantly, simultaneously pulled in two different directions, offering two alternative readings of his own story, as he is torn between the ethos of romance and the economy of exchange. 'Freya of the Seven Isles' is also narrated by a duplicitous voice and revolves on what Girard has described as 'mimetic' or 'triangular desire' which marks the shift from a Romantic to a Modernist sensibility. I believe that what is parti-cularly significant about these two stories is their underlying ethical stance, which ultimately involves an endorsement of the ostensibly debased or subverted genre.

Closely related to Conrad's treatment of romance and the generic schizophrenia in his work is the 'Woman Question', which is also related to the inscription of subjectivity and the dynamics of writing. In Chapter 5, 'Addressing the Woman', I deal with 'The Planter of Malata', written at about the point which critics mark as the onset of Conrad's 'decline', and with 'The Tale', written near the end of his writing career. The analysis offered in this chapter is psycho-textual rather than psychoanalytic: what is defined as a form of 'pathology' at work in the text is related to the dynamics of both subjectivity and writing. In both stories Masculinity is defined in relation to a Feminine Otherness; both seem to revolve on questions of reality and fiction, truth and lies, facts and illusion—turning the gender conflict into an epistemic struggle. Both these stories, I would argue, are ultimately about the encounter of authorial subjectivity with its own blind spot.

As we shall see, the crisis of metaphysics, the crisis of authority, and the crisis of subjectivity are inextricably related. Edward Said has noted 'how compulsively the whole complex of ideas associated with "the center" . . . keeps appearing in [Conrad's] work, especially if we remember that Conrad never lets us forget that written narrative transcribes a told narrative that draws attention to itself as a process of getting close and closer to the center.'[7] But the centre, we know, is only an ever receding home or destination. It does not hold. With the loss of the privilege granted to self-presence, the privilege of subjectivity which is 'the ether of metaphysics', as Derrida writes, we enter the Nietzschean realm: when the desire for metaphysical grounding is recognized as a mere form of nostalgia, the author is deprived of the prerogative of 'transgredience' in relation to the text, and subjectivity turns from a premise to a question in the text. It is at this junction that Modernism is born.

[7] Edward Said, 'Conrad: the Presentation of Narrative', in *The World, The Text, and the Critic* (London: Faber, 1984), 96.

PART I

On the Edge of the Subject

I

The Heterobiography of
Joseph K. Conrad

'No border is guaranteed, inside or out.'[1]

THE CONCEPT OF 'heterobiography', to be used here as an *ad hoc* rather than a legislative principle, revolves on the experience of liminality in more than one way. When a fictional text is scanned for autobiographical traces, the distinction between the onto-logical status of the historical subject who has authored the work and that of the fictional characters 'within' the work is usually honoured. The former is perceived as related to the latter through echoes and reflections: fictional renderings of historical events; textual representations of 'real' psychological states of mind, relationships, and dilemmas. The edges of the text, the borderlines separating the somatic from the semiotic corpus, the real historical from the fictional, are thus carefully preserved and accentuated.

The first swerve offered by the term 'heterobiography' is a Derridean conception of 'a text without edges', a probing of the jurisdiction of frames and borderlines, where 'the supposed end and beginning of a work, the unity of a corpus, the title, the margins, the signatures, the referential realm outside the frame' are no longer hermetically sealed off from each other.[2] We will follow an isomorphic relationship spiralling across or spilling over the edges of both text and subject: between Conrad's *Under Western Eyes* and Dostoevsky's *Crime and Punishment*[3]; between

---

[1] Jacques Derrida, 'Living On: Borderlines', in *Deconstruction and Criticism*, ed. Harold Bloom (London: Routledge and Kegan Paul, 1979), 78.

[2] Derrida, 'Living On: Borderlines', 83–4.

[3] *Under Western Eyes* (1911; London: Dent, 1923); Fyodor Mikhail Dostoevsky, *Crime and Punishment* (1866), trans. David Magarshack (Harmondsworth: Penguin, 1951).

Razumov and Haldin; between the narrator of *Under Western Eyes* and Razumov; between Conrad and Dostoevsky. It is this isomorphic relationship—a dynamics of permeation rather than an empirical correspondence of 'fiction' and 'biography'—which energizes the text and overruns its edges.

The refusal of conceptual borderlines is organically related to the substance of this discussion, as the kind of authorial 'presence' which boils over and across these boundaries is paradoxically marked by a reversal of what is usually associated with the traditional, humanistic sense of the term. *Under Western Eyes* is explicitly, insistently *non-autobiographical*: not only does it lack the parameters of the illocutionary act which would qualify for the term; it also reiterates, in various ways which I will presently note, its own adamant refusal of this label.[4] This recalcitrance notwithstanding, the text does seem to show all the internal symptoms of autobiographical writing: the will to autonomy, to unity, and to 'apartness', an attempt at integrating a past life and a present self, an 'anguished justification of a life'—the full syndrome of autobiography which seems to affect the author as it does the fictional subjects.[5]

'One of the most striking aspects of Conrad's writing is the intensity of his presence in it,' writes David R. Smith in his impressive scholarly study of the *Under Western Eyes*, which he describes as 'the most autobiographical' of Conrad's novels.[6] Smith, Carabine, and others attempt to disclose 'the figure behind the veil', the 'inner man', the authorial subject behind or beneath the layers of fiction.[7] The assumption underlying this project of excavation is that there is an authentic authorial presence—autonomous, centred, self-enclosed—behind the veil, an inner

[4] See Elizabeth Bruss, *Autobiographical Acts* (Baltimore, Md: Johns Hopkins University Press, 1976); and 'Eye for I: Making and Unmaking Autobiography in Film', in *Autobiography: Essays Theoretical and Critical*, ed. James Olney (Princeton, NJ: Princeton University Press, 1980), 296–320.

[5] John Sturrock, *The Language of Autobiography* (Cambridge: Cambridge University Press, 1993), 101–9.

[6] David R. Smith, 'The Hidden Narrative: The K in Conrad', in *Joseph Conrad's Under Western Eyes*, ed. David R. Smith (Hamden, Conn.: Archon, 1991), 39–40.

[7] See David R. Smith, 'The Hidden Narrative', 56; Keith Carabine, 'The Figure Behind the Veil: Conrad and Razumov in *Under Western Eyes*', in *Joseph Conrad's Under Western Eyes*, ed. David R. Smith (Hamden, Conn.: Archon, 1991), 12.

core of a priori selfhood, which is textually re-presented in the text, waiting to reveal itself to the astute reader.

Hence the second swerve offered by 'heterobiography', the suspicious quotation marks around subjectivity itself. While 'autobiography', as traditionally conceived, aspires to a territorial enclosure of the self, 'heterobiography' points to the inevitable a-topia of subjectivity, to the permeability of its borderlines. Rather than claim a territory which is the property of the self, the text opens up what turns out to have been a precarious enclosure. Heterobiography thus calls for a different strategy, a peristaltic rather than an archaeological approach: rather than attempt to disclose the 'figure behind the veil', the hidden presence of the author in his work, I would point to a recurrent pattern, a pattern made up of alternative resistance and invasion, cutting across the borderlines between the textual and the historical subject.

The Derridean notes of this introduction are undoubtedly loud and clear. What is perhaps less obvious is the extent to which the concept of heterobiography emerges, just as forcefully, from the work of Mikhail Bakhtin, which also revolves, albeit in a more ambivalent manner than Derrida's, around the question of border-lines: the borderlines of a text, the borderlines of a culture, and the borderlines of a subject.[8] Bakhtin's work on discursive polyphony, all too often flattened in critical discussions and reduced to a bland tag for benign pluralism, is an early formulation of Derrida's 'differance'. Far from a comfortable accommodation of diversity, it stands for the eruption of otherness in the same, for the permeability of cultural, textual, and psychic borderlines:

A domain of culture should not be thought of as some kind of spatial whole, possessing not only boundaries but an inner territory. A cultural domain has no inner territory. It is located entirely upon boundaries.[9]

---

[8] For a more detailed treatment of Bakhtin's deconstructive strategies and his ambivalent position in relation to the Postmodernist context, see Daphna Erdinast-Vulcan, 'Borderlines and Contraband: Bakhtin and the Question of the Subject', *Poetics Today*, 18 no. 2 (1997), 251–69.

[9] M. M. Bakhtin, 'Content, Material and Form in Verbal Artistic Activity' (written and scheduled for publication in 1924; first published in the Soviet Union in 1975), in *Art and Answerability: Early Philosophical Essays by M. M. Bakhtin*, trans. and notes by Vadim Liapunov, ed. by Michael Holquist and Vadim Liapunov, supplement translated by Kenneth Brostrom (Austin: Texas University Press, 1990), 274.

A person has no internal sovereign territory, he is wholly and always on the boundary: looking inside himself, he looks *into the eyes of another* or *with the eyes of another*. . . . I receive my name from others and it exists for an other (self-nomination is imposture).[10]

Few critics have read Conrad's *Under Western Eyes* without commenting on its glaring resemblance to Dostoevsky's *Crime and Punishment*.[11] The ubiquity of structural, thematic, and verbal parallels in the two novels is anything but subtle: Conrad seems to have appropriated Dostoevsky's work without any attempt to disguise or tone down his indebtedness to the Russian writer. Indeed, it is precisely this uninhibited, insolent quality of the appropriation which makes it so interesting. The nature of this connection is all the more puzzling in view of the massive biographical evidence of Conrad's hostility to Dostoevsky and what he believed him to represent. In his letter to Garnett on 27 May 1912, Conrad writes: 'I don't know what Dostoevksky stands for or reveals, but I do know that he is too Russian for me. It sounds

---

[10] M. M. Bakhtin, 'Toward a Reworking of the Dostoevsky Book' (1961), in *Problems in Dostoevsky's Poetics* (1929; 2nd ed. 1963) trans. and ed. Caryl Emerson, introd. Wayne C. Booth (Minneapolis: University of Minnesota Press, 1984), Appendix II, 287–8, italics in source).

[11] The entire volume of critical commentary on this subject is impossible to cover. A partial list of notable contributions should begin as early as 1930 with Gustav Morf's *The Polish Heritage of Joseph Conrad* (London: Sampson Low, 1930).The discussion of Conrad's relationship with Dostoevsky was taken up and developed by Jocelyn Baines in *Joseph Conrad: A Critical Biography* (London: Weiderfeld and Nicolson, 1960), 361–72; Eloise Knapp Hay, *The Political Novels of Joseph Conrad* (Chicago: University of Chicago Press, 1963), 280–313; R. E. Matlaw, 'Dostoevskij and Conrad's Political Novels', *American Contributions to the Fifth International Congress of Slavists*, vol. I (The Hague, 1963), 213–33; A. Fleishman, *Conrad's Politics* (Baltimore, Md: Johns Hopkins University Press, 1967); Andrzej Busza, 'Rhetoric and Ideology in Conrad's *Under Western Eyes*', in *Joseph Conrad: A Commemoration*, ed. N. Sherry (London: Macmillan, 1976); Jeffery Berman, 'Introduction to Conrad and the Russians,' *Conradiana* 12, no. 1 (1980), 3–12; Bernard C. Meyer, 'Conrad and the Russians,' *Conradiana*, 12, no. 1 (1980), 13–21; M. Wheeler, 'Russia and Russians in the Works of Conrad,' *Conradiana*, 12, no. 1 (1980), 23–36; L. R. Lewitter, 'Conrad, Dostoevsky, and Russo-Polish Antagonism,' *Modern Language Review*, 79 (July 1984), 653–63; Aaron Fogel, 'The Anti-Conversational Novel', in *Coercion to Speak* (Cambridge, Mass.: Harvard University Press, 1985), 180–218; Carola Kaplan, 'Conrad's Narrative Occupation of/by Russia in *Under Western Eyes*', *Conradiana*, 27, no. 2 (1995), 97–114; Keith Carabine, *The Life and the Art: A Study of Conrad's 'Under Western Eyes'* (Amsterdam: Rodopi, 1996), 64–96.

to me like some fierce mouthings from pre-historic ages.'[12] Richard Curle comments on Conrad's 'real hatred for Dostoevsky', and claims it was due to 'an appreciation of [Dostoevsky's] power. . . . It was the depth of an evil influence. Dostoevsky represented to him the ultimate forces of confusion and insanity arrayed against all that he valued in civilization. He did not despise him as one despises a nonentity, *he hated him as one might hate Lucifer and the forces of darkness.*'[13] The problem is still further complicated by the evidence that Conrad was, in fact, an avid reader of Dostoevsky's work.[14]

How then are we to understand Conrad's blatant use of the work of a writer for whom he had expressed such intense personal hostility? Conrad's earlier critics have often resorted to the formula of parody. Conrad, they argued, has taken up Dostoevsky's themes in order to rewrite, demythologize, and displace them, to 'challenge Dostoevsky on his own ground' and to offer a Western alternative to what is perceived as 'Russian' politics, culture, and psychology.[15] More recent discussions, however, have recognized the complexity of this relationship: the interplay of Polish nationalism and Pan-Slavism, the mixture of strong psychological affinities and an equally intense personal antipathy; the problematic relationship between Conrad and his father, who was a distinctly Dostoevskian figure; and the author's memory of his parents' ideological legacy. Singular difficulties emerge and frustrate any attempt to reduce Conrad's attitude to Dostoevsky into any neat, clear-cut formulation. What becomes obvious on a reading of these diverse discussions is the infusion of a psychic element into a cultural-ideological struggle and the utter inseparability of the private from the public realm,.

I would suggest that what is at issue here may be a case of fratricide rather than patricide. It is not the Oedipal 'anxiety of influence', sometimes invoked to describe Conrad's relationship with Dostoevsky, but the equally archetypal sibling rivalry which led to the first documented murder in Western culture. Both

---

[12] *Letters from Joseph Conrad, 1895–1924*, ed. E. Garnett (London: Nonesuch Press, 1928), 248.

[13] *The Last Twelve Years of Joseph Conrad* (New York: Doubleday; 1928), 26, my emphasis.

[14] Paul Kirschner, *Conrad: The Psychologist as Artist* (Edinburgh: Oliver and Boyd, 1968) 252–64.   [15] Baines, *A Critical Biography*, 361.

Dostoevsky and Conrad are primarily concerned with questions of ethics and authority. Both are deeply aware of the crisis of modernity, the relativization, and the precarious nature of man-made ethical constructs. But unlike Dostoevsky, whose work, even at its most polyphonic, ultimately bows down before the need for the Word, Conrad is already far beyond the consolations of metaphysics, unable to accept the 'doctrine of expiation through suffering', which he believed to be 'a product of superior but savage minds':

It is a doctrine that, on the one hand leads straight to the Inquisition and, on the other, shows the possibilities of bargaining with the Almighty. . . . Moreover, there isn't any expiation. Each act in life is final and inevitably produces its consequences despite all the weeping and gnashing of teeth and the sorrow of weak souls who suffer the terror that seizes them when confronted with the results of their own actions. As for myself, I shall never need be consoled for any act of my life, and that is because I am strong enough to judge my conscience instead of being its slave as the orthodox believers would persuade us to be.[16]

The slightly hollow ring of the last sentence is not accidental. At the age of thirty-four Conrad must have known that few people can boast of being strong enough to need no consolation, and fewer still can be the judges of their own conscience and retain their humanity. His ostensible anti-Dostoevskian thrust has probably had its origins in the bitter resentment of an exile—in a metaphysical, not a political sense—against a fellow writer still securely fastened to the umbilical cord of transcendence, whose protagonists can turn to a divine authority for absolution and mercy. Having cut that umbilical cord, Conrad could still feel the raw spot of amputation. This is the pain we see reflected in the anguished quest of his protagonists—not least of Marlow, his surrogate—for a 'sovereign power enthroned in a fixed standard of conduct'.[17] Conrad's essential predicament, the conflict between his temperamental need for the metaphysical dimension, for grounding and borderlines, and his overwhelming sense of the loss of that dimension, is at the heart of his hostility to

---

[16] A letter to Marguerite Poradowska, written on 15 September, 1891. *The Collected Letters of Joseph Conrad*, vol. 1 (1861–1897), ed. Frederick R. Karl and Laurence Davies (Cambridge: Cambridge University Press, 1983), 95.

[17] *Lord Jim* (1900; London: Dent, 1923), 50.

Dostoevsky, the fierce quarrel which runs through *Under Western Eyes*.[18] Dostoevsky was for him, however much he may have denied it, an Abel figure, a brother whose gift has been acknowledged by the ultimate Father. It is the absence of the Father, or his silence, that Conrad and his fictional surrogates have to grapple with.

To begin on the presumed edge of the text, we turn to the epigraph. 'I would take liberty from any hand as a hungry man would snatch a piece of bread.' This slightly crooked quotation of Natalia Haldin, a character within the text, upsets the usual structuring function of an epigraph.[19] Whereas an epigraph marks the borderlines of the text by gesturing towards another text which serves as an anchor of meaning, this epigraph points inwards, blurring the very edges of the text. What does it mean for an 'author' to quote one of his 'characters'? Which is the 'original' utterance, the one we hear in the voice of Natalia Haldin 'inside' the text, or the 'authorial' utterance 'outside' the text? Who is quoting whom? Whose voice do we hear? Where is the borderline between the story, the narrative, the text, the book?

In 'Living On: Borderlines' Derrida points to a similar strategy of textual contraband, a 'structure which deprives the text of any beginning and of any decidable edge or border':

What appeared to be the beginning and the upper edge of a discourse will have been merely part of a narrative that forms a part of the discourse . . . The starting edge will have been the quotation (at first not recognizable as such) of a narrative fragment that in turn will merely be quoting its quotation. For all these quotations, quotations of quotations with no original performance, there is no speech act not already the iteration of another.[20]

Inexorably, inextricably, the question of textual borderlines—of quotation, translation, and the proper name—is entangled with the dynamics of subjectivity: the borderlines between the somatic

---

[18] It seems to me that G. Morf, the earliest commentator on this relationship, was essentially right in arguing that 'at heart, [Conrad] was a mystic, like Dostoevskij,' and that his manifest hostility to his predecessor derives from his need to deny an identification with 'a mind to which he was akin' (*The Polish Heritage*, 85, 93).

[19] The verbal phrase Natalia Haldin actually uses is 'snatch at' which suggests an abortive action (*UWE*, 135). This may well be yet another twist in the process we are concerned with.   [20] 'Living On: Borderlines', 93, 96.

and the semiotic, between the real and the fictional, between presence and re-presentation. Quotation—an 'intra-atomic penetration of discourses', to use the Bakhtinian idiom—is the neoplasm which disrupts the self-contained purity of both text and subject, producing the peristaltic ripple which traverses the borderline of *Under Western Eyes*.[21]

Having dealt elsewhere with the workings of what I then called the process of 'doubleness' in the novel, I would like to recapitulate briefly the motions of what I now see as a form of peristalsis towards heterobiography.[22] The protagonist and the narrator in the novel, I have argued, both go through a dissolution of autonomy in the course of the narrative. Both of them attempt at the outset to stake out a Western territory of rational, carefully bounded selfhood through the exclusion of the Russian, irrational other. In the case of Razumov, that other is Haldin. In the case of the narrator, the other is Razumov himself, now in the position of the 'Russian Other' for the old teacher of languages. But neither of them can retain that internal sovereign territory for long: in a thoroughly Dostoevskian manner, the voice of the excluded Other stealthily invades their own discourse, re-accents or restructures it, changing its original orientation and meaning, and turning it into a 'double-voiced' discourse, a word with a 'sideward glance' towards an alien consciousness.[23] Autonomy turns into heteronomy. The *I* is traversed by the voice of the other; the Western Eye/*I* becomes an ear, the only organ which, as Freud reminds us, cannot easily be shut off.

In Bakhtin's fragmented notes 'Toward a Reworking of the Dostoevsky Book' there is an oblique reference to 'non-self-sufficiency'. Self-consciousness, according to Bakhtin, is 'not that which takes place within, but that which takes place on the boundary between one's own and someone else's consciousness, on the threshold. And everything internal gravitates not toward itself but is turned to the outside and dialogized, every internal

---

[21] A heterobiographical comment: I had originally conceived the relationship in terms of an 'enzymatic' action. The metaphor of the 'neoplasm'—less benign than my own formulation, more radical, intrusive, and charged with a deep personal significance—was suggested by my friend, Sarah Gilead. I wish to thank her for this and for much else besides.

[22] For a more detailed account, see Daphna Erdinast-Vulcan, *Joseph Conrad and the Modern Temper* (Oxford: Oxford University Press, 1991), 110–27.

[23] Bakhtin, *Problems in Dostoevsky's Poetics*, 211.

experience ends up on the boundary, encounters another, and in this tension-filled encounter lies its entire essence.'[24] The conception of intersubjectivity as prior to and constitutive of subjectivity may shed some light on another brief note, a few pages later, concerning 'the threshold, the door, and the stairway. Their chronotopic significance.'[25] The staircase is the chronotope of subjectivity for Conrad as well. Whatever his conscious intention may have been, having set out to 'capture the very soul of things Russian',[26] he ended up with an extremely Dostoevskian novel, not only in the striking resemblance between Raskolnikov and Razumov, the similar plot-lines, and the verbal intertextual echoes. It is a Dostoevskian novel first and foremost because of the textual dynamics of subjectivity which seem to operate 'within' it, on its borderlines, and 'outside it'. We will follow the motion of the ripple from 'inside' out.

Razumov, the bastard son of Prince K—, is a man who has fathered himself, who has named himself the man of reason through the exclusion of Russian messianic mysticism. But his betrayal of Haldin, the epitome of this Russian otherness, draws him into a Dostoevskian vicious circle: The need to confess, the religious idiom in which he couches his ostensibly rational act of betrayal, using the voice of the other to betray him, set the scene for a gradual invasion of his property rights, of the territory of selfhood he has staked out for himself. His subsequent mental soliloquies are invariably oriented towards the discourse of the other, and his professed affinity with the secular, rational West gives way to the incurable need for a father, for an author who would name him and an authority which would give him a context for ethical action.

He embraced for a whole minute the delirious purpose of rushing to his lodging and flinging himself on his knees by the side of the bed with the dark figure stretched on it; to pour out a full confession in passionate words that would stir the whole being of that man to its innermost depths; that would end in embraces and tears; in that incredible fellowship of

[24] Ibid., 287.   [25] Ibid., 299.
[26] Letter to John Galsworthy, written on 6 Jan., 1908. *The Collected Letters of Joseph Conrad*, vol. 4 (1908–1911), ed. Frederick R. Karl and Laurence Davies (Cambridge: Cambridge University Press, 1990), 8.

souls—such as the world had never seen. It was sublime. (*Under Western Eyes*, 40)

The extremely Dostoevskian rhetoric might have been intended as a parody of the latter's style but, as we shall soon see, it has turned into a double-edged weapon in Conrad's hands. The line between parody, quotation, and graft is dangerously thin. What might have been an attempt to contain and reject Dostoevsky by means of parodistic stylization turns into a graft, an unmarked quotation. In his need for an author and for a sovereign authority, Razumov undergoes a 'conversion' (*Under Western Eyes*, 30) and joins the ranks of other defeated Russian intellectuals who have given up their individual autonomy:

In Russia, the land of spectral ideas and disembodied aspirations, many brave minds have turned away at last from the vain and endless conflict to the one great historical fact of the land. They turned to autocracy for the peace of their patriotic conscience as a weary unbeliever, touched by grace, turns to the faith of his fathers for the blessing of spiritual rest. Like other Russians before him, Razumov, in conflict with himself, felt the touch of grace upon his forehead. (*Under Western Eyes*, 34)

This passage is an obvious echo of Conrad's diagnosis of the 'Russian curse' a few years earlier:

Some of the best intellects of Russia, after struggling in vain against the spell, ended by throwing themselves at the feet of that hopeless despotism as a giddy man leaps into an abyss.[27]

No explicit reference is made here, and yet, as Najder convincingly argues, the passage is obviously a critical allusion to Dostoevsky, a jab at the naïve enthusiasm shown by the Garnetts and their milieu for all things Russian.[28] Razumov, then, is a Dostoevskian hero, not only because of the obvious resemblance of circumstances, background, and plot. Like the feverish characters in a Dostoevsky novel, he too has been infected with Russian transcendentalism and fallen into what Conrad perceived as the Dostoevskiean 'abyss'. The most obvious symptom of Razumov's conversion is, of course, the ubiquitous phantom of Haldin, which

---

[27] 'Autocracy and War' (1905), in *Notes on Life and Letters* (London: Dent, 1924), 99.

[28] Zdzilaw Najder, *Joseph Conrad: A Chronicle*, trans. Halina Carrol-Najder (Cambridge: Cambridge University Press, 1983), 309.

grows more and more substantial until it becomes almost a character in its own right. Razumov, the Westernized man of reason, learns to accept this ghostly apparition, and gradually assimilates the identity and the voice of the other.[29]

But that dissolution of borderlines is most evident in Razumov's rhetoric, which gradually gives way to the impassioned messianic discourse of the excluded other. The process begins, as we have seen, when Razumov resorts to the idiom of religiosity in his attempt to justify the act of betrayal. When Razumov later comes to Geneva he infiltrates the revolutionist circles. It is thus realistically conceivable that he should sound like Haldin in his professed contempt for the obtuse complacency of the West (*Under Western Eyes*, 189, 191), his impatience with theories, his talk of 'the sacrifice of many lives' (212), and of starving young men in Russia (221, 227). These lines are ostensibly no more than a ventriloquist's trick as Razumov manipulates the puppet revolutionary behind which the 'authentic' self is hiding. But the discourse of the other gradually takes over and the invisible quotation marks which enclose Razumov's utterances fade away, as the words take on the same messianic tone, the same passionate religiosity which they had in Haldin's voice. When Haldin first describes Ziemianitch, the incurable romantic drunkard as 'a bright Russian soul', Razumov responds with derision. He echoes the words of the other but re-accents them parodistically and contemptuously:

That was the people. A true Russian man. Razumov was glad he had beaten that brute—the 'bright soul' of the other. Here they were: the people and the enthusiast. (*Under Western Eyes*, 31)

Later on, however, when he makes his final confession, he refers to 'that individual, the much ill-used peasant, Ziemianitch . . . a man of the people—a bright Russian soul' (365). The mocking quotation marks are no longer there. The ventriloquist has accepted the voice of the puppet.

---

[29] The process begins with Razumov's unconscious enactment of Haldin's imprisonment and torture, continues through an increasing physical resemblance to the dead man who becomes a 'sharer of his mind' (*Under Western Eyes*, 230; see also 246), and culminates in a full acceptance of the other's role and a ritualistic enactment of his last hours.

A similar dissolution of boundary lines takes place in the frame narrative, between the narrator and his protagonist. What we seem to have here is a fully embodied narrative voice, the voice of a subject who is totally *there* for us: timid, pompous, pedantic, greyish. But the subject of the action is annihilated in the act of telling. The old teacher of languages, who repeatedly marks himself as a non-presence, refuses to become an embodied character. Though deeply in love with Natalia Haldin, the teacher persistently disqualifies himself for the role of a lover, insisting on his position as an outsider, a non-participant in the drama he narrates. This emotional withdrawal culminates in a figurative death, when the narrator realizes that he has virtually ceased to exist for the other characters (*Under Western Eyes*, 346–7).

The anonymous narrator's convoluted asides, his anxious disqualification of himself as a potential lover and as a character, are Dostoevskian in the extreme. Like Dostoevsky's underground man, or Golyadkin in *The Double*, he insists on his sovereignty and autonomy as the author of his own mode of life. But his definition of himself is invariably refracted through the eyes of others; he constantly anticipates—or imagines—their response to him (as an elderly foreigner who should stay out of their lives) and responds to it by an emotional withdrawal (*Under Western Eyes*, 179, 185). There seems to be an odd correlation between his performative insistence and his non-presence, an inverted Cartesian formula of 'I tell, therefore I am not'. His own sense of belatedness, of being a mere shadowy presence beside the despised other whose story he has undertaken to tell, is yet another symptom of the same categorical disruption. Into his anxious enclosure of selfhood, there creeps an annihilating sense of non-being.

Like Razumov, the old teacher of languages predicates his identity on his Western outlook and the exclusion of the Eastern other who is, in his case, featured by Razumov. What he claims to offer is a sane, rational, and balanced viewpoint, radically different from and hostile to that of the Russians, which he condemns for its 'propensity of lifting every problem from the plane of the understandable by means of some sort of mystic expression' (*Under Western Eyes*, 104). He repeatedly and naggingly reverts to the unbridgeable gap between the Western and the Russian frame of mind which, he claims, makes it almost impossible for him to understand the protagonists or to communicate their story to the Western reader (see *Under Western Eyes*, 25, 67, 163, 169, 202, 287, 293, 377).

But the ostensible 'otherness' of Razumov and of the other Russians gradually wears thin as the reader realizes that the old teacher of languages has, in fact, much in common with the apparently incomprehensible alien spirit.[30] With the arrival of Razumov the old teacher of languages is given an opportunity to enter his own story, as it were, to become a character rather than a mere observer. 'The Westerner in me was discomposed,' he admits, when he follows Razumov about (*Under Western Eyes*, 317). But the Westerner in him is not merely discomposed. It also decomposes, or at least begins to crumble, from the moment he meets Razumov, the unacknowledged rival in a duel he will never fight. Oddly enough, it is only at this point, halfway though his story, that he mentions his own childhood in Russia (*Under Western Eyes*, 187). This incidental reference opens up a crack in the teacher's assumed Western enclosure. His discourse is penetrated by that of the other, and the boundaries between the character zones seem to dissolve.

Even on the structural level, beyond the edges of the narrative, there seems to be an unresolved ambiguity in the relationship between the narrator and his protagonist. The pedantic citation of documents and sources, the careful demarcation of the story and the narrator's comments on it, are suddenly loosened in part III, where the narrator often 'walks into' his own story, and the frequent shifts from Razumov's viewpoint to his own are veiled and baffling (*Under Western Eyes*, 198, 200, 289, 291). In a novel so overtly obsessed with cultural boundaries and points of view, this cannot be a mere technical flaw. The dissolution of the structural borderlines between the narrator and his protagonist is yet another symptom of heteronomy.[31]

---

[30] The resemblance between Razumov and the narrator has been noted and discussed in numerous critical studies of the novel: both men are lonely and 'English' in their reticence, both were born in Russia but claim an affinity with the West, both are initially the exponents of rationality, of 'evolution not revolution', and both are, of course, in love with Natalia Haldin. The resemblance is never recognized or acknowledged by the narrator, but as the story unfolds, he gradually learns to perceive this voluntary self-enclosure as a form of exile, an absence in himself and in what he represents.

[31] One instance of this structural dissolution is the view from the bridge, where the Western eyes of the narrator and those of Razumov, the Eastern 'other', seem to register

Once again, the symptoms of heteronomy are primarily discursive. The narrator's initial sweeping condemnation of the Russian outlook with its passionate mysticism, gradually seems to waver as he loses the tone of conviction, the pedantic pomposity of his utterance, and the assumption of detached superiority. A distinct tinge of contempt for his own mode of existence, as one of the 'staid lovers calmed by the possession of a conquered liberty', seeps into his reflections (*Under Western Eyes*, 164; see also 318). It is highly symptomatic that the narrator should undertake the translation of Razumov's diary, that he should entertain what Derrida calls 'the [impossible] dream of translation without remnants, a metalanguage that would guarantee "free flow" between "entry language" and "exit language" . . . between semantic radicals properly bordered'.[32] Translation too probes the question of autonomy and boundary lines. The narrator's illusory linguistic containment of the other is hollowed out by his repeated disclaimers of any affinity or understanding between the discourse of East and West. The dissolution of borderlines is complete when the old teacher of languages finally drops the translator's pose and begins to quote Razumov, when his own language takes on the colouring of the other's. The movement is thus reversed: instead of appropriating the other's discourse, he actually translates his own language into that of the other. His own discourse is expropriated, along with his proper name.

One notable instance of this dissolution is the narrator's attitude to Geneva, the paragon of administered Western rationality. The attitude of the self-proclaimed Westerner, who should have been proud of his city, sounds unaccountably similar to that of Razumov himself, who thinks of Geneva as 'the very perfection of mediocrity attained at last after centuries of toil and culture' (*Under Western Eyes*, 203–4), 'the respectable and passionless abode of democratic liberty, the serious minded town of dreary hotels, tendering the same indifferent hospitality' (*Under Western Eyes*, 357). This same note of contempt is echoed in the narrator's own description of his city as 'comely without grace and

the same impressions of the swift, headlong current (*Under Western Eyes*, 197–8). Razumov, left alone, seems to echo the previous thoughts of the narrator, but one should remember that the narrator has read and translated Razumov's diary before the narrative begins, and it is therefore he who echoes his own protagonist.

[32] Derrida, 'Living On: Borderlines', 119–20

hospitable without sympathy' (*Under Western Eyes*, 141), 'in-different and hospitable in its cold, almost scornful toleration—a respectable town of refuge to which all these sorrows and hopes were nothing' (*Under Western Eyes*, 338); He is just as contemp-tuous towards the Swiss couple 'whose fate was made secure from the cradle to the grave by the perfected mechanism of democratic institutions in a republic that could almost be held in the palm of one's hand' (*Under Western Eyes*, 175). Whose voice are we listening to?

And so with the author. Conrad's author's note, written eight or nine years after the first publication of *Under Western Eyes*, sounds as though it were written by the old teacher of languages himself.

It is the result not of a special experience but of general knowledge, fortified by earnest meditation. My greatest anxiety was in being able to strike and sustain a note of scrupulous impartiality. My obligation of absolute fairness was imposed on me historically and hereditarily, by the peculiar experience of race and family, in addition to my primary conviction that truth alone is the justification of any fiction which makes the least claim to the quality of art or may hope to take its place in the culture of men and women of its time. I had never been called before to a greater effort of detachment; detachment from all passions, prejudices and even from personal memories. (*Under Western Eyes*, p. viii)

How should one read the ambivalent message of this note with its pedantic, pompous diction and its excessive rhetoric? Conrad disclaims all personal knowledge and involvement on the one hand but admits, in the very same sentence, that it is precisely that intimate personal knowledge that made the task so difficult for him.

The answer has already been partly suggested above. There is no doubt that Conrad was indeed deeply hostile to Russia. His national and personal history left him very little choice in this matter, and he was perfectly capable of being ferociously articulate about this 'hereditary enemy' of his family and country. He too had insisted—like his narrator and his protagonist—on his essential otherness, maintaining that the 'formative forces' which had acted upon him 'at the most impressionable age' were 'purely

Western';[33] He rejected the label of 'Slavonisn' which he defined as a 'Byzantino-theological conception of life, with an inclination to perverted mysticism' and claimed that he belonged to 'an outpost of Westernism with a Roman tradition';[34] he insisted that

The Poles, whom superficial or ill-informed theorists are trying to force into the social and psychological formula of Slavonism, are in truth not Slavonic at all. In temperament, in feeling, in mind, and even in unreason, they are Western, with an absolute comprehension of all western modes of thought, even of those which are remote from their historical experience. . . . Between Polonism and Slavonism there is not so much hatred as a complete and ineradicable incompatibility.[35]

Like the old teacher of languages, Conrad too insists on the unbridgeable gap between Russia and the West:

This pitiful fate of a country held by an evil spell, suffering from an awful visitation for which the responsibility cannot be traced either to her sins or to her follies has made Russia as a nation so difficult to understand. . . . Hence arises her impenetrability to whatever is true in Western thought. Western thought, when it crosses her frontier, falls under the spell of her autocracy and becomes a noxious parody of itself. Hence the contradictions, the riddles of her national life, which are looked upon with such curiosity by the rest of the world. The curse had entered her very soul; autocracy, and nothing else in the world, has moulded her institutions, and with the poison of slavery drugged the national temperament into the apathy of a hopeless fatalism. It seems to have gone into the blood, tainting every mental activity in its source by a half-mystical, insensate, fascinating assertion of purity and holiness.[36]

The author—like the narrator and the protagonist of his novel—protests too much. The very quality of Conrad's rhetoric in this essay, supposedly a serious attempt at a rational political analysis, is highly symptomatic: he denounces the Russian temperament, but sounds more 'Dostoevskian' than ever in his

---

[33] In the same letter, however, Conrad adds, as an afterthought, 'this is the truth as far as I know. Mais, après tout, vous pouvez avoir raison. Men have but very little self knowledge, and authors especially are victims of many illusions about themselves. I put before you my claim to Westernism for no other reason but because I feel myself profoundly in accord with it'. A letter to Charles Chasse, 31 Jan., 1924, in Gerard Jean-Aubry, *Joseph Conrad: Life and Letters* (Garden City, NY: 1927), 336–7.

[34] Ibid., 289.

[35] 'A Note on the Polish Question' (1916), in *Notes on Life and Letters* (London: Dent, 1924), 135–6.   [36] 'Autocracy and War', 98.

ferocious supercharged language, in his demonization of the land, and in his metaphoric excesses. If translation can be defined as 'the movement of a language over the border into another',[37] the border itself—that line of cultural demarcation which Conrad has so firmly drawn—is worn to invisibility by these crossings and recrossings.

But deep and unbridgeable as it may be, this cultural rift alone is not sufficient to account for the intensity of Conrad's psychic investment in the novel. I would argue that what is at stake here is no less than the question of subjectivity itself.

Consciousness offers itself to thought only as self-presence, as the perception of self in presence. And what holds for consciousness holds here for so-called subjective existence in general. Just as the category of the subject cannot be, and never has been, thought without the reference to presence . . ., so the subject as consciousness has never manifested itself except as self presence. The privilege granted to consciousness therefore signifies the privilege granted to the present. . . . *This privilege is the ether of metaphysics*, the element of our thought that is caught in the language of metaphysics.[38]

The cultural rivalry which revolves on the metaphysical question of boundary lines ripples out deep into the realm of subjectivity. When the axiom of pure presence is no longer given, and the metaphysical structure wobbles, it is but a short step to an all-out deconstruction of the staked-out autonomy of the self, of property rights, and of the proper name. 'The question,' writes Derrida, 'is whether there is a kernel intact somewhere or other.' It is a question which holds for metaphysics as it does for language or for the proper name. Derrida's answer is that 'The desire for the intact kernel is desire itself, which is to say that it is irreducible . . . There is no intact kernel and there never has been one. That's what one wants to forget and to forget that one has forgotten it.'[39] The question of the intact kernel of subjectivity, of the proper name which resists translation but is inescapably caught up in the workings of differance, is the question of heterobiography.

Conrad's preoccupation with names and signatures, both his

[37] 'Living On: Borderlines', 77.

[38] Jacques Derrida, 'Differance' (1968), in *Margins of Philosophy*, trans. Alan Bass (Chicago: University of Chicago Press, 1982), 16; italics added.

[39] 'Roundtable on Translation', in *The Ear of the Other*, ed. Christie V. McDonald, trans. Peggy Kamuf (New York: Schocken, 1985), 115.

own and his characters', and his Protean need to define and redefine himself are clearly at work here.[40] In an attempt to map the 'semiotics of identity' in the novel, David R. Smith has followed the occurrence of K's jotted along the margins of the manuscript of *Under Western Eyes*, some of which are super-imposed with an R, for traces of the 'hidden narrative', the narrative of Conrad's guilt:

Conrad orphans Razumov, gives him a phantom father who is identified only as 'Prince K—'. Insisting on the distinction between the Eastern K and the Western C, he first introduces us to his protagonist as, 'Cyril son of Isido—Kyrilo Sidorovitch—Razumov.' Razumov, like Dostoevsky's Razumichin, takes his name from a root which suggests the mind, reason, whereas Kyrilo is utterly Slav, the name of St. Cyril, author of the Cyrillic alphabet, so that Razumov is *homo duplex* even in name, as was Conrad whose *nom de plume* was divided between the prudent self of his family tree (his first name was taken from Josef Bobrowksi, his maternal grand-father) and the fiery nationalist self (Konrad was taken from Konrad Wallenrod, hero of the Polish epic). Moreover, not only is each split between conceptions of rational accommodation and patriotic passion, each is divided between East and West.[41]

How poignant the irony, when the author, who insists, as though his life depended on it, that the novel is not, absolutely not, an autobiographical production, frames the text with scrib-blings of his proper name—not that of his chosen, translated self, but the slavic K, the initial of the excluded other who speaks in and through him. It would seem, then, that Smith's insightful study may be taken as evidence for the 'semiotics of *non*-identity', of *hetero*- rather than *auto*-biography. The resemblance between Conrad and Razumov, the historical and the fictional subject, lies not only in the ambivalence of their political or cultural affilia-tions but in their attempt to name and author themselves. Both these cultural exiles try to translate their names. Both will eventually acknowledge the affinity of *traduttore* and *traditore*, the proximity of translation and betrayal.

Shortly after the completion of the novel Conrad had a mental breakdown, aptly described by Jeffery Berman as a 'Dostoevskean

---

[40] This obsession with names has been noted by Frederick R. Karl in *Joseph Conrad: The Three Lives* (London: Faber, 1979), 22.

[41] David R. Smith, 'The Hidden Narrative', 44.

crisis'. Raskolnikov's breakdown as rendered in Dostoevsky's voice, and that of Conrad, the living writer, in the voice of his wife, are strikingly similar. Conrad 'lay with his eyes closed and his arms folded, repeating snatches of orders in an Eastern language'; he was 'mixed up with the scenes' of the complete manuscript which he did not allow anyone to touch, and 'held conversations with the characters'.[42] Here, on the unfinished edge of the text, when the semiotic blends into the somatic, is where we have to stop. In acting out an unacknowledged affiliation with Dostoevsky's tormented character—a behavioral quotation of the excluded other—Conrad was true to the motto of his familial coat of arms, *usque ad finem*, as he took the Dostoevskian logic of polyphony all the way through. Having let the other slip through the boundary lines of his painfully constructed topos of the I/eye, having been defeated in his project of autonomy (self-nomination), he may have eventually become more Dostoevskian than Dostoevsky himself.

[42] Jessie Conrad, *Joseph Conrad and His Circle* (London: Jarrolds, 1935) quoted in Jeffery Berman, *Writing as Rescue* (New York: Astra Books, 1977), 146–7.

2

The Seductions of the Aesthetic

The statement, 'I'm a man' . . . at most can mean no more than, 'I'm like
he whom I recognize to be a man, and so recognize myself as being such.'
In the last resort, these various formulas are to be understood only in
reference to the truth of 'I is an other', an observation that is less
astonishing to the intuition of the poet than obvious to the gaze of the
psychoanalyst.[1]

To be embodied, to become more clearly defined, to become less, to
become more limited, more stupid.[2]

FOLLOWING THE 'HETEROBIOGRAPHICAL' orientation of the
previous chapter, I will now turn to 'The Secret Sharer' and study
the story through its relation to *Under Western Eyes*. I believe that
here too we can see the same isomorphic paradigm which overruns
the boundaries of the text: both the fictional and the historical
subjects, I would argue, are constituted within the same vectorial
parallelogram, in a no man's land between an aesthetic and an
ethical mode of being. Our point of departure is, once again, a
reconstructed Bakhtinian theory of subjectivity. Bakhtin did not
propose a theory of the subject or, for that matter, any other grand
theory. To attempt a distillation of a conceptual system out of his
eclectic surviving essays would involve both circumstantial and
immanent difficulties: problems of access, translation, and attribution are compounded by what appears to be a temperamental
aversion to the academic proprieties of system-building. But if all
the above may lead to the dismissal of the project as unfeasible on
historical or biographical grounds, it becomes all the more

[1] Jacques Lacan, 'Aggressivity in Psychoanalysis' (1948). In *Ecrits: A Selection*
(1966), trans. Alan Sheridan (London: Tavistock, 1977), 23.
[2] Bakhtin, 'Notes made in 1970–1', in *Speech Genres and Other Late Essays*, trans.
Vern W. McGee, ed. Caryl Emerson and Michael Holquist (Austin: University of Texas
Press, 1986), 147.

challenging when one realizes that the suspicion of systematicity is, in fact, fundamental and built into Bakhtin's philosophical outlook.[3] The project is further complicated by changes at the receiving end as well: the canonization of Bakhtin as a prophet of Postmodernity, based on his writings of the 1930s and 1940s, is giving way to a more complex conception of his work with the belated publication of his earlier writings. The Bakhtinian corpus, as we now have it, seems to be fraught with ambivalence: on the one hand, a surprisingly avant-garde conception of the human psyche as a network of discourses; on the other, an equally forceful religious cross-current, a deep, incurable nostalgia for grounding.

True to his suspicion of abstract, universal conceptual systems, Bakhtin's point of departure for the relational process which he calls 'architectonics' is the phenomenal, embodied subject. Subjectivity, for him, is an ongoing event, a 'meeting of two movements on the surface of a human being that consolidates or gives body to his axiological boundaries'.[4] These two 'movements', or modalities of consciousness, are extrapolated from the aesthetic relation of 'author' to 'hero': within the modality which Bakhtin calls *I-for-myself* (hero) the subject can never become a given object for itself, can never coincide with itself, must always reach out beyond itself as 'yet-to-be':

I can remember myself, I can to some extent perceive myself through my outer sense, and thus render myself in part an object of my desiring and feeling—that is, I can make myself an object for myself. But in this act of self-objectification I shall never coincide with myself—I-for-myself shall continue to be in the act of this self-objectification, and not in its product. . . . I am incapable of fitting all of myself into an object, for I exceed any object as the active subiectum of it.[5]

The impossibility of self-representation from within—whether spatially, temporally, or axiologically—requires the second constituent 'movement', the modality of *I-for-the-other*. The integral

---

[3] I am referring to a paper given by Prof. Vitali Makhlin at the 7th International Bakhtin conference in Moscow in June 1995, which significantly addressed Bakhtin's work in terms of 'a theory which surpasses theoreticism' and a 'system which surpasses systematicity'.

[4] 'Author and Hero in Aesthetic Activity', in *Art and Answerability: Early Philosophical Essays by M. M. Bakhtin*, trans. and notes by Vadim Liapunov, ed. Michael Holquist and Vadim Liapunov; supplement translated by Kenneth Brostrom (Austin: University of Texas Press,1990), 91.   [5] Ibid., 38.

subject, as Bakhtin refers to it, is authored through a reflective consciousness, through the framing gaze of a transgredient other/author positioned outside and beyond the subject. It is only the authored consciousness which is a closed, given totality. Only through the eyes of the others can the subject be given an objectified solidity of existence.[6]

Several significant aspects of Bakhtin's architectonics of the subject ought to be highlighted here: first, the identification of the *I-for-the-other* mode with aesthetics. 'The aesthetic', according to Bakhtin, is not an abstract conceptual category; it is a powerful psychic modality, as relevant to the study of subjectivity as it is to the study of texts:

It is only in a life perceived in the category of the *other* that my body can become aesthetically valid, and not in the context of my own life as lived for myself, that is, not in the context of my self-consciousness.[7]

Conversely, the position of *I-for-myself* is identified with an ethical modality, a non-coincidence in principle of 'is' and 'ought'. Against that 'whole, integral human being', aesthetically framed by the transgredient other, Bakhtin positions the 'ethical subiectum' who is 'nonunitary in principle'.[8]

The *subiectum* of lived life and the *subiectum* of aesthetic activity which gives form to that life are in principle incapable of coinciding with one another.[9]

The ethical *subiectum* is present to itself as a task, the task of actualizing himself as a value, and is in principle incapable of being given, of being present-on-hand, of being contemplated: it is I-for-myself.[10]

As I have suggested elsewhere, the relationship of these two modalities in Bakhtin's work is far from settled, and any attempt to homogenize the Bakhtinian corpus would have to account not only for the apparent transition from the aesthetic to the ethical, most evident in Bakhtin's altered perception of Dostoevksy's work between 'Author and Hero' (1924) and *Dostoevsky's Poetics* (1929), but with several knots of ambivalence within each of these two phases as well.[11]

---

[6] 'Author and Hero in Aesthetic Activity', 126.
[7] Ibid., 59, italics in source.
[8] Ibid., 83; see also 118.   [9] Ibid., 86.   [10] Ibid., 100; see also 109.
[11] 'Bakhtin's Homesickness: a Late Reply to Julia Kristeva', *Textual Practice* 9, no. 2 (1995), 223–42.

Most significant for the present discussion is Bakhtin's apparently seamless transition from a psychological frame of reference with a strong Lacanian note to a frame of reference relating to 'axiological boundaries'. Bakhtin writes of the 'dark chaos of my inner sensation of myself'; of the 'boundless, "darkly stirring chaos" of needs and dissatisfactions, wherein the future dyad of the child's personality and the outside world confronting it is still submerged and dissolved';[12] and of the constitution/authoring of the subject by the transgredient other/author.:

For self-consciousness, this integral image [of the self] is dispersed in life and enters the field of seeing the external world only in the form of fortuitous fragments. And what is lacking, moreover, is precisely external unity and continuity; a human being experiencing life in the category of his own *I* is incapable of gathering himself by himself into an outward whole that would be even relatively finished. . . . the point . . . is . . . the absence in principle of any unitary axiological approach from within a human being himself to his own outward expressedness in being. . . . In this sense one can speak of a human being's absolute need for the other, for the other's seeing, remembering, gathering, and unifying self-activity—the only self-activity capable of producing his outwardly finished personality. This outward personality could not exist, if the other did not create it.[13]

If this inability of the subject to perceive its own spatial and temporal boundary lines (the back of its head, the moment of its death) is obvious to the point of triviality, the axiological translation of this spatio-temporal perspective is far more disturbing. The 'self', in Bakhtin's terms, is that 'possible other who is with us when we look at ourselves in the mirror, when we dream of glory, when we make plans for our life; the possible other who has permeated our consciousness and who often guides our acts, our value judgments, and our vision of ourselves'.[14] Selfhood, then, is no longer synonymous with authenticity.

Bakhtin's aestheticized, *I-for-the-other* mode of consciousness, and Lacan's concept of the mirror stage are, as I have noted above, strikingly similar:

The *mirror stage* is a drama whose internal thrust is precipitated from insufficiency to anticipation—and which manufactures for the subject, caught up in the lure of spatial identification, the succession of

<hr>

[12] 'Author and Hero', 50.   [13] Ibid., 35–6.   [14] Ibid., 152.

phantasies that extend from a fragmented body-image to a form of its totality that I shall call orthopaedic—and lastly, to the assumption of the armour of an alienating identity, which will mark with its rigid structure the subject's entire mental development.[15]

For Lacan too, the mirror stage is not a developmental phase, outgrown and discarded at infancy, but a paradigmatic mode of psychic operation which 'reveals in demonstrative fashion the tendencies that then constitute the reality of the subject'.[16] Lacan too is highly suspicious of this psychic mode which constitutes the ego and the 'illusion of autonomy to which it entrusts itself'. Most strikingly, perhaps, Lacan also related the mirror stage to the appearance of the double.[17]

Bakhtin, however, is committed to an axiological conception of the subject. He cannot let go of the subject position which enables us to act out of a sense—illusory as it may be—of oneness, a bonding of I-for-myself and I-for-the-other. This is where the forensic aspect of subjectivity comes in, for it is the sense of internal coherence and agency which allows us to make ethical choices in the real world. Ideally, to paraphrase Bakhtin, these two 'movements' whose tensile relationship constitutes the subject-in-process, should balance and offset each other: the 'possible other' should normally be assimilated into the subject's yet-to-be mode of consciousness rather than framing and 'consummating' it to the point of impotence:

All these moments or constituents of our life that we recognize and anticipate through the other are rendered completely immanent to our own consciousness, are translated, as it were, into its language: they do not attain any consolidation and self-sufficiency in our consciousness, and they do not disrupt the unity of our own life—a life that is directed ahead of itself toward the event yet-to-come, a life that finds no rest within itself and never coincides with its given, presently existing makeup.[18]

[15] Lacan, 'The Mirror Stage as Formative of the Function of the I as Revealed in Psychoanalytic Experience' (1949), in *Ecrits: A Selection*, 4.
[16] 'The family' [1938], quoted in John Muller and and William J. Richardson, *Lacan and Language* (New York: International Universities Press, 1982), 30. 'The Family' is a transitional paper between Lacan's work on paranoia and the paper on the mirror stage, where the clinical observations are extended from the developmental to the 'ontological' sphere.   [17] Lacan, 'The Mirror Stage', 3.
[18] 'Author and Hero' 16.

In order to live and act, I need to be unconsummated, I need to be open for myself—at least in all the essential moments constituting my life; I have to be, for myself, someone who is axiologically yet-to-be, someone who does not coincide with his already existing makeup.[19]

The disintegration of this precarious vectorial balance, the take-over of the aestheticized, authored self, results in a loss of what Bakhtin calls 'the inner stance', a form of paralysis, uncannily presented as an emergence of a 'double':

[when] these reflections [i.e. the consciousness of the self as an other, as perceived through the eyes of the other] do gain body in our life, as sometimes happens, they begin to act as 'dead points', as obstructions of any accomplishment, and at times they may condense to the point where they deliver up to us a double of ourselves out of the night of our life.'[20]

This last point takes us to the process of subjectivity in 'The Secret Sharer', the complex interaction between these two modalities of consciousness, which boils over the borderlines of the text into the territory of the authorial subject. To understand the process, we should study the text against *Under Western Eyes*, its 'other' text. The circumstances in which the short story was written, in the midst of the novel, as it were, obviously beg the juxtaposition, but studies of the relationship between these two works have so far been confined to a thematic level predicated on issues of commit-ment, betrayal, and loyalty, which seem to emerge in both these texts.[21] It seems to me that while there is, in fact, a mechanism of compensation at work here, this mechanism goes much deeper than the wish to balance or offset the 'message' of the novel; that the short-lived therapeutic function which the story may have had for its author derives from the relational dynamics within and between these texts.

As we have just seen, *Under Western Eyes* is 'heterobiographical'

---

[19] Ibid., 14; see also 16.

[20] Ibid., 15–16; see also 59–60, 152 on the 'usurping double'.

[21] Steve Ressler, for example, considers the short story as an 'affirmative', if not altogether problem-free version of the novel and analyses the relationship primarily in terms of thematic compensation: 'The Secret Sharer', he argues, offers hope where *Under Western Eyes* is irredeemably pessimistic; the narrator of the story is free from the burden of Conradian scepticism or the moral pressure which weigh Razumov down; and the emphasis in the short story is on courageous, self-authenticating action rather than on moral consciousness. 'Conrad's "The Secret Sharer": Affirmation of Action', *Conradiana*, 16, no. 3 (1984), 195–214.

in that it is structured by its relationship with Dostoevsky's *Crime and Punishment*. The same relational paradigm which links the novel with its 'other' text obtains within the text, between Razumov and Haldin; on the border of the text, between the narrator and Razumov; and outside the text, between Conrad and his own Eastern 'other'. Intertextuality and intersubjectivity coalesce when the voice of the other frustrates the desire for autobiography, invades the territory of the self and subverts its claims to sovereignty. The subject, like the text, is—to use a Bakhtinian formulation—'wholly and always on the boundary'.[22]

Taking this line a step further, I would argue that 'The Secret Sharer' enacts the return of autobiographical desire. If, as I have speculated, the invasion of the subject by the voice of the other in *Under Western Eyes* was not only the structuring principle in the novel but the catalyst for the author's collapse on its completion, 'The Secret Sharer' was written in an attempt to reclaim the ground lost in the writing of the novel, to regain the (non-existent) internal territory of the subject and its sovereignty. If in *Under Western Eyes* the boundaries between hero and author, self and other, are transgressed often enough to invalidate the very concept of an inner territory (cultural or psychic), the narrator of 'The Secret Sharer' tries—with a degree of *méconnaissance* which applies to the author himself—to aestheticize and frame himself; to reclaim, or rather fabricate, an autonomous topos of subjectivity.

It is hardly surprising that 'The Secret Sharer' should have become so widely anthologized, given its extremely neat structural and formal symmetries, its ostensible treatment of ethical questions, and its equally ostensible concern with psychology, all within the very manageable scope of a short story. But this combination of narrative mastery and apparent thematic weightiness, striking as it undoubtedly is, has produced a rather disturbing work, whose formal elegance 'not only aestheticizes but actually anaestheticizes the call for ethical action'.[23] There is much about the narrator's interpretation of his own motivation and state of

---

[22] M. M. Bakhtin, 'Toward a Reworking of the Dostoevsky Book' (1961), in *Problems of Dostoevsky's Poetics* (1929; 2nd ed. 1963), ed. and trans. Caryl Emerson, introd. Wayne C. Booth (Minneapolis: University of Minnesota Press, 1984), Appendix II, 287.

[23] Cedric Watts, 'The Mirror-tale: an Ethico-structural Analysis of Conrad's "The Secret Sharer"', *Critical Quarterly*, 19, no. 3 (1977), 36.

mind which is unconvincing; the conflict of loyalties in which he is caught is not resolved by any clear-cut choice; the ostensible act of liberation (whether of himself or of the fugitive is unclear) is highly ambivalent or downright morally suspicious; and the triumphant cadences on which the narrative concludes sound rather hollow when one realizes that the elegance of the resolution is aesthetic rather than ethical. The narrator Captain has put the lives entrusted to him at risk in the most outrageous way in order to save the life of his secret sharer; his future standing with his justly mistrustful crew is by no means assured; and it is only through an amazing stroke of undeserved good fortune (rather than navigational mastery) that his final act does not end disastrously for his ship and her crew.

However, even readers who have refused to be anaestheticized by the neat structural symmetries of the story have only addressed the narrator's unreliability, exempting the author under the implicit assumption that there must be a good moral to a good story; that behind, or above, or below the conflicting elements there is an authorial/ authoritative principle of organization; that the ambivalence of the narrative can be relegated to one phase in the dialectics of art and is eventually resolved on a higher, more sophisticated level of authorial construction.[24] Neat as such a resolution would be, there is little in the story to warrant it. The text seems to endorse the position of the narrator by default: there is no rhetorical dissociation of the story from the narrative; no authoritative embodied other who would dispute or challenge the narrator's interpretation and judgment; no hint of retrospective self-doubt in the narrator's discourse; no point of anchorage for that wishful assumption of higher organization.

Like *Under Western Eyes*, its 'other' text, 'The Secret Sharer' explores the idea of borderlines, divisions, and boundaries. But the ubiquity of border states in the story, discussed in an excellent study by James Hansford, does not necessarily indicate an inner rift which needs to be mended as Hansford suggests.[25] I believe

---

[24] For a sampling of these 'suspicious' readings, see Cedric Watts, 'The Mirror-tale'. David Eggenschwiler, 'Narcissus in "The Secret Sharer": a Secondary Point of View', *Conradiana*, 11, no. 1 (1979): 23–40; Michael Murphy, '"The Secret Sharer": Conrad's Turn of the Winch', *Conradiana* 18, no. 3 (1986), 193–200.

[25] James Hansford, 'Closing, Enclosure and Passage in "The Secret Sharer"', *The Conradian*, 15, no. 1 (1990), 30–55.

that it is precisely the obverse, a state of psychic 'borderlessness', which lies at the core of the narrator's anxiety; that the obsession with boundaries and their inscription is a symptom of the narrator's need to stake out a spurious territory of selfhood. The man who feels like 'a stranger' to himself is already deeply troubled at the outset of the narrative by his inability to make out the lines of division between land and sea, between rocks and ruins:

On my right hand there were lines of fishing stakes resembling a mysterious system of half-submerged bamboo fences, incomprehensible in its division of the domain of tropical fishes, and crazy of aspect as if abandoned for ever . . . there was no sign of human habitation as far as the eye could reach. To the left a group of barren islets, suggesting ruins of stone walls, towers, and block houses. . . . I saw the straight line of the flat shore joined to the stable sea, edge to edge, with a perfect and unmarked closeness. (91)

The narrative moves in a cinematic fashion from the panoramic (the view of the land) to the scenic (the ship and her crew), and finally closes up on the perceiving individual. But that movement, normally designed to place and orientate the subject, only compounds the sense of physical and psychological disorientation as it removes all the potential points of reference outside the self and positions the narrator within three concentric circles of uncertainty: the mysterious aspect of the physical surroundings, the unknown ship and her crew, and his own self as captain.[26]

It is this spatial anxiety, this threatening loss of 'selfhood', which generates the need to reinscribe the lines of division, to frame the self as an integral, distinct object. In *Under Western Eyes* the staircase—that threshold where subjects cross and invade each other's spaces—acquires chronotopic significance, strikingly similar to that which predominates in Dostoevsky's *Crime and Punishment*.[27] In 'The Secret Sharer', however, there is no staircase. There is a stepladder which can be pulled up or lowered down into the water at the narrator's will. It is not a permanent avenue for the subject's traffic with the other, but a means of

---

[26] In his reading of the story, Jeremy Hawthorn has rightly noted the 'split between perceiving and perceived self'. *Multiple Personality and the Disintegration of Literary Character*' (London: Edward Arnold, 1983), 85. It is, I believe, an observation that can apply not only to the process within the text, but to the dynamics of subjectivity 'outside' it.

[27] Bakhtin, 'Notes Toward a Reworking of the Dostoevsky Book', 299.

enclosure for the subject.[28] The very same 'anxiety of border-lessness' is shared, as I will argue later, by the author himself.

Put into a Bakhtinian frame of reference, the narrator's initial state of mind is clearly that loss of the 'inner stance', which is the enabling condition for all action.

A man who has grown accustomed to dreaming about himself in concrete terms—a man who strives to visualize the external image of himself, who is morbidly sensitive about the outward image impression he produces and yet is insecure about that impression and easily wounded in his pride—such a man loses the proper, purely inner stance in relation to his own body. He becomes awkward, 'unwieldy,' and does not know what to do with his hands and feet. This occurs because an indeterminate *other* intrudes upon his movements and gestures.[29]

Like other Conradian characters—most notably Lord Jim—who have lost the 'inner stance', the narrator would revert to an aesthetic modality of consciousness. In order to recover a sense of his own selfhood, he would try to objectify and 'author' himself exotopically as an 'other', an object of perception, a hero in a text—whole, autonomous, and clearly delineated. He would need, in other words, to devise a human mirror for himself.

With Leggatt's arrival on board, the human mirror material-izes. There is very little in the narrated events to justify the sense of inexorable fate, the mysterious coincidences, and the sugges-tions of the uncanny with which the narrative is so heavily fraught. These effects are produced entirely by the narrator's insistence on the bond of doubleness which seems to exist, a priori, between himself and the fugitive. Both men are young and similarly built; they have both been to the same school and are members of the same social class. But the resemblance ends there, and would certainly not justify the assumption of double-ness or the structural symmetry which is so heavy-handedly imposed on the narrative.[30] The narrator's observation of the

---

[28] The narrator's pretence of deafness in his exchange with the skipper of the *Sephora* (118–19) may also be related to this 'undoing' of *Under Western Eyes*. If Razumov's literal deafness marks the ultimate invasion of the other's discourse (as literary clairvoyance is often accompanied by a literal blindness), the narrator's pretence recoils on him as it ironically serves to accentuate the impotence of his willed self-enclosure.   [29] 'Author and Hero', 59–60.

[30] This has been discussed in detail by Eggenschwiler in 'Narcissus in "The Secret Sharer"'.

general physical resemblance between himself and his 'double' is suspiciously overblown:

He had concealed his damp body in a sleeping suit of the same grey-stripe pattern as the one I was wearing and followed me like my double on the poop. Together we moved right aft, barefooted, silent. (100)

My sleeping suit was just right for his size. (100)

The shadowy, dark head, like mine, seemed to nod imperceptively above the ghostly gray of my sleeping-suit. It was, in the night, as though I had been faced by my own reflection in the depth of a sombre and immense mirror. (101)

A few minutes after their first encounter, the narrator begins to refer to Leggatt—with no qualifying quotation marks in the text—as 'my double', my 'other self', the 'secret sharer', etc. (104, 105, 109, 111, 114, 115 ff.). It is precisely that insistence, the 'overkill' effect of the narrative, which calls for a suspicious reading and produces what appears to be a generic ambiguity in the text.[31] But the sense of the uncanny which looms so large over the story is epistemological rather than ontological: Leggatt, the man, is real enough. It is the perception of Leggatt as the Captain's double which corrodes the substance of the tale.

The projection of identities goes both ways. The narrator Captain looks at his 'double' believing that 'anybody would have taken him for me' (115), superimposing this fabricated inter-changeability on his dealings with the skipper of the *Sephora* and with his own crew (119–20). The more interesting and less explicit process which takes place is the Captain's willed identific-ation with the fugitive. It is, in fact, *he* who takes on the other man's identity; it is *he* who becomes, in fact, the mirror of the other so that the other might become his 'double'. In his need to objectify himself, to view himself from without in the absence of

[31] In his discussion of the *doppelgänger* motif in the story Paul Coates argues that 'The Secret Sharer' is 'a key example of the way in which the transition from realism to modernism generates uncertainty in writers'. Conrad, he writes 'cannot decide whether his doubling should be discreetly latent (realistic) or manifest (proto-modernist); driven towards the modernist problematic by the independent logic of his subject-matter, he shies away from direct confrontation with it. His work is laboured and indecisive, hovering between realism and fantasy, unable either to unite them to separate them'. *The Realist Fantasy: Fiction and Reality since Clarissa* (New York: St Martin's Press, 1983), 115.

that 'inner stance' which is the necessary condition for all action, he fabricates and literally stage-manages this doubleness as he begins to mime the gestures of the other.

He rested a hand on the end of the skylight . . . and all that time did not stir a limb, so far as I could see. . . . One of my hands, too, rested on the end of the sky-light; neither did I stir a limb, so far as I knew. It occurred to me that if old 'Bless my soul—you don't say so' were to put his head up the companion and catch sight of us, he would think he was seeing double, or imagine himself come upon a scene of weird witchcraft; the strange captain having a quiet confabulation by the wheel with his own gray ghost. (103)

Like Gentleman Brown in *Lord Jim*, another fictitious double who preceded Leggatt by a decade, the outlaw intuitively plays on this assumed doubleness, and the Captain narrator readily and uncritically responds:

You know well enough the sort of ill-conditioned snarling cur—He appealed to me as if our experiences had been as identical as our clothes. And I knew well enough the pestiferous danger of such a character [i.e. the dead man] where there are no means of legal repression. And I knew well enough that my double there was no homicidal ruffian. I did not think of asking him for details, and he told me the story roughly in brusque, disconnected sentences. I needed no more. I saw it all going on as though I were myself inside that other sleeping-suit. (101–2)

Neither a reliable character witness nor an impartial judge in his readiness and need to acquit Leggatt, the narrator seems to be oddly insensitive to the distinct note of callousness in the other's account:

It's clear that I meant business, because I was holding him by the throat still when they picked us up. He was black in the face. . . . I wonder they didn't fling me overboard after getting the carcass of their precious ship-mate out of my fingers. (103)

Though clearly aware of the temperamental and moral disparity between the fugitive and himself, the narrator Captain chooses to suppress it. But his occasional slips indicate that he is, in fact, conscious of Leggatt's potential for violence.[32] His reaction to a

[32] Murphy rightly notes that narrator wilfully suppresses the Skipper's different version of the incident on board the *Sephora*, judging it 'unworthwhile' to record it. Murphy, 'Conrad's Turn of the Winch', 196.

near discovery (when the steward enters the bathroom unexpectedly and there seems to be no way to avert an encounter) indicates the extent of his self-deception: 'My voice dies in my throat and I went stony all over. I expected to hear a yell of surprise and terror, and made a movement, but had not the strength to get on my legs. Had my second self taken the poor wretch by the throat?' (120). This is clearly at odds with his repeated assertion that 'my double there was no homicidal ruffian.'

When the skipper of the *Sephora* comes on board, the narrator meets his tenacious adherence to the law with derision:

His obscure tenacity on that point had it something incomprehensible and a little awful; something, as it were, mystical, quite apart from his anxiety. . . . Seven-and-thirty years at sea, of which over twenty of immaculate command, and the last fifteen in the *Sephora* seemed to have laid him under some pitiless obligation. (119)

The young Captain narrator cannot see that he too should have been under the same 'pitiless obligation' which comes with the position of command. Having invested his sense of selfhood in this 'double', the narrator reduces the terms of the ethical dilemma into a bogus equation:

It was all very simple. The same strung-up force which had given twenty-four men a chance, at least, for their lives, had, in a sort of recoil, crushed an unworthy mutinous existence. (125)

Eggenschwiler notes that his equation is reversed at the end of the story, when the narrator risks the lives of the crew to save the life of one man.[33] But this equation is unacceptable even if one chooses to believe Leggatt's version of the murder. If the supreme value of the communal ethos is that of discipline (hence the unworthiness of the 'mutinous existence' and the justification for the killing), isn't Leggatt himself guilty of mutiny in his refusal to let the law take its course?

In his need to 'find refuge in the other and to assemble—out of the other—the scattered pieces of [his] own givenness, in order to produce from them a parasitically consummated unity' ('Author and Hero', 126), the narrator has trapped himself within the aestheticized mode of consciousness. The other has become, in

---

[33] David Eggenschwiler, 'Narcissus in "The Secret Sharer"', 32, 35.

Bakhtin's terms again, a 'usurping double', forcing the narrator to articulate a position in conflict with the communal ethos to which he is committed by vocation. The fabricated mirror-relationship born out of the psychic need for self-objectification now becomes a question of what Bakhtin would call 'axiological authority'. What, we should ask, is the source of axiological authority for the subject who is inevitably constructed within the narrative of the other? What kind of agency may be assumed if there is no such thing as an autonomous, sovereign topos of subjectivity? What guarantees do we have for the benevolence of the authorial Other?

Though fully aware of the seductions of aesthetics, Bakhtin, unlike many of his Postmodernist successors, views the need for a meta-narrative as incurable.[34] In his search for an anchor which would lend some axiological validity to the narrative of the other, the 'authored' or 'aestheticized' mode of being, which he recognizes as an inevitable constitutive movement of subjectivity, Bakhtin makes a rather wobbly distinction between the 'fabricated' Other whose axiological authority is entirely fortuitous and spurious, and the Other as the potential communal narrator of one's story:

What renders the other an authoritative and inwardly intelligible author of my life is the fact that this other is not fabricated by me for self serving purposes, but represents an axiological force which I confirm in reality and which actually determines my life.[35]

The other who possessed me does not come into conflict with my I-for-myself, so long as I do not sever myself axiologically from the world of others, so long as I perceive myself within a collective (a family, a nation, civilized mankind). In this case the axiological position of the other within me is authoritative for me; he can narrate the story of my life and I shall be in full inner agreement with him. So long as my life proceeds in indissoluble unity with the collective other, it is interpreted, constructed, and organized . . . in the plane of another's possible consciousness of my life; my life is perceived and constructed as a possible

---

[34] The recognition that 'a person's consciousness awakens wrapped in another's consciousness' is one of the consistent themes of Bakhtin's work down to his very last writings.('Notes made in 1970–71', 138). For an illuminating discussion of this disturbing aspect of Bakhtin's work see Caryl Emerson's 'Problems with Baxtin's Poetics', *Slavic and East European Journal*, 32, no. 4 (1988), 503–25; and Ann Jefferson, 'Bodymatters: Self and Other in Bakhtin, Sartre and Barthes', in *Bakhtin and Cultural Theory*, ed. Ken Hirschkop and David Shepherd (Manchester: Manchester University Press, 1989), 152–77.   [35] 'Author and Hero', 153.

story that might be told about it by the other to still others (to descendants). My consciousness of a possible narrator, the axiological context of a possible narrator, organizes my acts, thoughts, and feelings where, with respect to their value, they are involved in the world of others.[36]

But neither the voice of the communal narrator nor his axiological authority are strong enough to trigger an *anagnorisis*. The apparent turning-point in the story is reached when the time comes for the ship to get under way and for the Captain to take action. To understand the sense of paralysis which overwhelms him at this point, we should turn once again to the Bakhtinian diagnosis of what he describes as the loss of the 'inner stance' in terms of a bodily action performed in space:

Inner sensation of self remains the foundation—the proper world of action—during intense external action: it dissolves within itself or subordinates to itself everything that is externally expressed, and it does not allow anything external to complete itself in a stable intuitable given either within or without myself. Focusing on one's own exterior in performing an action may even prove to be fatal, a force that destroys the action. Thus when one has to perform a difficult and risky jump, it is extremely dangerous to follow the movement of one's own feet: one has to collect oneself from within and to calculate one's own movements—again from within. . . . The external image or configuration of an action and its external, intuitable relation to the objects of the outside world are never given to the performer of the action himself, and if they do irrupt into the action-performing consciousness, they inevitably turn into curbs or 'dead points' of action.[37]

If we may translate the spatial into an axiological frame of reference, as Bakhtin clearly does, if becomes clear that the Captain narrator has reached the 'dead point' of action.

It's to no commander's advantage to be suspected of ludicrous eccentricities. But I was also more seriously affected. There are to a seaman certain words, gestures, that should in given conditions come as naturally, as instinctively as the wincing of a menaced eye. A certain order should spring to his lips without thinking; a certain sign should get itself made,

---

[36] 'Author and Hero', 155. The smooth assimilation of Bakhtin into the Postmodernist canon is somewhat incongruous in view of his explicit ideological position on this issue, which is decidedly on the conservative side. A strikingly similar view of the narrative of communality as a substitute for metaphysical narratives has been offered by Alasdair MacIntyre in *After Virtue* (1981; 2nd ed., London: Duckworth, 1985).   [37] 'Author and Hero', 44–5.

so to speak, without reflection. But all unconscious alertness had abandoned me. (126)

In order to set himself free from a psychic paralysis, the narrator Captain paradoxically needs to take the assumption of doubleness to its ultimate conclusion. The floppy white hat which he puts on the exposed head of his 'double' becomes a metaphoric vehicle for that cast-off identity.

All at once my strained, yearning stare distinguished a white object floating . . . I recognized my own floppy hat. . . . Now I had what I wanted—the saving mark for my eyes. But I hardly thought of my other self, now gone from the ship. . . . The hat was meant to save his homeless head from the dangers of the sun. And now—behold—it was saving the ship, by serving me for a mark to help out the ignorance of my strangeness. (142)

Miraculously and improbably, the trope of identity becomes a mark of distinction. The discarded hat is no longer a vehicle for transposed identities, but a distinct physical object whose very separateness from the perceiving subject turns it into a reference point outside the self, an aid marking the position of the ship, enabling the narrator to recover his subject position as a member of the community.

If one feels uncomfortable with this triumphant and neat conclusion of the narrative, it is no doubt because of the double bind which seems to operate here. The young Captain narrator seems at last to reject the aestheticizing fantasy of selfhood, to realign himself with the voice of the authorial/authoritative collective other. But at the very point where he sets out to exorcize the double, the narrative swerves once again in the direction of the uncanny: the ship is not saved through his navigational skills but by a most unlikely miracle, which belongs to the same order of phenomena as the appearance of the mysterious double, the improbable avoidance of discovery, and other projections of fantasy. The exorcism of the usurping double is not a truly liberating act; it is little more than an empty gesture performed by a narrator who is still deeply captivated in the realm of the aesthetic.

The extrapolation of subjectivity from the textual to the biographical site requires some theoretical orientation regarding the vexed question of authorial presence and representation and the relationship between the writing and the written subject. As in *Under Western Eyes*, the form of authorial presence which permeates the text and overruns its boundaries is 'heterobiographical' precisely in that it does not represent an intact kernel of selfhood but points to the very absence of that kernel, a form of desire for self-presence which is the ultimate metaphysical need. Far from a discovery or a recovery of selfhood through a *rite de passage*, the text is an abortive gesture towards an empty topos of subjectivity.

The composition of the story has been dated by Keith Carabine, in an admirable feat of critical sleuthing, as the three weeks between the first and the nineteenth of December, 1909. 'Given the evidence of the manuscripts, we can safely presume Conrad began the story on or just after his fifty-second birthday, December third, and completed the holograph by the fifteenth.' Carabine adds in a footnote, 'I favor his birthday if only because Conrad seems to have been fond of symbolic gestures.'[38] I would suggest that the full significance of that symbolic gesture is all the more striking when one relates it to Conrad's 'quest for completeness or inner unity' and to the 'tenuousness of [his] sense of self' as diagnosed by Bernard C. Meyer:

That Conrad was intensely preoccupied by mirrors and reflections needs no emphasis. Undoubtedly his most explicit 'mirror' story is 'The Secret Sharer' which is, in essence, the story of a double or mirror image of the self. . . . What is implied in 'The Secret Sharer', and for that matter in all of Conrad's kindred tales, is the complementary role played by the 'Other', the double, or the mirror image in rounding out the incomplete self of the protagonist.[39]

In a letter to William Rothenstein on 15 November 1909, shortly before the writing of 'The Secret Sharer', Conrad wrote: 'Twenty months have gone already over a novel and now I must finish it—or I am totally undone.'[40] This is as neat an inversion as any analyst may wish for, as Conrad was to be psychologically 'undone' just when he finally did finish the novel. On the completion of *Under Western Eyes* Conrad had a serious nervous break-

[38] Keith Carabine, '"The Secret Sharer": a Note on the Dates of its Composition'. *Conradiana*, 19, no. 3 (1987), 210, 212.

[39] Bernard C. Meyer, *Joseph Conrad: A Psychoanalytic Biography* (Princeton: NJ: Princeton University Press, 1967), 321.

[40] Joseph Conrad, *Collected letters*, ed. Frederick R. Karl and Lawrence Davis, vol. 4 (Cambridge: Cambridge University Press, 1990) 290.

down. The process of writing had opened a crack in his psychic and cultural inner space, that 'sovereign territory' he had tried— like his protagonist—to stake out for himself. The tortured, drawn-out process of writing, and Conrad's inability to bring the novel to a close, indicate the enormity of the psychic threat it entailed for the author, the danger which materialized in a psychotic crisis when the novel was finally finished. 'The Secret Sharer' was written on the brink of that breakdown as a futile gesture of self-enclosure, a last-ditch attempt to shore up the subject position which had crumbled in the writing of the novel.

Judging by Conrad's reports of a regained 'sense of confidence' and a 'marked mental improvement' shortly after the completion of the story, it appears that the writing did have a distinctly (albeit temporary) beneficial effect on Conrad's health and state of mind, an effect which is undoubtedly due to at least in part to a sense of accomplishment, but might have something to do with the different relational dynamics set in this short piece.[41] The most interesting letter in this respect is the one written to Pinker on 12 December 1909: 'I am now feeling as well as I have not felt since the Lord Jim days—which were the last good ones.'[42] The allusion to *Lord Jim* is highly significant: Jim is the proto-Conradian character who aestheticizes himself, who perceives himself as a literary hero, and whose failure in action is related to his consciousness of the self as an other.[43] On 17 December 1901 Conrad wrote a letter to the painter William Rothenstein:

Here I've been 2 years writing a novel which is not yet finished. Two Years! Of which surely one half has been illness complicated by a terrible moral stress. Imagine yourself painting with the Devil jogging your elbow *all the time*. . . . [Conrad apparently refuses Rothenstein's offer to visit him.] I speak to you here as to a second self and thus I cannot conceive you taking it ill. Perhaps I am unreasonable. But to-day in the second week of my 52nd year, a failure from the worldly point of view and

---

[41] A letter to Galsworthy on 10 Dec. 1909: 'I have been working rather well of late. I took off last week to write a short story. Razumov is really nearing the end . . . I am aware of a marked mental improvement', *Collected Letters*, vol. 4, 294. A letter to Galsworthy on 14 Dec. 1909: 'I've just finished the story—12000 words in ten days. Not so bad. I had to lay aside Razumov for a bit tho' I didn't think it would take 10 days. No great harm done tho! Doing something easy has given me confidence', *Collected Letters*, vol. 4, 296. [42] *Collected Letters*, vol. 4, 298.

[43] For a relevant discussion of *Lord Jim* see Daphna Erdinast-Vulcan, *Joseph Conrad and the Modern Temper* (Oxford: Oxford University Press, 1991), 34–47.

knowing that there can be no change—that this must go on *usque ad finem*—I may perhaps be allowed a little unreason.[44]

It was not unusual for Conrad to transpose his fiction into his letters, and the mere use of the phrase 'second self' in a letter during the writing of the story is not puzzling in itself. What is more interesting is the relationship which had prompted the use of the expression. Rothenstein was a friend, but he was not closer to Conrad than many others, and surely not closer than Galsworthy, to whom Conrad wrote at the same time. Why, then, did Conrad use this epithet for Rothenstein rather than for his closest friend? I believe that the answer lies in the same need which has prompted the writing of the story. William Rothenstein had painted Conrad's portrait in the summer of 1903, when Conrad was beginning to emerge and receive recognition as a public figure.[45] Rothenstein had, in Bakhtin's terms, 'consummated' Conrad: in painting his portrait he had given him form and substance; he had—quite literally—framed him and fixed his ever-elusive selfhood for the world and for himself to see. Rothenstein must have been for Conrad that other whose excess of vision he needed to regain a sense of a unified subject.

A similar conclusion might be drawn in view of Conrad's references to 'The Secret Sharer' in his letters of that time as 'very characteristic Conrad' and 'a good specimen of Conrad'.[46] This is not merely sales talk. The writer who had more than once fiercely objected to being labelled and tagged as 'a writer of the sea' was now setting up a non-existent 'Conradian' essence which readers would presumably be able to recognize. Conrad's references to himself in the third person, from 'outside', as it were, may be seen as further evidence of this need to objectify and frame his authorial persona. Another interesting document is the letter written by Conrad to Edward Garnett on 5 November 1912, shortly after the publication of the story:

---

[44] *Collected Letters*, vol. 4, 299– 300.

[45] Zdzislaw Najder, *Joseph Conrad: A Chronicle* trans. Halina Carroll-Najder (Cambridge: Cambridge University Press, 1983), 292.

[46] A letter to Pinker, undated but probably written on Wednesday, 15 Dec. 1909, *Collected Letters*, vol. 4, 298; a letter to Perceval Gibbon, written on 19 Dec. 1909, *Collected Letters*, vol. 4, 301.

'The Secret Sharer' between you and me is *it*. Eh? No damned tricks with girls there. Eh? Every word fits, and there is not a single uncertain note. Luck, my boy, pure luck.[47]

This is an odd letter for Conrad to write, not so much in what it says, but in its tonality and rhetoric. The voice we hear sounds entirely out of character. It is not the familiar Conradian voice with its elaborate courtesy and refinement, its careful qualifications and modulations, and its formality, which sometimes borders on stiffness even when writing to friends. What we have here seems to be the voice of another persona: its nearly vulgar bluffness, its deliberate colloquialism, and its emphatic cockiness make it sound like the utterance of a ventriloquist's dummy, a puppet which becomes a character on its own. I believe that this change of voice is another symptom of the author's need to counter the absence of subject position and set up a persona for himself. 'The Secret Sharer' is a last-ditch attempt to mend the fences, to enclose and frame the sovereign territory of the self which, as Conrad was to learn very shortly afterwards, is entirely and inescapably permeable.

To conclude this discussion, we should turn once again to the subject in process. The story, I have argued, is both a symptom and a diagnosis. Its symptomatic quality lies in the placebo effect of self-enclosure: the isomorphic relationship between the narrator's spurious attempt to frame and objectify himself through a fabricated mirror image; and the author's abortive attempt to shore up a 'very characteristic Conrad' against the invasion of the Eastern other. But the story is also a diagnosis of the role of metaphysics in the dynamics of subjectivity. Metaphysics, to reverse the Derridean formula, is the ether of subjectivity. Taken only one step further, the 'aesthetic' modality, the enabling condition for Bakhtin's 'authored' subject, can be extended to what is conventionally taken as a metaphysical framework, 'a powerful *point d'appui*' outside the subject.[48]

An aesthetic event can take place only when there are two participants present; it presupposes two noncoinciding consciousnesses. . . . When

---

[47] *Letters from Joseph Conrad*, ed. Edward Garnett (London: Nonesuch Press, 1928), 263.   [48] 'Author and Hero', 31.

the other consciousness is the encompassing consciousness of God, a religious event takes place (prayer, worship, ritual).[49]

A whole, integral human being is the product of the aesthetic, creative point of view and of that point of view alone. . . . A whole, integral human being presupposes an aesthetically active subiectum situated outside him (we are abstracting from man's religious experience in the present context).[50]

'The Secret Sharer' is indeed a good story with a good moral. But it is not yet another compact version of the *Bildungsroman*, a coming into one's own.[51] What it offers is a perception of subjectivity as a Möbius strip, where the desire for an illusory kernel of being, an 'aestheticized' or 'authored' selfhood, traverses and surfaces through an ethical, 'yet-to-be' mode of consciousness, which offers no respite from responsibility. The tensile relation between these two modalities may be the missing link in the Postmodernist critique of the transcendental subject. The need for grounding is a concomitant of our innate non-self-sufficiency; it emerges out of our very constitution as discursive, responsive beings, creatures who live on their borderlines. The need to be authored and authorized from without cannot easily be thrown overboard as dead metaphysical ballast. Having lost our moorings, the need for anchorage is still with us.

---

[49] 'Author and Hero', 22.   [50] Ibid., 82–3.

[51] Paul Coates argues that 'Conrad's story is too ready to give hostages to the moralism that sees in it merely a *rite de passage*; he interprets the decomposition of the personality as merely a temporary phase—teething troubles of the captain's first command—detached from the deeper level at which there exist fundamental rifts in the structure of character. Conrad hides the trail that leads from his captain-hero to the self-conscious narrators of modernist fiction' (116). I believe that this critique should be directed at the interpreters of the story rather than at the author. Josiane Paccaud's-Huguet's discussion, to take just one instance, is couched in Lacanian terminology, but concludes on a note which is totally alien to Lacan's work, with a presentation of the resolution as an 'achievement of selfhood'. 'Under the Other's Eye: Conrad's "The Secret Sharer"'. *The Conradian*, 12, no. 1 (1987), 62.

PART II

The Strange Short Fiction

I

Writing and Fratricide

CONRAD'S AUTHOR'S NOTE to *Tales of Unrest* begins with a long and rather peculiar anecdote of a 'common steel pen' with which, he claims, both *An Outcast of the Islands* and 'The Lagoon' were written.

> I thought the pen had been a good pen and that it had done enough for me, and so, with the idea of keeping it for a sort of memento on which I could look later with tender eyes, I put it into my waistcoat pocket. Afterwards it used to turn up in all sorts of places, at the bottom of small drawers, among my studs in cardboard boxes, till at last it found permanent rest in a large wooden bowl containing some loose keys, bits of sealing wax, bits of string, small broken chains, a few buttons, and similar minute wreckage that washes out of a man's life into such receptacles. I would catch sight of it from time to time with a distinct feeling of satisfaction till, one day, I perceived with horror that there were two old pens in there. How the other pen found its way into the bowl instead of the fireplace or wastepaper basket I can't imagine, but there the two were, lying side by side, both encrusted with ink and completely undistinguishable from each other. It was very distressing, but being determined not to share my sentiment between two pens or run the risk of sentimentalizing over a mere stranger, I threw them both out of the window into a flower bed—which strikes me now as a poetical grave for the remnants of one's past. But the tale remained. (pp. v–vi)

This odd, apparently pointless, and not very amusing anecdote, ostensibly introduced to flavour the preface with a picture of the author in his slippers (with the domestic inventory of cufflinks, sealing wax, etc.), deserves some further consideration. The hyperbolic, overcharged rhetoric deployed in the telling of a rather trivial little story—the 'horror' at finding two pens instead of one; the 'distress' of sharing the sentiment between them; the 'risk' of sentimentalizing over a mere stranger—as well as the startling violence of the final gesture, clearly point to a deeper personal significance. 'The Lagoon', Conrad's first short story,

according to his author's note (but not according to his
biographers or his collected letters!), also marks the end of what
he calls his 'first phase', the 'Malayan phase with its special
subject and its verbal suggestions'. Between *An Outcast of the
Islands* and 'The Lagoon', Conrad tells us, there has been 'no
change of pen', both figuratively and literally. But that good old
pen, which had served the author so well, well enough to deserve
the status of a favourite memento, is thrown out at some unspecified point later, when the author suddenly realizes that it
has produced its own clone.

The concept of cloning emerges again in Conrad's author's note
to *An Outcast of the Islands* (1896), written shortly before 'The
Lagoon' and, according to the author's testimony, with the very
same pen: '*An Outcast of the Islands* is my second novel in the
absolute sense of the word; second in conception, second in execu-
tion, second as it were in its essence.' Conrad goes on to tell how
he was induced to write the novel by Richard Garnett's suggestion,
following the publication of *Almayer's Folly*, that he should 'write
another':

Had he said, 'Why not go on writing,' it is very probable he would have
scared me away from pen and ink forever; but there was nothing either to
frighten one or to arouse one's antagonism in the mere suggestion to
'write another'. . . . And thus a dead point in the revolution of my affairs
was insidiously got over. The word 'another' did that. (7–8)

What is the meaning of 'second in the absolute sense of the word'?
It would seem that what we have here is, in fact, a confession of
bad faith: *An Outcast of the Islands* is perceived by its author not
only as a second novel in terms of chronological sequence; it is
'another' novel, a literary sibling or clone of the previous one.

'Karain' too was initially meant to be 'something like "The
Lagoon" but with less description. A Malay thing . . . [which]
will be easy and may bring in a few pence'.[1] Indeed, more than any
other pair of Conrad's short stories, 'The Lagoon' (completed in
August 1896) and 'Karain' (completed in April 1897) can easily
be read as literary clones. Both stories are set in lush, exotic,
Malay scenes; both are narrated by white men who are 'unbelievers'; both stories involve an act of betrayal and fratricide

---

[1] A letter to Garnett on 7 Feb. 1897, *Collected Letters*, vol. 1, 338.

committed out of love for a woman who is to remain inaccessible; and both deal with native heroes, haunted by guilt, driven away from their homelands, who tell their respective ghost stories to the white men. But these apparent literary clones, only eight or nine months apart, are, in fact, wholly antagonistic siblings. In this chapter I shall offer a reading of 'Karain' as a literary assassination of its own prototype, and as a transitional point in the psycho-textual dynamics of Conrad's work.

Shortly after the submission of 'The Lagoon' for publication, Conrad wrote to Garnett:

I've sent a short thing to the Cornhill. A Malay tells a story to a white man who is spending the night in his hut. It's a tricky thing with the usual forest river-stars-wind sunrise, and so on—and lots of secondhand Conradese in it. I would bet a penny they will take it. There is only 6000 words in it so it can't bring in many shekels. Don't You think I am a lost soul? Upon my word I hate every line I write.'[2]

This is not just the usual Conradian gesture of self-deprecation. 'The Lagoon' is indeed a rather crude specimen of Conrad's exoticism at its worst:

The narrow creek was like a ditch: tortuous, fabulously deep; filled with gloom under the thin strip of pure and shining blue of the heaven. Immense trees soared up, invisible behind the festooned draperies of creepers. Here and there, near the glistening blackness of the water, a twisted root of some tall tree showed amongst the tracery of small ferns, black and dull, writhing and motionless like an arrested snake. . . . Darkness oozed out from between the trees, through the tangled maze of the creepers, from behind the great fantastic and unstirring leaves; the darkness, mysterious and invincible; the darkness scented and poisonous of impenetrable forests'. (188–9)

There is more, much more, of the same in the few pages which make up the story. Conrad was right, for once, in his judgement of his own work. But the author's use of the phrase 'secondhand Conradese' should give us pause. Years later, in his author's note to *Tales of Unrest*, Conrad wrote: 'I have lived long enough to see ['The Lagoon'] most agreeably guyed by Mr. Max Beerbohm in a volume of parodies entitled "A Christmas Garland," where I found myself in very good company. I was immensely gratified. I began to believe in my public existence. I have much to thank "The Lagoon" for' (p. vi).

Conrad was not being entirely facetious here, just as he had not been entirely cynical a few years earlier in referring to his own writing as 'secondhand Conradese'. I would suggest that his notorious 'will to style', as Jameson calls it, was not only a strategy of aesthetic containment, demarcating the world of the text from material and historical realities; nor was it only a literary variety of impressionism, a mode of cultivated ambiguity, as seen by many other readers.[3] At this early point in his career, when he was about to discard one identity option—the marine officer—purchased with great difficulties over a long period of time, for another still uncertain and difficult redefinition of himself as a writer against tremendous odds, Conrad's stylistic mannerisms were also a strategy for the containment of authorial subjectivity, a fingerprinting of the text. A self-parody, 'secondhand Conradese', was one way of claiming a public persona for himself. A parody written by another was even better: it meant that there was indeed a mode of writing which readers would recognize as his own; that his convoluted style with its figurative excess, its adjectival insistence, and its cultivated opacity has become a hallmark of authorial presence. It is perhaps symptomatic that years later, when Conrad wrote of his first steps as a writer, he invoked Novalis: 'It is certain my conviction gains infinitely the moment another soul will believe in it.'[4]

It is the same need to inscribe the authorial persona which underlies the pseudo-ethnographic stance of this short story, which exhibits all the symptoms of 'primitivist' discourse; marking a sharp division between the Western white observer and the native who turns into an object of curiosity and knowledge; deploying the tropology of mysticism and magic; setting up a participative relationship with nature; and presenting the native hero as emotional, childlike, and untamed.[5] The narrative

[3] Frederic Jameson, 'Romance and Reification', in *The Political Unconscious* (London: Methuen, 1981), 206–80.

[4] *A Personal Record* (1908; London: Dent, 1923), 14. The earliest study of Conrad's need to manufacture and manage a public persona for himself through his fiction is Edward Said's *Joseph Conrad and the Fiction of Autobiography* (Cambridge, Mass.: Harvard University Press, 1966).

[5] For a detailed study of primitivist discourse, see Marianna Torgovnick, *Gone Primitive* (Chicago: University of Chicago Press, 1990). Torgovnick takes Conrad to

throughout the text insists on the motionless, timeless quality of the setting. The scenery is a finished painting, framed, static, unchanging. It is as though the story takes place in some mythical region beyond history, beyond the experience of the white observer or that of the reader.

The forests, sombre and dull, stood motionless and silent on each side of the broad stream . . . bunches of leaves enormous and heavy, that hung unstirring. . . . in the stillness of the air every tree, every leaf, every bough, every tendril of creeper and every petal of minute blossoms seemed to have been bewitched into an immobility perfect and final'. (187)

The local people, presented through what appears to be free, indirect discourse, are universalized stereotypes of primitive 'natives'. Their discourse is made up of aphorisms and ready-made formulas of superstition:

They disliked Arsat, first as a stranger, and also because he who repairs a ruined house, and dwells in it, proclaims that he is not afraid to live amongst the spirits that haunt the places abandoned by mankind. Such a man can disturb the course of fate by glances or words . . . white men care not for such things, being unbelievers and in league with the Father of Evil, who leads them unharmed through the invisible dangers of this world. To the warnings of the righteous they oppose an offensive pretence of disbelief. (190)

Though supposedly different from the local people by virtue of his strangeness, their hostility, and his friendship with the white man, Arsat is, in fact, as faceless as the other natives, unindividuated, entirely true to type. The same stilted, wooden quality of rhetoric is evident in Arsat's brief dialogue with the white man and in his account of his life-story.

task for what she claims is 'a cheat'. Writing of *Heart of Darkness* she argues that 'the novella wants to have it both ways: to criticize language and yet to take refuge in the gorgeousness of Conrad's own language . . . [which] is finally unable to transcend the very western values it attacks.' (153). Conrad's tropes, she claims, 'convey only stale, familiar ideas about Africa and the west's relation to it. The words flirt with a radical critique of certain western values, but stop short. *Heart of Darkness*, like Marlow, goes only so far' (154). Torgovnick points to the substitution of 'female' for 'primitive' in Conrad's work, and to the circularity between these concepts, which, she argues, is symptomatic of Western thinking, and argues, rightly, I believe, that 'the west's fascination with the primitive has to do with its own crises of identity, with its own need to clearly demarcate subject and object even while flirting with other ways of experiencing the universe' (157).

But the narrative is not only cliché-ridden and stilted: it becomes downright offensive in the description of the relationship between the unnamed white man and the native: 'he liked the man who knew how to keep faith in council and how to fight without fear by the side of his white friend. He liked him—not so much perhaps as a man likes his favourite dog—but still he liked him well enough to help and ask no questions to think sometimes vaguely and hazily in the midst of his own pursuits, about the lonely man and the long-haired woman' (191–2). Even the form of sympathy which the white man is said to feel for Arsat is abstract, impersonal, and diffuse, dissolving into empty grand rhetoric:

the fear and fascination, the inspiration and the wonder of death—of death near, unavoidable, and unseen, soothed the unrest of his race and stirred the most indistinct, the most intimate of his thoughts. . . . In that fleeting and powerful disturbance of his being the earth enfolded in the starlight peace became a shadowy country of inhuman strife, a battle-field of phantoms terrible and charming, august or ignoble, struggling ardently for the possession of our helpless hearts. An unquiet and mysterious country of inextinguishable desires and fears. (193–4)

Apart from that vague, abstract, emotional stirring at the proximity of death, there is no real exchange between these two men, and no concrete, individuated response to the other in his grief. The white man remains an observer, impervious to ghosts and superstitions, unable to feel with the other, securely fastened in his armour of 'unbelief'.

An enclave of exoticism with its *National Geographic* glossiness, a realm of magic and illusion, constituted by an archaic and alien discourse—'The Lagoon' is a spectacle for the entertainment of the observing (imperial, white, male) reading/writing/narrating subject, who thus secures a stable sense of his own subjectivity against that exotic foil. Otherness is bounded and framed, cordoned off, as it were.[6] It is the same strategy which

---

[6] In traditional ethnographic writing, too, the other is described as a 'stable, changeless and typified entity which act[s] as a permanent foil for English identity and English selves . . . . . the predominant metaphors in anthropological writing and the prominent practices in terms of the activity of anthropology—participant observation, systematic data collection, cultural description—all imply a process of looking at, examining, "objectifying" and "collecting". This visualism . . . the voyeurism, the act of looking, is, of course, the act of othering'. Henrietta Moore, 'Master Narratives: Anthropology and Writing', in *What is an Author?* ed. Maurice Biriotti and Nicola Miller (Manchester: Manchester University Press, 1993), 191–213, at 208.

becomes evident in 'real' contemporary ethnographic accounts, as studied by Henrietta Moore, where the topography of self and other is 'thoroughly textualized, based on Victorian "Boy's Own" stories; where the central theme is that of "a heroic white man penetrating a dark continent at great personal risk", drawing on images of quest, adventure, and control';[7] where the relationship between 'self' and 'other' in such discursive practices is typically marked by the fear of 'going native'. That underlying fear, writes Moore, is 'ultimately a fear about the erasure of difference, and in that erasure the loss of self. The self constitutes and defines itself through the "detour of the other", and for this process to take place the other must exist and, if it does not exist, it must be created. Crudely put, stable selves require stable others. The instability of self and other accounts for the sense of vulnerability and panic which characterizes anthropological fieldwork for many anthropologists'.[8]

The symptomatic nature of 'The Lagoon' tells much about the desire of the authoring subject. It is the same paradigm which structures the relationship 'within' the story, between the white man and Arsat; on the borderlines of the story, between the narrative voice and that native otherness; and 'outside' the text, between the author and his work. Conrad's descriptive tactics, his use of the disembodied narrative voice, his quasi-anthropological stance, his deployment of primitivist tropes, and the fixed otherness of the scene with its motionless, lush exoticism, can be read as an attempt to construct a public persona through a project of 'othering'. Delineating the boundary lines between 'us' and 'them', the narrative firmly inserts the authorial figure in his position as the subject who knows when it posits the other as 'a good object of knowledge, the docile body of difference'.[9] Needless to say, the transferability of the paradigm invalidates the notion of inside and outside.

---

[7] Moore, 'Master Narratives', 198. For references of related interest, see Brian W. Shaffer, *The Blinding Torch: Modern British Discourse and the Discourse of Civilization* (Amherst: University of Massachusetts Press, 1993); John W. Griffith, *Joseph Conrad and the Anthropological Dilemma* (Oxford: Oxford University Press, 1995). Griffith notes Conrad's relatedness to contemporary anthropological writing, and to the work of his friend Hugh Clifford, himself a travel writer and author of ethnographic fiction, but does not go beyond Clifford's observations, and does not mention 'The Lagoon' or 'Karain'. [8] Moore, 'Master Narratives', 199.
[9] Homi Bhabha, *The Location of Culture* (London: Routledge, 1994), 31.

Nothing would have been easier for Conrad than to make a home for himself in that quasi-ethnographic mode of adventure writing. He did not.[10] Putting away the good old steel pen with which 'The Lagoon' was written, he had chosen, in fact, to discard the logic of cloning, of sameness, of absolute self-identity. The cultural anxiety, compounded by the author's underlying private fear of psychic dissolution, is certainly there, but Conrad's mature work, which is, in fact, a proto-deconstructive subversion of the very possibility of self-definition, offers very little by way of compensation. Its main interest lies not in its therapeutic function (which would have been the case if we could read it as a solid articulation of subjectivity), but in its persistent failure of articulation. Conrad's figural excess did not fully abate in his subsequent work, but rather than an authorial signature, a synecdoche for the presumed 'whole Conrad', it became a strategy for the blurring of boundary lines between the observing subject and the observed other, between civilization and savagery, between culture and nature, between self and other. *Heart of Darkness*, with its notorious adjectival insistence, is structured—or destructured—precisely on this dissolution of boundary lines. Written only three years after 'The Lagoon', it is as far as writing can get from the neat enclosure of otherness which marked the short story.

In his reading of *Heart of Darkness* in relation to ethnographic writing, James Clifford notes the biographical and temperamental resemblance between Conrad and Bronislaw Malinowski, the founder of 'modern anthropology'.[11] Both were displaced Poles 'condemned by historical contingency to a cosmopolitan European identity; both pursued ambitious writing careers in England. . . . the two exiles shared a peculiarly Polish cultural distance, having been born into a nation that had since the eighteenth century existed only as a fiction—but an intensely believed, serious fiction—of collective identity.'[12] Clifford focuses on Malinowski's *Trobriand Diary*, written while he was in the field,

[10] For a study of Conrad's position within this generic context, I would refer the reader to Andrea White's *Joseph Conrad and the Adventure Tradition* (Cambridge: Cambridge University Press, 1993).

[11] James Clifford, 'On Ethnographic Self-Fashioning: Conrad and Malinowski', in *The Predicament of Culture: 20th Century Ethnography, Literature, and Art* (Cambridge, Mass. Harvard University Press, 1988), 92–113.

[12] Clifford, *The Predicament of Culture*, 98.

collecting material for the ground-breaking *Argonauts of the Western Pacific*, but discovered only after his death in 1967. The *Diary*, documenting the author's anxiety in his encounter with the primitive other, his hostility towards his 'subjects', his sexual ambivalence, and the precariousness of his own sense of identity, shattered the public persona Malinowski had projected successfully throughout his career. There is, perhaps, no better testimonial to Conrad's presence in Malinowski's diary, which often echoes or explicitly quotes *Heart of Darkness*, than the last words of this painful private document—'truly, I have no character at all'—which might have been written by Conrad as well.[13]

Both Conrad and Malinowski were therefore particularly vulnerable to situations of cultural liminality, but Malinowski never did become 'the Conrad of anthropology'. The *Trobriand Diary*, read by Clifford as the torn-off supplement of Kurtz's report—'both an act of censorship and of meaning creation, a suppression of incoherence and contradiction'—is, after all, a private document, not meant for the readers who had valorized this figurehead of modern anthropology.[14] This sense of avoidance is angrily and beautifully described by Marianna Torgovnick, who argues that 'The Malinowski of the Diary understands fully the universe of transcendental homelessness—and the furious desire for the primitive it helps to produce,' but 'the Malinowski of the published ethnographies surveys the world with cool authority; it is his home, his oyster, cradling pearls of wisdom.'[15] Malinowski could not go as far as Conrad, his model, did twenty years earlier; he could not openly recognize his own writing as a process of 'fictional self-fashioning'.[16] It is only when we realize how high the stakes were, how psychically dangerous such a recognition might have been, that we can fully appreciate the kind of courage it took for Conrad to move from 'The Lagoon' to *Heart of*

---

[13] Geoffrey Galt Harpham has followed Clifford's line and taken it a step further, claiming that 'Conrad's Polish experience . . . the experience of dominating and being dominated, of being implicated in power on both sides' which had given him 'singular access to a position of . . . [what Homi Bhabha calls] "hybridity" outside of and beneath the dualism of same and other, a non-position founded on discontinuity, heteroglossia, and non-fixity.' *One of Us: The Mastery of Joseph Conrad* (Chicago: The University of Chicago Press, 1996), 49–50.

[14] Clifford, *The Predicament of Culture*, 96, 112.

[15] Torgovnick, *Gone Primitive*, 231.

[16] Clifford, *The Predicament of Culture*, 110.

Darkness. 'Karain' can be read as a turning-point, a deconstruction of the logic of sameness and identity on which its ostensible prototype is premised.

As in the best of Conrad's fiction, the focus of the text is not on its ostensible 'kernel'—i.e. the protagonist's story of brotherhood, betrayal, and guilt—but on the dynamics of storytelling. What makes 'Karain' so interesting (or strange, in the terms of this study) against the neat enclosure of otherness in 'The Lagoon', is the unresolved tension between two perceptual sets or spheres: the island and the schooner; the stage and the real world; superstition and rationality; East and West. The narrator's attempt to privilege his own perceptual system, to contain the other within the realm of the exotic, the mythical, or the theatrical, is constantly thwarted as his Western, rational, realistic, perceptual orbit is constantly breached.[17] It is this invasion of otherness, when the boundary lines between self and other begin to crack, which energizes the story and turns it into an important landmark on Conrad's way to *Heart of Darkness,* as he first steps out of the stagnant safety of 'The Lagoon' into the troubled waters of Modernism.

Most clearly, the two perceptual spheres are demarcated in space: Karain's kindgom on land and the white men's schooner at sea. Karain himself occupies a liminal position in between: having been chief of the stockade at the 'mouth of the river' (29), he had dealt with the Dutch traders in the past, and can now negotiate with the British white men who are his friends. He too makes the distinction between the two spheres: the schooner serves him as a haven of 'unbelief', impermeable to the ghost which haunts him. When the crisis finally breaks, he saves himself

---

[17] In *Joseph Conrad and the Fiction of Skepticism* (Stanford, Ca.: Stanford University Press, 1990), Mark A. Wollaeger notes the perceptual division in the story and the fact that the narrator 'ultimately ignores everything that conflicts with his established construction of the world. He prefers . . . to attribute his more unusual impressions to moments of imaginative vision, which he can then dismiss as mere fancy. In this he remains blind to the further significance of the central fact that it is Karain's imaginative transformation of the coin that restores his equilibrium', and that 'the boundaries defined by "superstition" break down' as the story unfolds (48). However, Wollaeger treats this division as a dialogue between 'skepticism' and 'belief' and confines the conflict to the epistemological level. I would argue that what we have here goes much further than the question of whether or not one believes in the supernatural; that what makes the story so interesting is the isomorphic relationship between the cracks in the narrator's resistance and the current of authorial subjectivity.

by crossing the boundary into their sphere: 'I came here . . . I leaped out of my stockade as after a defeat' (24). The leap out of the stockade, reiterated later in the story, will echo later in *Lord Jim*. In both these works it is a willed transformation of identity through a transition to a different perceptual sphere, closely related to the 'exilic' state of the authorial subject.[18] The ghost cannot come into the white men's sphere: 'He cannot come here—therefore I sought you. You men with white faces who despise the invisible voices. He cannot abide your unbelief and your strength' (24). But even as he seeks asylum, acknowledging the power of Western rationality, there is an edge of contempt in his address: 'your people who live in unbelief; to whom day is day, and night is night—nothing more, because you understand all things seen, and despise all else! To your land of unbelief, where the dead do not speak, where every man is wise, and alone—and at peace!' (44).

Time too appears to signify differently in these two spheres. Against the mythical, timeless quality of the invading presence, the narrator recalls the reassuring tick of the chronometers in the cabin: 'the silence became so profound that we could distinctly hear the chronometers in my cabin ticking along with unflagging speed against one another' (23); 'We three white men, looking at the Malay, could not find one word to the purpose amongst us—if indeed there existed a word that could solve the problem. . . . And then again there was a silence, the feeble flash of water, the steady tick of chronometers' (45). As we shall see, these chronometers, marking Western Greenwich time, are not powerful enough to serve as a barrier against that other mode of perception.

The very first sentences of the story undermine the traditionally authoritative position of the narrator: 'We knew him in those

---

[18] Writing on Jim's famous 'leap' from the deck of the *Patna*, identified by many readers as symbolic of Conrad's emigration from 'Partia', or Poland, Harpham notes that the actual leap does not occur before the reader's eyes. It is a kind of 'chasm' in the text. Conrad, Harpham argues, 'was drawn to jumping as a form of action that took the form of a gap' (*One of Us*, 58). Michael Seidel notes that 'The word *exile* derives from *ex* ("out of") and the Latin root *salire* ("to leap"). . . . Joseph Conrad understood this intuitively when as a young man he made what he called his exilic "jump": "I verily believe mine was the only case of a boy of my nationality and antecedents taking a, so to speak, standing jump out of his racial surroundings and associations." [*A Personal Record*, London: Dent, 1923, 121]. The experience split him in two, made him, as he put it, into "Homo duplex," a sailor and a writer whose extraterritorial perspective worked to sooth his exilic conscience.' *Exile and the Narrative Imagination* (New Haven and London: Yale University Press, 1986), 1.

unprotected days when we were content to hold in our hands our lives and our property.' One would expect a distinction between those days and the narrative present to follow, leading to a state of relative security and prosperity which is the traditional vantage-point of reminiscences. But what follows is: 'None of us, I believe, has any property now, and I fear that many, negligently, have lost their lives' (3). If anything, it seems that the position of the narrator and his friends has now become more precarious. This initial paradox undermines the traditional assumption of the 'wisdom of the storyteller', subverting the authority of the narrator, who presents himself as a kind of failure. The line of demarcation between this anecdote of the narrator's distant youth and the narrative present is also blurred by the very literal invasion of the Malay scenery into the newspaper print: 'The few who survive are not yet so dim-eyed as to miss in the befogged respect-ability of their newspapers the intelligence of various native risings in the Eastern Archipelago. Sunshine gleams between the lines of those short paragraphs . . . the printed words scent the smoky atmosphere of today faintly' (3). The characters and lines of newspaper print—the processed, cerebral, hollowed-out render-ing of experience—seem to evaporate against the sensual reality of that episode.

Throughout the story, the narrative stance seems to waver between unqualified adoration for the hero and amused scepti-cism; between a willing suspension of disbelief at Karain's magni-ficent regal performance and an urge to expose and flatten the show by cutting Karain down to his 'real' size. The natives are initially described as an undifferentiated mass of faces, bronzed bodies, variegated colours of sarongs and turbans. Karain appears like a deity, not physically described but circumscribed by his people's adoration: 'They were Karain's people—a devoted following. Their movements hung on his lips; they read their thoughts in his eyes; he murmured to them nonchalantly of life and death, and they accepted his words humbly, like gifts of fate.' Immediately afterwards, however, the narrative plunges into irony, deflating the deified description through the use of parallel syntactic structure: 'He was the ruler of three villages on a narrow plain; the master of an insignificant foothold on the earth—of a conquered foothold that, shaped like a young moon, lay ignored between the hills and the sea' (4).

From this point onwards the narrator's description of Karain and his kingdom is steeped in theatrical imagery, insisting on the ficticiousness and unreality of it all. But the narrator's ironic position is not quite secure. In spite of himself, he seems to be drawn into Karain's show, collapsing the precious distinction between appearance and reality, between the primitive hero's illusion and the Westerner's knowledge of facts:

It was the stage where, dressed splendidly for his part, he strutted, incomparably dignified, made important by the power he had to awaken an absurd expectation of something heroic going to take place. . . . . He was ornate and disturbing . . . he presented himself essentially as an actor, as a human being aggressively disguised. His smallest acts were prepared and unexpected, his speeches grave, his sentences ominous like hints and complicated like arabesques. He was treated with the solemn respect accorded in the irreverent West only to the monarchs of the stage, and he accepted the profound homage with a sustained dignity seen nowhere else but behind the footlights and in the condensed falseness of some grossly tragic situation. It was almost impossible to remember who he was—only a petty thief of a conveniently isolated corner of Mindannao, where we could in comparative safety break the law against the traffic in firearms and ammunition with the natives. (6–7)

There seems to be a series of about-faces here regarding the narrator's position: from ironic amusement at Karain's theatrical bearing to a reluctant admission of its power over the spectators; from a mocking reference to the stage and the footlights, back to an admission of being swept by the illusion; from a reminder of who Karain 'really' is (not a king but a petty thief) to a casual revelation of the narrator's own less than respectable position as a gunrunner.

The very landscape appears to be part of the stage set for Karain's performance:

In many successive visits we came to know his stage well—the purple semicircle of hills, the slim trees leaning over houses, the yellow sands, the streaming green of ravines. All that had the crude and blended colouring, the appropriateness almost excessive, the suspicious immobility of a painted scene; and it enclosed so perfectly the accomplished acting of his amazing pretences that the rest of the world seemed shut out forever from the gorgeous spectacle'. (7)

But this is a far cry from the immobile lush exoticism of 'The Lagoon'. A layer of irony seems to separate the narrator's voice from the narrative description, a sense of uncomfortable self-consciousness closely related to the initial ambivalence of the narrative stance. Nature itself seems to collaborate in the creation of what the narrator insists is a mere spectacle or illusion: 'he summed up his race, his country, the elemental force of ardent life, of tropical nature' (7). 'He appeared utterly cut off from everything but the sunshine, and that even seemed to be made for him alone' (8).[19]

As in 'The Lagoon', the narrative is completely uninhibited in its use of the pathetic fallacy. If anything, it becomes overwhelmingly powerful here. By the end of the narrative, the elements themselves seem to echo Karain's state of mind. The crisis is announced by storm signals: 'The afternoon was sultry. Ragged edges of black clouds peeped over the hills, and invisible thunderstorms circled outside, growling like wild beasts' (20). Karain's breakdown is accompanied by the outbreak of the storm: 'Before sunset the growling clouds carried with a rush the ridge of hills, and came tumbling down the inner slopes. Everything disappeared; black whirling vapours filled the bay, and in the midst of them the schooner swung here and there in the shifting gusts of wind' (21); and his eventual recovery coincides with the clearing of the weather: 'the sun had risen beyond the hills, and their long shadows stretched far over the bay in the pearly light. The air was clear, stainless, and cool' (51). But the 'participative' quality of the relationship between man and nature is no longer an alienating feature of another perceptual sphere; it seems to be part of a power which the white narrator will eventually have to recognize outside the orbit of his cultivated rational position.

Obtuse as he is, the narrator cannot sustain his superior pose of Western scepticism, and his initially grudging aesthetic appreciation of what he insists is Karain's 'performance' gradually

---

[19] Christopher Gogwilt, who reads 'Karain' as a 'deeply disturbing and unsettling experience of crossed cultural purposes', rightly notes 'the complexity of Conrad's construction of a sentimental retrospective point of view striving to achieve the effect of a simple tale of adventure' and the 'self-consciousness about the artificiality of the exoticism in the narrator's account', suggesting that 'it is this exaggeration that introduces the details that disorient the exotic scene. The landscape is too composed'. *The Invention of the West* (Stanford, Ca: Stanford University Press, 1995), 46, 48.

dissolves against his genuine admiration of the man's real stature and power. Though still couched in theatrical imagery, the description shifts to a different mode. The narrative voice seems to be taken over by native rhetoric at this point, describing Karain's virtues in terms more appropriate to epic panegyrics than to the reality principle on which the narrator pretends to operate.

He gave them wisdom, advice, rewards, punishment, life or death, with the same serenity of attitude and voice. He understood irrigation and the art of war—the qualities of weapons and the craft of boat-building. He could conceal his heart; had more endurance; he could swim longer, and steer a canoe better than any of his people; he could shoot straighter, and negotiate more tortuously than any man of his race I knew. He was an adventurer of the sea, an outcast, a ruler—and my very good friend. I wish him a quick death in a stand-up fight, a death in sunshine; for he had known remorse and power, and no man can demand more from life. Day after day he appeared before us incomparably faithful to the illusions of the stage, and at sunset the night descended on him quickly like a falling curtain. (8–9)

Questions of subjectivity seem to mushroom in the process of the narrative. Is self-perception or the perception of others constitutive of subjectivity? Is there a kernel of subjectivity apart from one's appearance to others? Is self-definition determined by a definition of or by the other? Like other Conrad characters, the narrator protests too much.

As the deconstructive process goes on, the narrator's stance is further eroded. Karain believes, or pretends to believe, that the white men are actually more respectable than they appear to be, delegates of their Queen rather than gunrunners. 'I fancy that to the last he believed us to be emissaries of Government, darkly official persons furthering by our illegal traffic some dark scheme of high statecraft. Our denials and protestations were unavailing' (12). Like previous distinctions between appearance and reality, the opposition between state emissaries and gunrunners becomes much weaker when one realizes later that the illegal traffic is, in fact, run by 'respectable people sitting safely in counting houses' (19). The ideological implications of this collapsed distinction will become more explicit in the narrator's ambiguous preface to Marlow's account of the journey into the heart of darkness, when he recalls 'all the men of whom the nation is proud, from Sir Francis Drake to Sir John Franklin, knights all, titled and untitled—the

great knights-errant of the sea. . . . Hunters for gold or pursuers
of fame, they had all gone out on that stream, bearing the sword,
and often the torch, messengers of the might within the land,
bearers of a spark from the sacred fire' (*Heart of Darkness*, 53–4).

Initially, the narrator's grudging admiration and real affection
for Karain is hedged by racial condescension: 'We came to like
him, to trust him, almost to admire him. He was plotting and
preparing a war with patience, with foresight—with a fidelity to
his purpose and with a steadfastness of which I would have
thought him racially incapable. He seemed fearless of the future,
and in his plans displayed a sagacity that was only limited by his
profound ignorance of the rest of the world. We tried to enlighten
him, but our attempts . . . failed to discourage his eagerness to
strike a blow for his own primitive ideas.' Along the same lines, he
goes on to talk with contemptuous affection of Karain's 'childish
shrewdness', his 'absurd and unanswerable' replies, and his potential for falling prey to 'a concentrated lust of violence which is
dangerous in a native' (18). Shortly afterwards, however, that
racist edge is explicitly withdrawn: 'There are those who say
that a native will not speak to a white man. Error. No man will
speak to his master; but to a wanderer and a friend, to him who
does not come to teach or rule, to him who asks for nothing and
accepts all things, words are spoken by the camp-fires, in the
shared solitude of the sea, in riverside villages, in resting-places
surrounded by forests—words are spoken that take no account of
race or colour. One heart speaks—another one listens' (26). Even
more interesting than the explicit withdrawal is the kind of rhetoric which takes over the narrative. The urbane, amused, distant
voice of the narrator is transformed into the voice of the other,
with its biblical cadences, its syntactic appositions and parallels,
and its aphoristic tonality.

What the narrator fails to note is the fact that it is he and his
friends who provide the guns and the powder for the conflagration
which might be the ruin of their friend's little kingdom; they are
not essentially different from the Dutch traders who had taken
advantage of native wars to gain access to the land (28). When
Karain tells the white British people about those other white men,
presumably different from themselves, he expresses contempt for
the local people in Java, where 'every man you meet is a slave' and
'the rulers live under the edge of a foreign sword' (31). Telling

them of the initial failure of his pursuit of the Dutchman, he adds: 'these Dutchmen are all alike' (32). This inversion of the racist expression, usually heard from white people in reference to the colonized population, should give us pause. The narrator does not seem to realize that he and his friends are also potentially 'all alike' in the eyes of the local people; that they too ply their trade in the service of imperial interests; that the 'foreign sword' may well be theirs.[20]

Clearly, then, the narrator is not a privileged listener. Though singled out by Karain by virtue of his past experience in this part of the world, it is not he but Hollis, the youngest man, who reaches out to the other. When Karain appears in the schooner, soaking wet and wild-eyed, in the midst of the storm which rages over both perceptual spheres, it is Hollis who says: 'give him a dry sarong—give him mine; it's hanging up in the bathroom' (22). The fact that Hollis should wear the native garment and offer his sarong to Karain immediately puts him in a better position to understand the other man. He obviously does not need to set up barriers of culturally marked apparel between himself and the other; his offer of a sarong is a token of recognition; he accepts the other on the other's terms (22). Not surprisingly, it is Hollis who responds to the native's rather contemptuous description of the white people in apparent agreement: '"Capital description," murmured Hollis with the flicker of a smile' (44).

At the end of the story, it is Hollis who seems to empathize most powerfully with Karain's state of mind, while Jackson looks aside, and the narrator positions himself as an observer, listening again to the reassuring ticking of his Western time:

He moved not. He stared fixedly past the motionless head of Hollis, who faced him, as still as himself. Jackson had turned sideways, and with elbow on the table shaded his eyes with the palm of his hand. And I looked on, surprised and moved; I looked at that man, loyal to a vision,

[20] Jeremy Hawthorn has treated the reversal of the gaze in the story and the movement 'from an objectifying and one-way looking *by* Europeans *at* natives to a reciprocal and intimate exchange of looks'. The most significant point is that 'those guns which surround Jackson's gaze [in the last episode of the story, when the white men stand in front of the shop window of a firearms merchant] suggest that imperialism decides what is *real* and what is *illusory* by means of force. The gaze of the European comes accompanied by the power of weaponry.' 'Power and Perspective in Joseph Conrad's Political Fiction: The Gaze and the Other', a paper given at the Joseph Conrad Conference in Potchefstroom and Capetown, South Africa, April 1998, 15–16.

betrayed by his dream, spurned by his illusion, and coming to us unbelievers for help—against a thought. The silence was profound; but it
seemed full of noiseless phantoms, of things sorrowful, shadowy, and
mute, in whose invisible presence the firm, pulsating beat of the two
ship's chronometers ticking off steadily the seconds of Greenwich Time
seemed to me a protection and a relief. (40)

Even the narrator's genuine sympathy for the other man's plight
takes the form of cultural exclusion: 'It was evident that he had
been hunted by this thought along the very limit of human
endurance, and very little more pressing was needed to make
him swerve over into the form of madness peculiar to his race'
(45). When Karain resentfully rejects his advice to 'live and
forget', the narrator cannot go beyond his own sense of reality:
'It was amazing. To him his life—that cruel mirage of love and
peace—seemed as real, as undeniable, as theirs would be to any
saint, philosopher, or fool of us all.' Again, it is Hollis who takes
the other's viewpoint: '"You won't soothe him with your
platitudes"' (44).

It is in the final act of redemption performed by Hollis, presented in the narrative as an amusing if cheap trick played on a
superstitious native, that the two perceptual spheres eventually
clash. The apparently paradoxical construction of the act as 'no
play' and Hollis's request of his friends to 'lie a little' is less of an
oxymoron than it seems (46). Producing a gilt Jubilee sixpence
stamped with the Queen's image, Hollis says: '"A charm for our
friend. . . . The thing itself is of great power—money, you
know—and his imagination is struck."' He then turns to Karain
with a deliberately ambivalent reference to the Imperial power:
'"This is the image of the Great Queen, and the most powerful
thing the white men know. . . . She commands a spirit, too—the
spirit of her nation; a masterful, conscientious, unscrupulous,
unconquerable devil . . . that does a lot of good—incidentally.
. . . a lot of good . . . at times—and wouldn't stand any fuss
from the best ghost out for such a little thing as our friend's
shot"' (49–50).

If the act is indeed 'no play', then what we have here is a
conception of value very different from our habitual notions. To
understand its significance we should turn for a moment to the
work of Georg Simmel, a cultural philosopher and Conrad's contemporary. In an essay written in 1907, Simmel defines exchange

as 'the purest and most concentrated form of all human inter-
actions', which enacts 'the economic realization of the relativity of
things'. The conception of value, on which every mode of
exchange is predicated, is a thoroughly relative one, entirely determined by cultural systems. Even more pertinent is Simmel's
concept of value as produced by sacrifice: 'Economic value as
such does not inhere in an object in its isolated self-existence,
but comes to an object only through the expenditure of another
object which is given for it.' The value of an object in any human
transaction is therefore determined by the sacrifice required to
obtain it. [21]

Hollis's lie is not a lie. If we do not fetishize the coin as an
object whose value inheres in itself but view it instead as a token
of value within a cultural system, we should realize that it is,
indeed, the 'most powerful thing white men know'. But it is not
merely the relativization of culture which is at stake here. If the
value of an object is determined by the magnitude of the sacrifice
it entails for the person aiming to obtain it, as Simmel suggests,
Hollis himself makes a move into a different economy, an economy
of gift-giving, when he parts with the silk ribbon and the piece of
leather, both evidently gifts of love from the girl he has left back
home, saying: '"I'll give him something I'll really miss"' (50).
Hollis's gift, whose value inheres in the sacrifice of the *giver*, is
magnificent indeed. It may well be the container—the little
leather pouch tied with the silk ribbon—rather than the thing
contained which makes the charm so potent for Karain.

Hollis's gesture is a symbolic redemption of his Malay friend
primarily in that it restructures the relationship and relativizes the

---

[21] Georg Simmel, 'Exchange' (1907), in *On Invividuality and Social Forms*, ed.
Donald N. Levine (Chicago and London: University of Chicago Press, 1971), 43–69,
at 43, 69, 54. Writing of Simmel's work in relation to Adam Smith's *The Wealth of
Nations*, Christopher Herbert pursues the implications of this conception: 'Once such
a schema is established, value can never again be conceptualized and fetishized as a
positive term, but only taken as a contingent and indeterminate one, subject to
potentially endless interpretation; and desire by the same token can no longer signify
a direct psychological grappling of individuals onto tangible realities but only a
phenomenon of a system of symbolic relations. Value always depends on one's point
of vantage and is impossible to grasp except as a conventionalized fiction of a particular
social system. . . . There is no way to pry value apart from the symbolic medium which
represents it in a given culture. It has no other existence.' *Culture and Anomie:
Ethnographic Imagination in the Nineteenth Century* (Chicago: University of Chicago
Press, 1991), 96.

positions of these men, exposing the underlying likeness of their ostensibly separate spheres: '"every one of us, you'll admit, has been haunted by some woman . . . And . . . as to friends . . . dropped by the way . . . Well! . . . ask yourselves"' (47).[22] The sight of the box with Hollis's tokens of love—the girl's portrait, the silk ribbon, the narrow white glove, the dried flowers, the letter—is powerful enough to move the narrator out of his entrenched Western scepticism: 'Amulets of white men! Charms and talismans! Charms that keep them straight, that drive them crooked, that have the power to make a young man sigh, an old man smile. Potent things that procure dreams of joy, thoughts of regret; that soften hard hearts, and can temper a soft one to the hardness of steel. Gift of heaven—things of earth' (48). Again we should note that as he acknowledges the resemblance, the narrator unconsciously slides into what has been presented as the native idiom.

Their gunrunning days over, the narrator and his friends go back home, back to the security of their own perceptual sphere, where illusion and reality can presumably be told apart. But this sense of security is invaded again a few years later, when the narrator accidentally meets his old mate Jackson in London. This time the encounter takes place at the very heart of Western civilization. Jackson is as 'magnificent as ever' with his head 'high above the crowd' (53). Stopping before the shop window of a firearms merchant, with his face near the glass, Jackson recalls the story of Karain. At that moment, it is not his friend's reflection that the narrator sees in the glass but that of 'another man, powerful and bearded, peering at him intently from amongst the dark and polished tubes that can cure so many illusions' (53–4).[23]

It is Jackson, who seems to have taken on Karain's features and his aura of magnificence, who brings up the question of reality and illusion:

[22] Hollis's gesture is also a an act of redemption in that it symbolically reverses the act of his Malay friend. Karain had betrayed Pata Matara for the sake of a woman— Hollis gives up a precious object related to heterosexual love for the sake of male camaraderie. I would agree with Harpham, who has dealt with the transition from homosociality to homoeroticism in Conrad's work more explicitly and convincingly than any other reader I know, but this is beyond the scope of the present discussion.

[23] The reverberation of this ambiguous reflection in *Heart of Darkness* (London: Dent Uniform Edition, 1923, 156) is not incidental.

'I wonder whether the charm worked—you remember Hollis's charm, of course. If it did . . . never was a sixpence wasted to better advantage. Poor devil! I wonder whether he got rid of that friend of his. Hope so. . . . Do you know, I sometimes think that—'

I stood still and looked at him.

'Yes . . . I mean, whether the thing was so, you know . . . whether it really happened to him. . . . What do you think?'

'My dear chap,' I cried, 'you have been too long away from home. What a question to ask. Only look at all this.' (54)

Holding on to his sense of reality as tenaciously as ever, the narrator still cannot accept the suggestion that his mode of perception, his own kernel of subjectivity as that of an 'unbeliever', is less solid than he would like it to be. Trying to make Jackson face 'reality', he points to the busy streets around them:

The broken confusion of roofs, the chimney-stacks, the gold letters sprawling over the fronts of houses, the sombre polish of windows, stood resigned and sullen under the falling gloom. . . . Innumerable eyes stared straight in front, feet moved hurriedly, blank faces flowed, arms swung. Over all, a narrow ragged strip of smoky sky wound about between the high roofs, extended and motionless, like a soiled streamer flying above the rout of a mob. (54–5)

But Jackson refuses to be drawn in: ' "I'll be hanged if it is yet as real to me as. . . . as the other thing . . . say, Karain's story." ' (55). The narrator, as obtuse as ever, opts for a sarcastic dismissal of the other man's conversion: 'I think decidedly, he had been too long away from home' (55).

Conrad too had been away from home, 'away' in the most fundamental sense possible. Having turned exile into a mode of being and writing, he was particularly vulnerable to the question of culture and subjectivity, and his writing at its best articulates this essential homelessness through a process of relativization, which is as relevant to the author as it is to his characters. Following our reading of the two stories 'against' each other, we should now go back to the nexus of writing and subjectivity, the isomorphic relationship which operates throughout Conrad's work. The shift from 'The Lagoon' to 'Karain'—or rather, the demolition of the former by the latter—can be read as a paradigm shift, a transition from the realm of sameness and identity to the realm of alterity, which is analogous to what we have described earlier as the dynamics of 'heterobiography'.

The tale told by the native to the white man in both these texts is a story of fratricide, a betrayal which leads to the death of a close friend or brother for the sake of a woman who remains inaccessible. The betrayer then becomes a fugitive, persecuted by the ghostly presence of his own sense of guilt. The story is, in fact, a version of the Cain–Abel theme, an enduring cultural myth which runs through the cultural evolution of the West. The moral force of the theme, as Ricardo J. Quinones writes in his impressive historical study, lies in the fact that it addresses 'a breach in existence, a fracture at the heart of things'.[24]

Intrinsically the theme is devoted to presenting the stark and basic fact of division, division that is so unyielding as to become part of the essential matter of existence itself. . . . The fraternal context of the Cain–Abel story means that division becomes more emotionally vibrant as the tragedy of differentiation. Such differentiation is painfully realized at the moment of the offering, when one of the brothers has his essential nature endorsed over that of the other brother. The arbitrariness of preference thus compounds the tragedy of differentiation and brings home the fact of division in a way that is particular to the Cain–Abel theme. . . . Unity of whatever sort—familial, tribal, even personal—the virtual starting point of the theme, proves to be elusive and even illusory. However much we may wish them to be so, no two things can ever be equal. (9)

The sacrificed brother has thus greater possibilities for indicating a lost portion of the self, a self that is abandoned, sundered, the twin, the double, the shadowy other, the sacrificed other that must be gone and yet can never be gone.

As we have already noted, the betrayed and slain other—brother or best friend—in both these stories is perceived as an ideal version of the self, a paragon of masculinity:

There was no better paddler, no better steersman than my brother . . . there was no braver or stronger man in our country than my brother . . . he was strong. He was brave. He knew not fear and no fatigue . . . my brother! ('The Lagoon', 199)

[24] Ricardo J. Quinones, *The Changes of Cain: Violence and the Lost Brother in Cain and Abel Literature* (Princeton, NJ: Princeton University Press, 1991), 3, 9, 11, 12.

[Pata Matara] was great amongst us—one of those who were near my brother, the Ruler. He spoke in council, his courage was great, he was the chief of many villages. . . . When his sword was carried into a campong in advance of his coming, the maidens whispered wonderingly under the fruit-trees, the rich men consulted together in the shade, and a feast was made ready with rejoicing and songs. He had the favour of the Ruler and the affection of the poor. He loved war, deer hunts, and the charms of women. He was the possessor of jewels, of lucky weapons, and of men's devotion. He was a fierce man; and I had no other friend. ('Karain', 29)

As in the case of Abel, the innocent brother whose offering was accepted by God, the slain other is perceived as the better man; the betrayal is a denial of plenitude, of a wholeness and innocence of being. The crime of fratricide is directed at that sense of primal innocence, unity, or sameness. Cain's banishment is, therefore, the enactment of this breach or separation which is the condition of subjectivity. As Quinones says:

The Cain–Abel story is potent because it presents the first offering, the first venture out of the self, out of an undifferentiated and unconscious communion, and into an objective world. Brotherhood, where young innocence and communion are epitomized, will increase the pain of difference. The offering quite naturally then forms the first definition of character; it is a fundamental presentation of the self. How vulnerable the offerer is and how massively crushing can rejection be.

But the mythical subtext is not contained within the story—as in the case of *Under Western Eyes*, it boils over the edges of the narrative. 'Karain' relates to 'The Lagoon' as Cain does to Abel— it articulates the disruption of an illusory sameness; it opens up the boundary lines between self and other; it invalidates the desire of enclosed subjectivity. Indeed, it would seem that the Lacanian formulation of subjectivity can be modified and reinscribed through the biblical myth: the rejected offering marks the loss of the imaginary realm of unity and plenitude. The slaying of Abel is the inaugural moment of entry into the symbolic order. As human subjects we are all the descendants of Cain—it is not the quest with its teleological promise but the banishment which structures our mode of being.

It is the same moment which structures the psycho-textual dynamics of authorial subjectivity as well. Conrad's 'cloning tactics'—the 'will to style', the use of primitivist discourse, the quasi-ethnographic stance—were born out of the need to delineate his own authorial identity, to ratify it through repetition and reiteration, which are the guarantees of sameness. But *Homo Duplex* that he was, Conrad was at least subliminally aware of the duplicity, the *méconnaissance* entailed in any willed act of self-constitution and containment. His ultimate inability to clone his work, to become identical to the authorial persona of the exotic adventure writer, must have been fraught with the deepest anxiety. It is not a coincidence that *The Rescuer*, begun shortly after 'Karain', was not completed until twenty years later under a different title.[25] Whether or not it was Conrad's engagement with the sea which had provided him, as Geoffrey Harpham maintains, with 'a powerful model of such general concepts as the essential likeness of unlike things, the permeability of distinctions, the migration of identity as things become attached to or affiliated with their Others, the confusion of vision',[26] it is undoubtedly significant that crisis followed closely in the wake of an 'infernal' short story, as Conrad called it: not 'another' but an 'other' story, which had refused to guarantee its author's identity by becoming yet another literary clone.

As in the case of the biblical prototype and his literary progeny, the author has also sentenced himself to exile in the act of writing: having renounced the 'home' he had made for himself, where selfhood is securely framed and bounded, where the exotic other is fixed and knowable, he ultimately chose to leave the enclosure of 'The Lagoon' and began the long itinerary of a literary 'fugitive and vagabond', the voyage towards the heart of darkness which is the furthest away from any notional homecoming; from the secure posture of 'the subject who knows' to the much more precarious position of the subject in process, the subject who is always under erasure.

[25] *The Rescuer* was begun in March 1896, but completed as *The Rescue* only in 1919. [26] Harpham, *One of Us*, 102.

2

The Pathos of Authenticity

THE END, THAT sense of an ending which is the destination of all narrative, is the most appropriate beginning. In his essay on Henry James, Conrad wistfully comments on the 'usual methods of solution by rewards and punishments, by crowned love, by fortune, by a broken leg or a sudden death', which, he says, 'are legitimate inasmuch as they satisfy the desire for finality, for which our hearts yearn, with a longing greater than the longing for the loaves and the fishes of this earth. Perhaps the only true desire of mankind, coming thus to light in its hours of leisure, is to be set at rest.'[1] The desire for the end is not only the motor of narration. It is the incurable need for a final significance, appropriately related to the loaves and the fishes, and—just like them—no longer available in a secular world.

'Death,' says Walter Benjamin, 'is the sanction of everything that the storyteller can tell. He has borrowed his authority from death.' This startling claim is, in fact, quite close to Conrad's loaves and fishes:

The reader of the novels . . . [looks] for human beings from whom he derives the 'meaning of life.' Therefore he must, no matter what, know in advance that he will share their experience of death: if need be their figurative death—the end of the novel—but preferably their actual one. . . . The novel is significant, therefore, not because it presents someone else's fate to us, perhaps didactically, but because this stranger's fate by virtue of the flame which consumes it yields us the warmth which we never draw from our own fate. What draws the reader to the novel is the hope of warming his shivering life with a death he reads about.[2]

---

[1] Joseph Conrad, 'Henry James: an Appreciation' (1905), *Notes on Life and Letters* (London: Dent, 1924), 18–19.

[2] 'The Storyteller' (1936), in *Illuminations*, ed. and introd. Hannah Arendt, trans. Harry Zohn (London: Jonathan Cape, 1970), 101.

The structural dependence of narratives on that retrospective sense of significance and the Modernist 'crisis of closure' have been articulated in depth in the notable studies of Kermode, Brooks, and Ricoeur.[3] The invalidation of death—either figurative or literal—as a point of culmination which closes off the narrative of life and endows it with significance is a distinct feature of Modernist fiction. Its ethical open-endedness, the multiplicity of perspectives, voices, and judgements it offers, and its abdication of narrative authority may all be construed as forms of resistance to narrative closure. Kermode points to the tension between Reality, which is 'the sense we have of a world irreducible to human plot and human desire for order', and the ever-present need for significance which can only be answered by the imposition of 'narratives', of 'plots'. He writes of 'the need in a moment of existence to belong, to be related to a beginning and to an end', and suggests that it is the 'sense of an ending', immanent in every moment of our life, which endows it with fullness. In our need to live by a pattern rather than grope blindly in a reality which is entirely fragmented, contingent, and incoherent, 'we project ourselves . . . past the end, so as to see the structure whole, a thing we cannot do from our spot of time in the middle.'[4]

The Modernist narrative seems to have renounced the consolations of form and closure. 'Ends,' writes Peter Brooks, 'are no longer available.'[5] If the enormous narrative production of the nineteenth century, with its over-elaboration of and over-dependence on plots, may suggest an anxiety at the loss of a 'masterplot', the Modernist era is plagued by an intense suspicion and undermining of closural authority, an 'intense awareness of the epistemological and linguistic problems posed by story-telling.'[6] The structuring force of the end, the promise of a final coherence, give way to an acute self-consciousness, a subversion of narrative frames and boundaries and a mistrust of the predicative

---

[3] Cf. Frank Kermode, *The Sense of an Ending* (New York: Oxford University Press, 1967); Peter Brooks, *Reading for the Plot: Design and Intention in Narrative* (Oxford: Clarendon Press, 1984); Paul Ricoeur, *Time and Narrative*, vol. 2, trans. Kathleen McLaughlin and David Pellauer (Chicago: University of Chicago Press, 1984).

[4] *The Sense of an Ending*, 3, 8, 10. Kermode's recognition that even the writing of history involves 'the use of regulative fictions' and 'the imposition of plot on time' (43) has by now become, with the work of Hayden White and others, a cornerstone of contemporary historiography.   [5] Brooks, *Reading for the Plot*, 253.

[6] Ibid., 6–7, 236–7.

capacity of closure.[7] Problems of narrative closure seem to belong to an order of significance different from that of other Modernist strategies or 'devices', because narrative is, by definition, end-bound. Reading involves a process of 'retrospective patterning', a 'configurational act' which operates from the end backwards.[8] The very definition of plot—the concept of narrative—is inextricably bound to a sequential segmentation of events, with beginnings, middles, and ends, with causes and their effects, with a retroactive sense of coherence. The abdication of narrative closure—that form of resolution which creates a retrospective patterning of the whole—is tantamount to an abdication of the very essence of storytelling, of the very possibility of narrative significance. To paraphrase Ortega y Gasset, the theme of the Modernist narrative seems to be the collapse of narrativity.[9]

But narrative is not only a structure of aesthetic production. Narrativity is, as most Postmodernist thinkers have come to realize—paradoxically at the moment when all master-narratives have been invalidated—a cognitive structuring category of a Kantian magnitude. The very idea of selfhood, of a coherent sense of identity, is related to the possibility of narrativization:

We are forever telling stories about ourselves. In telling these self-stories to others we may, for most purposes, be said to be performing straightforward narrative actions. In saying that we also tell them to ourselves, however, we are enclosing one story within another. This is the story that there is a self to tell something to, a someone else serving as audience who is oneself or one's self. When the stories we tell others about ourselves concern these other selves of ours, when we say, for example,

---

[7] Ibid., 236–7, 253.

[8] See Barbara Herrnstein Smith, *Poetic Closure* (Chicago: University of Chicago Press, 1968); Paul Ricoeur, 'Narrative Time', in *On Narrative*, ed. W. J. T. Mitchell (Chicago: University of Chicago Press, 1981), 165–86.

[9] Like most such neat critical formulations, the above proposition is not entirely accurate. As the literary genre which is most closely related, historically and culturally, to Modernity, the novel has never really had an unproblematic relationship with reality. However, even among scholars who have rightly insisted on the need to qualify the assumption of a radical break between the nineteenth-century and the Modernist novel, there seems to be a fairly wide consensus that the narrative assumptions of fiction, particularly those concerned with framing and closure, did indeed change at the turn of the century. See Marianna Torgovnick, *Closure in the Novel* (Princeton NJ: Princeton University Press, 1981); D. A. Miller, *Narrative and Its Discontents: Problems of Closure in the Traditional Novel* (Princeton, NJ: Princeton University Press, 1981); Michael Bell, 'How Primordial is Narrative?' in *Narrative in Culture*, ed. Christopher Nash (London: Routledge, 1990), 175–96.

'I am not master of myself,' we are again enclosing one story within another. On this view, *the self is a telling*.[10]

Narrative and subjectivity are both structured by the desire for the end and the quest for the origin. Robert Con Davis, who proposes a Lacanian 'psychoanalytic anthropomorphism of the text', focuses on the role of the father, or rather the absence of the father, in narrative. Davis argues that 'a Freudian theory of certain laws of transformation suggests a paradigm for textuality — for the structural relations within a text. Since the operations of the psychoanalytic subject and the text are synonymous — rather, since textuality is an inscription of the subject — many of the same laws govern both.'[11] Davis discusses the paradigmatic status of the *Odyssey* in terms of this Lacanian psychopoesis: the father's absence, the son's quest, the recognition scene, and the reassertion of the law of the father are 'laws of transformation' which operate within the subject and the text alike.

Just as in Lacanian theory where the initial absence of the father inaugurates a desire for the father's function, and the child thereby becomes the embodiment of knowledge about the father (and the absence associated with him), the Odyssean son begins the epic as he gazes toward a fatherless horizon and answers Athena's question about what it is to know a father. The paternal absence at the beginning of the Odyssey, then, has a necessary structural function in the evocation of a lack, but this lack is not irrevocably bound to father figures. Absence can also be indicated in complex and indirect ways. . . . The development of narrative . . . is fully dependent on the structural absence that initiates it. . . . This lack . . . is an originary feature of every narrative.[12]

I would suggest that the Negative Theology of the Lacanian formula is merely the obverse of the same metaphysical paradigm. If the absence of the father — a metaphoric extension of the primordial *manque a etre* — is the lack which produces discourse, which triggers all narratives into motion, it is the assumption of an eventual homecoming which is ultimately the enabling condition of narrative closure. But this analogy between the textual

---

[10] Roy Shafer, 'Narration in the Psychoanalytic Dialogue', *Critical Inquiry*, 7 (1980); reprinted in Emanuel Berman (ed.), *Essential Papers on Psychoanalysis and Literature* (New York: New York University Press, 1993), 345. Italics added.

[11] Robert Con Davis, *The Fictional Father: Lacanian Readings of the Text* (Amherst: University of Massachusetts Press, 1981), 3.

[12] Davis, *The Fictional Father* 7–8.

dynamics of narrative and the psychic dynamics of paternity, predicated on a secure relationship of origins to ends, is ultimately dependent on a metaphysical frame of reference, a principle of authority in which the subject/text is firmly grounded. In the absence of that framework, the analogy collapses.

The framework collapses, but the desire remains. The need to insert oneself and one's private narrative into some 'transindividual order', a meta-narrative which would contain and unify the incoherent private one, is not obviated in the absence of religion.

The individual, we might say, makes raids on a putative masterplot in order to remedy the insufficiencies of his own unsatisfactory plot—unsatisfactory because unclosed and thus not fully coherent, unilluminated. It is as if the individual, in order to be able to narrate his life story to himself in such a way as to make it coherent and significant, had to reach back toward the idea of a providential plot which, for better or for worse, would subsume his experience to that of mankind, to show the individual as a significant repetition of a story already endowed with meaning.[13]

It is this nostalgia for the 'masterplot' of identity which produces the Modernist anxiety of authenticity, the quest for that notional 'downward movement through all the cultural superstructures to some place where all movement ends, and begins'.[14] It is this nostalgia which translates itself into a psycho-cultural anxiety about origins and ends, about paternity and death, about the viability of narrative order in life and in fiction.

On 25 July 1894, Conrad wrote to Marguerite Poradowska:

Man must drag the ball and chain of his individuality to the very end. It is the [price] one pays for the infernal and divine privilege of thought; consequently, it is only the elect who are convicts in this life—the glorious company of those who understand and who lament, but who tread the earth amid a multitude of ghosts with maniacal gestures, with idiotic grimaces. Which do you prefer—idiot or convict?[15]

Metaphorically extended, this impossible choice between two

[13] Brooks, *Reading for the Plot*, 280.

[14] Lionel Trilling, *Sincerity and Authenticity* (Cambridge, Mass.: Harvard University Press, 1971), 12.

[15] *The Collected Letters of Joseph Conrad*, ed. Frederick R. Karl and Lawrence Davies, vol. 1 (Cambridge: Cambridge University Press, 1983), 163.

modes of being—idiot or convict—is both a theme and a structuring principle which runs across the best of Conrad's mature
Modernist work, written during the first decade of the century.
But it is not really a matter of choice. The author who cannot will
himself into idiocy is willy-nilly a convict, imprisoned within his
own scepticism, sentenced to a lifetime of hard labour, anxiously
trying to quarry meaning out of the brute matter of existence.[16] In
what follows I would suggest, on the same forensic note, that one
may detect the 'voice prints' of that Modernist anxiety in one of
Conrad's earliest and most problematic short stories, a text which
is both a symptom and a diagnosis of the same cultural crisis. The
symptomatic nature of the story is evident in its ultimate failure;
the diagnostic power which turns it into a text of some cultural
significance lies in its apparent awareness of that failure.

'The Idiots', written in May 1896, during Conrad's honeymoon
in Brittany, has been almost unanimously treated by critics as an
embarrassing bit of juvenilia. In his author's note, written in the
summer of 1919, Conrad himself had, according to Najder,
dissociated himself from the story 'unobtrusively but quite
clearly', dismissing it as 'such an obviously derivative piece of
work that it is impossible for me to say anything about it
here'.[17] The story was subsequently described in Guerard's influential study as 'an amateur's desperate search for a "subject" after
a dismal experience of "writer's block"', a verdict which seems to
have foreclosed any further critical discussion.[18] The story did,

---

[16] See Daphna Erdinast-Vulcan, *Joseph Conrad and the Modern Temper* (Oxford:
Oxford University Press, 1991), 1–24, 139–56.

[17] Zdzislaw Najder, *Joseph Conrad; A Chronicle* (Cambridge: Cambridge University Press, 1981), 441; Joseph Conrad, *Tales of Unrest*, The Dent Uniform Edition
(London: Dent, 1923), author's note, p. vii.

[18] Albert Guerard, *Conrad the Novelist* (Cambridge, Mass.: Harvard University
Press, 1958), 95. One exception to this unanimous critical silence is a comment
made by Daniel Schwarz who, in trying to redeem the story from critical oblivion,
describes it as 'a penetrating study of emotional and moral idiocy', where 'the blighted
offspring are stark symbols of a community where family, clerical, and political
structures are undermined by the hypocrisy, selfishness, and vanity of those in positions
to provide moral leadership', and argues, with very little support from the text, that the
narrator's 'values' are 'a humanistic alternative' to those of the Ploumar parish which
fails 'to provide responsible care for the helpless children'. Schwarz's commentary itself
is a case in point, for in providing the story with a didactic message, a moral which is
obviously not to be found in the text, it exposes a sense of acute readerly discomfort
which does not derive from an aesthetic weakness in the text but from what is clearly an
ethical issue. Daniel R. Schwarz, Conrad: *Almayer's Folly to Under Western Eyes*
(London: Macmillan, 1980), 23–4.

however, draw some attention as a suggestive source of speculation for psycho-biographical or pathographical studies. Hardly a honeymoon piece, it is, no doubt, highly interesting if one takes the liberty of studying the author's psycho-sexual life. Bernard C. Meyer, for instance, has focused on the figure of the wife, the half-demented murderous woman who was to feature more fully in Conrad's later work as Winnie Verloc (the surrogate mother of another congenital idiot, who, like her early prototype, stabs the father-figure in a fit of fury).[19] It is probably Meyer's rather ruthlessly clinical discussion which Najder has in mind when he observes, a touch acerbically perhaps, that the story 'was to provide great fun for all Conrad's future psychoanalytical critics'.[20] I would argue that 'The Idiots' is indeed interesting mainly for its symptomatic significance, but the anxiety it articulates, in the most inarticulate manner, is not merely the private mental torment of a troubled individual trying to adjust to the marital state, but a much wider-reaching cultural malaise. I believe that the biographer's justified refusal of facile, sometimes vulgar psychoanalytic or pathobiographical speculation does not necessarily rule out the perception of symptomatic indications where psychic, textual, and cultural vectors are significantly related. The following discussion would question the still prevalent distinction between the psychic (private, subjective, internal) and the cultural parameters of human reality, and suggest that any such watertight compartmentalization is ultimately less productive than the rather messier practice of watching these enclosures intersect and blend into each other.

'The Idiots' is one of Conrad's most pointless stories. It is the story of a peasant couple whose children are all born mentally deficient, a story of remorseless, fortuitous disintegration. By the end of the story Jean-Pierre Bacadou and his wife, Susan, are both dead. No ending, it seems, can be more final and absolute. And yet, the story seems to remain unfinished. The absolute and final end does not yield the 'sense of an ending' which would endow the plot with significance, that retrospective illumination on which narratives—both traditional and Modernist—depend for their

---

[19] Bernard C. Meyer, *Joseph Conrad: A Psychoanalytic Biography* (Princeton, NJ.: Princeton University Press, 1967).
[20] Najder, *Joseph Conrad; A Chronicle*, 195.

ultimate justification. Stripped of all narrative scaffolding which would turn it into a neatly packaged unit of meaning, the story collapses into a meaningless tale of woe. It is a narrative without a proper ending, without a moral. The protagonist of 'The Idiots', like its author, is a citizen of a world which has been stripped of its narrative framework. Struck by the manifest and utter arbitrariness and randomness of his fate, he can find no 'narrative order', to use Musil's phrase, no construction which would endow his life with a sense of coherence. Desperately trying to place his life within some significant framework, Jean-Pierre Bacadou is temporarily deluded by the apparent pattern which seems to emerge out of the recurrent disasters that hit him. It is precisely this need to find some narrative order in life that moves him to the point of religious conversion. A man of strong anti-clerical convictions, he breaks down at the suggestion that there may, indeed, be some mechanism of reward and punishment which has determined his fate:

Jean-Pierre felt the [Republican, anti-clerical] convictions imbibed in the regiment torn out of his breast—not by arguments, but by facts. Striding over his fields he thought it over. There were three of them. Three! All alike! Why? Such things did not happen to everybody—to nobody he ever heard of. One yet—it might pass. But three! All three. Forever useless, to be fed while he lived and . . . What would become of the land when he died? This must be seen to. He would sacrifice his convictions. One day he told his wife—

'See what your God will do for us. Pay for some masses. (66–7)

Jean-Pierre Bacadou capitulates to the illusory significance of his tragedy, the narrative force generated by mere repetition, by the magic number of three. If textual closure is the ultimate goal of the text, its 'desire', to use Brooks' psychotextual terminology, the road leading to it often goes through the detour of 'repetitions serving to bind the energy of the text so as to make its final discharge more effective'.[21] Folk stories, fairy tales, mythological narratives, and other formulaic literary genres are typically structured on serial principles which generate a sense of significance through sameness and variation. It is the repetition of the event which turns the calamity into a potential 'story' which might yet end—as stories do—on a note of recognition and a reversal of

---

[21] Brooks, *Reading for the Plot*, 108.

fortune. But Bacadou's 'new credulity' is soon belied. Three priests in black soutanes come to the christening of the new baby, and Mme Lavaille, with her unique combination of piety and avarice, serves as her godmother. But the fourth child too turns out to be an idiot. It is at this point that Bacadou, cheated out of his precarious narrative, is moved to a gesture of hollow defiance. Rattling the iron bars of the church gates, he calls out: 'Hey there! Come out!' He too is a convict, realizing that the transcendental Being which is supposed to 'be there' is, like himself, a nobodaddy.

But the question of origins and ends—the question of metaphysics—is not merely a conspiracy of the clergy, a 'swindle of the crows', as Jean-Pierre naïvely believes, along with a number of quite sophisticated intellectuals much closer to home. The need for grounding—the primary metaphysical need—becomes painfully real with the fact of parenthood. In the narrative of human continuity the question of origin and destination is transformed into a question of paternity. It is this inescapable fact of life which smuggles the Trojan Horse of metaphysics into the very heart of a thoroughly disenchanted, secularized civilization. The sense of a totality larger than the self, a family, a community, or a nation, is the obvious alternative to religious faith. But Jean-Pierre Bacadou is not offered the comforts of any such alternative master narrative, communal or familial. One by one, all the conventional idealizations of peasant life—Nature, Community, Tradition—are demolished in the telling. There is no sense of significance to be found in the bleak landscape, the cynicism, the greed, and the indifferent callousness of the characters. The 'pathos of authenticity', to use Vattimo's phrase, fails to work.[22] Even 'the land', that altar at which Bacadou religiously serves, which seems to be invariably capitalized in his thoughts, can offer him nothing but its heavy, indifferent silence. It is the state of 'the land' which motivates him to get married soon after his return to the village:

'It is not for me that I am speaking,' insisted Jean-Pierre. 'It is for the land. It's a pity to see it badly used. I am not impatient for myself.' The

---

[22] Gianni Vattimo, *The End of Modernity* (1985; Baltimore: Johns Hopkins Press, 1988), 23. Vattimo uses the phrase in his 'apology for Nihilism', with reference to the 'resistance to the accomplishment of nihilism', which he defines as the 'reduction of Being to exchange value' in the absence of the 'terminal, interrupting instance of highest value (God)' (21). My own use of the phrase in a somewhat extended sense denotes the substitution of the religious with other forms of metaphysical ballast.

old fellow nodded over his stick. . . . The mother was pleased with her daughter-in-law. (59)

There is no transition from the discussion of the badly used land to the wedding, not a word about the courtship or the bride, not a word about love. The marriage is an offering to the land which is the ultimate, terminal value against which the lives of individuals are measured. It is also in terms of the service of the land that Jean-Pierre thinks of his retarded children a few years later:

All three. Forever useless, to be fed while he lived and. . . . What would become of the land when he died? (66)

He looked at the black earth, at the earth mute and promising, at the mysterious earth doing its work of life in death-like stillness under the veiled sorrow of the sky. And it seemed to him that to a man worse than childless there was no promise in the fertility of the fields, that from him the earth escaped, defied him, frowned at him like the clouds, sombre and hurried above his head. Having to face alone his own fields, he felt the inferiority of man who passes away before the clod that remains. (71)

Faced with the unresponsive earth, trapped into the 'antipathetic fallacy' which Watts has diagnosed as one of Conrad's 'absurdist techniques', Jean-Pierre Bacadou is stripped of the last metaphysical consolation.[23] There is no master plot which can subsume and justify this pointless tale of sorrows. It is, one might say, an 'idiot reality', a reality which resists narrativization with the indifferent force of brute matter.[24]

When the psychic and the cultural parameters of human reality intersect, it is hard to draw the line which marks the diagnosis from the symptom. The failure of paternity is not contained within the text; it spills over its borderlines and turns into a failure

---

[23] C. T. Watts 'Conrad's Absurdist Techniques: a terminology' *Conradiana*, 9: 2 (1977), 141–8.

[24] In *The Subject of Modernism: Narrative Alterations in the Fiction of Eliot, Conrad, Woolf, and Joyce* (Ann Arbor: University of Michigan Press, 1994), 71, 75, Tony E. Jackson offers a persuasive view of Conrad as a borderline figure between Naturalism and Modernism. 'The subject presupposed by realism remains presupposed by naturalism but is presupposed in an irreconcilably negative opposition to nature and society: thus the unremitting bleakness, the cruelty of the random coincidence, the inclusion of a final return that, far from being ameliorative, often enough presents an unredeemed fall into a death of which the only significance is its insignificance.' The most significant point for the present discussion is that the (incurable) desire for 'some form of redemption, merciful explanation, or final justification' emerges as desire when such modes of closure are no longer a 'fixed standard of storytelling'.

of narrative. If the reader, unlike the protagonist, may sometimes find a sense of communality in the very act of narration—implying a bond between an implicit authorial figure or an embodied narrator and his listeners—that meagre consolation is also denied us. The story begins as a personal reminiscence: 'We were driving along the road' (56). But the first-person narrator disappears with the beginning of the tale, and the omniscient narrative mode which seems to follow does not entail any comforts of providence and wisdom. The failure of the narrative is echoed in the failure of narration. The failure of paternity is ultimately the failure of authorship.

'The Idiots' is a dead end at the very beginning of what was to develop into a singular literary journey. Its symptomaticity points to a junction at which various authorial anxieties, both psychic and cultural, intersect and merge into a highly explosive mixture. It is the spring of 1896, when fatherhood becomes a real possibility, when the decision to become a professional, fully committed writer is about to be made. Having broken away from his own heritage, the familial and the communal narratives are no longer readily available to Conrad as a trans-individual narrative of continuity: he is about to become a father outside the familial narrative, a storyteller without the wisdom and the sanction of a meaningful literary death.

Shortly before he wrote the story, Conrad fell ill:

It remains unclear whether the difficulties with writing or other distressing factors were the cause (which seems likely) or the effect; at all events, Conrad fell ill suddenly. . . . 'he became more and more incoherent and rambling in his speech. . . . He raved in grim earnest, speaking only in his native tongue. . . . All that night Joseph Conrad continued to rave in Polish, a habit he kept up every time any illness had him in its grip.'[25]

Fourteen years later, upon the completion of *Under Western Eyes* (another work which revolves around similar issues), Conrad was afflicted by a similar reaction.

But the collapse of the narrative is overdetermined: its underlying anxiety is not only that of a particular uprooted individual. It is related to a much deeper sense of a cultural and epistemic crisis. When the metaphysical outlook is no longer viable, the

---

[25] Jessie Conrad, *Joseph Conrad and his Circle* (London: Jarrolds, 1935), 26; quoted in Najder, 198.

possibility of narrative framing becomes a mere aesthetic fiction, and the concept of paternity is thoroughly shaken. It is here that the cultural and the private realms blend into what I have called 'the anxiety of Modernism', which Conrad was to grapple with in the best of his work. Nineteenth-century narrative was typically 'the narrative of an attempted homecoming: of the effort to reach an assertion of origin through ending, to find the same in the different, the time before in the time after'.[26] The twentieth century, heralded by Nietzsche and Vaihinger, is the age of homesickness. 'It's a wise child that knows its own father,' says Telemachus to Athena. It is, to extrapolate, an idiot child who does not. The Modernist narrative is plagued by the suspicion that we are all idiots in that sense. When narrative ends can no longer signify and be true at the same time, the author can opt either for the silence of the idiot or for the forced conviction of the convict, the willed and desperate construction of meaning, 'as if', to use Vaihinger's paradigm, there were really a home to come back to. The central question of Modernism turns on the very possibility of any homecoming. The centrality of exile, the persistence of nostalgia, are all the symptoms of this Modernist ache, the suspicion that narratives—'real' narratives with beginnings and ends—are mere fictions. The narrative of the self, that construction which enables us to sustain a sense of coherent identity, is no exception to this.

In one of his most memorable letters to Cunninghame Graham, written just a few hours before the birth of his eldest son, Conrad seems to be at his bleakest best:

Life knows us not and we do not know life—we do not know even our own thoughts. Half the words we use have no meaning whatever and of the other half each man understands each word after the fashion of his own folly and conceit. Faith is a myth and beliefs shift like mists on the shore; thoughts vanish; words, once pronounced, die; and the memory of yesterday is as shadowy as the hope of to-morrow—only the string of my platitudes seems to have no end. As our peasants say; 'Pray, brother, forgive me for the love of God.' And we don't know what forgiveness is, nor what is love, nor where God is. Assez.[27]

---

[26] Brooks, *Reading for the Plot*, 110.
[27] Written on 14–15 Jan. 1898, in *Joseph Conrad's Letters to Cunninghame Graham*, ed. C. T. Watts (Cambridge: Cambridge University Press, 1969), 65.

Nothing, it seems, is left to the author of this bleak, hopeless message. Nothing but silence. But the dark conclusion of the letter is reversed by a curious postscript:

PS. This letter missed this morning's post because an infant of male persuasion arrived and made such a row that I could not hear the Postman's whistle. It's a fine commentary upon this letter! But salvation lies in being illogical. Still I feel remorse.[28]

The truth of this odd postscript outweighs, if only by the smallest of margins, the apocalyptic tone of the letter. Conrad, we know, had chosen to turn away from the dead end of his own lethal scepticism, to attend to the tiny voice of the infant and all it stood for rather than listen for the postman's whistle. A convict of his own making, he had apparently chosen—as if it were a matter of choice—to join the company of 'the elect', those cursed with the 'infernal and divine privilege of thought', those 'who understand and who lament'. Salvation, it seems, does lie in being illogical.

'Born Originals, how comes it to pass that we die Copies?' The question formulated by Edward Young in 1759 is a nutshell formulation of one of the most persistent concerns of European culture from the Enlightenment to the end of the era we now label 'Modernity'.[29] The nostalgic urge towards a lost authenticity is first articulated in Rousseau's *Discourse on Inequality* (1755). 'The desire to know correctly a state which no longer exists, and the desire to express one's awareness of the fictionality of such a state' are, as Leslie Brisman writes, 'the two great motivating powers behind Rousseau's work and that of the Romantic movement he is often credited with fathering.'[30]

Freud's *Civilization and Its Discontents* (1929) marks the end point of the very same itinerary.[31] It is the same 'anxiety of authenticity', inextricably bound up with the distinctly Modern

[28] Ibid.
[29] Edward Young, *Conjectures on Original Composition* (1759). Facsimile reprint (Leeds: Scholar Press, 1966), 42.
[30] Leslie Brisman, *Romantic Origins* (Ithaca and London: Cornell University Press, 1978), 11.
[31] Sigmund Freud, 'Civilization and its Discontents' (1929–30). *The Standard Edition of the Complete Psychological Works of Sigmund Freud*, trans. James Strachey, vol. 21. (London: Hogarth Press, 1961), 59–146.

sense of belatedness, which finds expression in both these works.[32] Rousseau writes of the historical developments which had 'civilized man and ruined the human race', which 'have succeeded in improving human reason while worsening the human species, making man wicked while making him sociable'.[33] Freud's postulate of the aim-inhibited libido as a condition of social existence seems to point in a similar direction, identifying the process of civilization against a loss of authenticity, a repression of the—to use a Rousseauean expression—the natural state of man:

It is impossible to overlook the extent to which civilization is built up upon a renunciation of instinct, how much it presupposes precisely the non-satisfaction . . . of powerful instincts.[34]

If civilization imposes such great sacrifices not only on man's sexuality but on his aggressivity, we can understand better why it is hard for him to be happy in this civilization. In fact, primitive man was better off in knowing no restrictions of instinct.[35]

Freud's view of culture is marked, as Lionel Trilling has noted, by an 'indignant perception', a simultaneous acknowledgement of the self as inextricably implicated in and formed by culture, and of the self as set against culture and in perpetual struggle with it:

It can of course be said that the indignation which an individual directs upon his culture is itself culturally conditioned. . . . Yet the illusion, if that is what it be, of separateness from one's culture has an effect upon conduct, and upon culture, which is as decisive as the effects of the illusion of free will. For Freud this separateness was a necessary belief.

---

[32] Rousseau's pivotal position in relation to Modernity has been a matter of unusual consensus in a field which is usually plagued by nuances of periodization and visibility. Jeoffrey Blainey, for instance, describes Rousseau as 'the conductor of the new orchestra of Nature', placing him at one end of what he calls 'the great seesaw' of Western culture; see *The Great Seesaw: A New View of the Western World 1750–2000* (London: Macmillan, 1988), 27. From a different perspective, Charles Taylor seems to agree that 'by the turn of the eighteenth century, something recognizably like the modern self is in process of constitution.' Although Taylor warns of the tendency to reduce Rousseau's work to a cult of primitivism and of the 'Noble Savage', he too recognizes his crucial role in the shaping of this self; *Sources of the Self: The Making of the Modern Identity* (Cambridge, Mass.: Harvard University Press, 1989), 185.

[33] Jean-Jacques Rousseau, *A Discourse on Inequality* (1755), trans. Maurice Cranston (London: Penguin Books, 1984), 116, 107.

[34] *Civilization and Its Discontents*, 97.   [35] Ibid., 113.

He needed to believe that there was some point at which it was possible to stand beyond the reach of culture.[36]

Trilling's own study of this 'standing quarrel between self and culture', written in the disillusioned wake of the 1960s, follows the fortunes of 'authenticity' from an ironic distance, albeit not without a certain note of wistfulness. Trilling views the centrality of the concept and its deployment in the 'moral slang of our day' as symptomatic of 'the peculiar nature of our fallen condition, our anxiety over the credibility of existence and of individual existences'. It is in literature, and particularly in Modernist literature, he argues, that we can find the most conclusive evidence of 'our modern demand for reminders of our fallen state'.[37]

Authenticity has not fared well under the cultural regime of Postmodernity. Indeed, it is arguable that one way of defining this regime is precisely through its hostility to the concept, or the myth of authenticity in the widest possible sense.[38] The Postmodernist crisis of subjectivity and its concomitant refusal of the Modernist concept of authenticity as derived from the opposition of self and culture opposition is clearly visible in Heidegger's work: 'authenticity', for Heidegger, is a radical openness or 'being-unto-death', a diametric reversal of the original sense of the term which is

---

[36] Lionel Trilling, 'Freud: Within and Beyond Culture', in *Beyond Culture: Essays on Literature and Learning* (New York: Viking Press, 1955), 108.

[37] Lionel Trilling, *Sincerity and Authenticity* (Cambridge, Mass.: Harvard University Press, 1971), 93, 105.

[38] In his study of Rousseau's work, Alessando Ferrara notes the paradoxical nature of this reversal:

> On [the] one hand, the spokesmen of poststructuralism, deconstructionism and philosophical postmodernism who most explicitly refer to the teachings of Nietzsche and Heidegger—Foucault, Derrida, Lyotard, Rorty—avoid using the term authenticity because to their sensibilities it conveys the illusory myth of a totalizing, harmonious, unitary self, which they seek to replace with the image of a fragmented, plural, centerless and irrevocably split subjectivity. Yet this image of the postmodern, centerless self is propounded in terms that imply that it carries a greater potential for authenticity than the early-modern image of the self-reflecting subject who is the master of its destiny. An authenticity *against* or *despite* the self or, in other words, a theme of authenticity played on the register of the *sublime* is here contrasted with the inauthenticity of the all-round notion of a *harmonious* authenticity'.

Modernity and Authenticity: A Study in the Social and Ethical Thought of Jean-Jacques Rousseau (New York: SUNY Press, 1993), 24–5.

predicated on a notional foundation or core of subjectivity.[39] It is not surprising that Gianni Vattimo, one of the most articulate spokesmen for Postmodernity, writes of 'the pathos of authenticity' as a residual nostalgia for the reappropriation of the *ontos on* which had 'vanished with the death of God', for an 'imaginary self that refuses to yield to the peculiar mobility, uncertainty and permutability of the symbolic'.[40] Vattimo's translation of the 'pathos of authenticity' into a Lacanian terminology is significant for the present discussion.[41] The Lacanian concept of subjectivity entails a recognition of the nostalgia for grounding and plenitude as an ever-shifting, never to be reached translation of desire. It is through the symbolic function, through language primarily, that the object of desire is both articulated and lost.

The 'paradigmatic literary expression of the modern concern with authenticity' is, according to Trilling, Conrad's *Heart of Darkness* which 'contains in sum the whole of the radical critique of European civilization that has been made by literature in the years since its publication'.[42] Marlow's reverence for Kurtz, Trilling argues, can be accounted for in terms of the latter's authenticity of being: 'By his regression to savagery Kurtz had reached as far down beneath the constructs of civilization as it was possible to go, to the irreducible truth of man, the innermost core of his nature, his heart of darkness. From that Stygian authenticity comes illumination.'[43] Indeed, the question of authenticity has remained an axis of interpretation in subsequent readings of the novella, so much so that it can serve as a watermark to gauge the professional readers' transition into Postmodernity as evidenced in

---

[39] As a discussion of this reversal is well beyond the scope of this chapter, I would refer the reader to *The Eclipse of the Self: The Development of Heidegger's Concept of Authenticity* by Michael E. Zimmerman (Athens, OH. and London: Ohio University Press, 1981); *Heidegger and the Philosophy of Mind* by Frederick A. Olafson (New Haven and London: Yale University Press), 1987.

[40] Vattimo, *The End of Modernity*, 23–5.

[41] The Postmodernist/Lacanian version of Freud has tended to dismiss (or rather, repress) the nature–culture opposition, and to place far greater weight on the inescapably cultural determination of the self. Freud's question as to whether we have 'a right to assume the survival of something that was originally there, alongside of what was later derived from it' (*Civilization*, 68) is currently read as a rhetorical invitation of emphatic denial.   [42] Trilling, *Sincerity and Authenticity*, 107.

[43] Ibid., 108. The ambivalence of Marlow's attitude, his perception of civilization as 'fraudulant and shameful' and his 'passionate commitment to civilization, just so it is the right sort' (108), remains unresolved.

the Poststructuralist turn of the 1980s, which has yielded numerous deconstructive versions of the 'authenticity paradigm'.[44]

The case study for the present discussion is Conrad's 'Falk', written at the very turn of the century nearly contemporaneously with *Heart of Darkness*. I believe that Conrad's ambivalent cultural position at the very edge of Modernity may become apparent through a two-layered reading of the story as an uncomfortable intersection of sensibilities: a 'Modernist' nostalgia for an 'authentic' core of subjectivity, and a sceptical sensibility which reaches well beyond the ironic stance of the 'strong Modernist', much closer to the cultural climate of Postmodernity. What I hope will emerge from these two incompatible readings, which I would call, as an *ad hoc* designation, 'vertical' and 'lateral'—is a genuine paradigm shift from the desire for authenticity (Trilling's 'downward movement through all the cultural superstructures') towards an alternative, 'relational' conception of subjectivity.[45]

'Falk' is framed as a 'reminiscence', an anecdote told at a gathering of veteran seamen, at a temporal and spatial distance from the episode itself. The narrator's initial description of the man he refers to as 'my friend, Hermann' is almost affectionate, if not exactly flattering. The narrator seems to be benevolently amused by this man who has the 'simple, heavy appearance of a well-to-do farmer, combined with the good-natured shrewdness of

---

[44] The first example of the 'authenticity paradigm' is Albert J. Guerard's classic reading of the novel as a psychological journey into the realm of libidinal unbridled energy which threatens to erupt through the thin surface of civilized restraint (*Conrad the Novelist* (Cambridge, Mass.: Harvard University Press, 1958). For examples of the 'inverted authenticity' paradigm, see Peter Brooks' *Reading for the Plot* (Oxford: Clarendon Press 1984); J. Hillis Miller, 'Heart of Darkness Revisited', in *Conrad's Heart of Darkness*, ed. Ross C. Murfin (New York: St Martin's Press, 1989). A notable instance of this transition is Perry Meisel's *The Myth of the Modern* (New Haven: Yale University Press, 1987). Following Trilling up to a point, Meisel agrees that 'if there is a recurrent structure to our modernist problematic, it is the structure of the retroactive production of lost primacy by means of evidence belatedly gathered to signify the presence of its absence' (1). This 'paradox of belatedness', Meisel argues, can yield a 'weak Modernism', a 'structure of compensation' attempting to oppose a lost plenitude to the Modernist wasteland; conversely, it can generate a 'strong Modernism' which ironizes and exposes—by thematizing and dramatizing—'the naked structure of our desire to discover such a transcendental realm' or origin (5, 7–8). On this scale, *Heart of Darkness* is read by Meisel as a model of epistemological and political decentring (239).

[45] For a discussion of *Heart of Darkness* along similar lines, see the section entitled 'The Failure of Metaphysics' in my *Joseph Conrad and the Modern Temper*, 86–108.

a small shopkeeper' (147–8) and his 'rustic' and 'homely' ship, which is 'a heavy, strong, blunt-bowed affair, awakening the ideas of primitive solidity, like the wooden plough of our forefathers' (148).

> This *Diana* of Bremen was an innocent old ship and seemed to know nothing of the wicked sea, as there are on shore households that know nothing of the corrupt world. And the sentiments she suggested were unexceptional and mainly of a domestic order. She was a home. All these dear children had learned to walk on her roomy quarter-deck. In such thoughts there is something pretty, even touching. (149–50)

But the endearing naïveté imputed to the ship—and metonymically to her owner and Captain—takes on an ambiguous meaning as the tonality of the narrative shifts from effusive sentimentality to a nearly audible, sarcastic sneer. The immaculate domesticity, regularity, and tidiness of life on board the *Diana*—the '*Diana* not of Ephesus but of Bremen', the narrator pointedly says (149)—initially perceived as emanations of innocent bliss, begin to elicit an overtly hostile response and are given a grotesque twist. Far from subscribing to these sentimental pieties regarding this 'exemplary family' (153), the narrative adopts the domestic jargon only to put it between invisible, sardonic quotation marks, as the narrator refers to 'the state of Karl's dear little nose' (151), to 'Excellent Mrs. Hermann's baggy cotton gowns' (152), and to the 'air of civic virtue' with which the 'worthy Hermann' looks at his offspring (153).

The family laundry, hanging on the poop to dry, is metonymically suggestive: 'The afternoon breeze would incite to a weird and flabby activity all that crowded mass of clothing, with its vague suggestions of drowned, mutilated and flattened humanity. . . . There were long white garments, that taking the wind fairly though their neck openings edged with lace, became for a moment violently distended as by the passage of obese and invisible bodies' (149). It is impossible to reconcile this description, misanthropic on a Swiftian scale, with the narrator's initial designation of Hermann as 'my friend'.

Significantly, the narrator's relationship with Hermann has grown out of an incident of theft. The energetic but failed pursuit of the thief who has stolen the narrator's savings, and Hermann's subsequent expressions of outrage and sympathy, mark the beginning of this odd friendship. Hermann's respect for property and his veneration of propriety are the two distinctive traits of what Freud describes as an 'anal' character. '*Orderly, parsimonious* and *obstinate*', Hermann answers the Freudian definition to the very last adjective. Freud, we should remember, relates thrift to the sublimation of the anal instinct (retention) and views excessive cleanliness as a reaction-formation which expresses itself as the rejection of 'dirt'.[46]

The ontogenetic is closely related to the phylogenetic itinerary in Freud's work: 'we cannot fail to be struck,' he writes, 'by the similarity between the process of civilization and the libidinal development of the individual.'[47] Following the same logic, Erich Fromm associates the same cluster of 'anal' traits with a distinctly capitalist mode of production and socio-cultural organization. The excessively high premium placed on bodily cleanliness is, according to Fromm, a form of environmental control which, combined with the virtues of thrift and competition, is instrumental in shaping the ethos of capitalism. It is, Fromm argues, the economic basis which determines the pedagogic (and ultimately the psychological) superstructure.[48]

It is thus only appropriate that Hermann should be described as 'a caricature of a shopkeeping citizen in one of his own German comic papers' (181–2). His decision to let the girl marry Falk is entirely mercenary. The thought of having to put up the money for her passage home after she has outgrown her usefulness as an unpaid governess carries more weight than his outrage at the idea of cannibalism (168). The happy household with its 'meticulous neatness' turns from a sanctuary of 'guileless peace' and 'arcadian felicity' (157) into an apotheosis of bourgeois existence, with its sense of self-righteousness, its stale proprieties, and its mercenary concerns.

---

[46] Freud, 'Three Essays on the Theory of Sexuality' (1904–5). *The Standard Edition of the Complete Psychological Works of Sigmund Freud*, trans. James Strachey, vol. 7 (London: Hogarth Press, 1953), 125–243; 'Character and Anal Erotism' (1908). *The Standard Edition of the Complete Psychological Works of Sigmund Freud*, trans. James Strachey, vol. 9 (London: Hogarth Press, 1959), 167–75.

[47] Freud, 'Civilization', 97.

[48] Erich Fromm, 'Character and Social Progress', in *Escape from Freedom* (1941; New York: Avon, 1965), 304–27.

Falk, the narrator's designated 'enemy', seems to stand for a different evolutionary phase of humanity.[49] Strong, inarticulate, and self-sufficient, he seems to be of the same ilk and stature as Old Singleton, Gaspar Ruiz, and other elemental, quasi-epic characters in Conrad's fiction who stand for a 'natural' human species: powerful, unreflexive, and anterior to culture.[50] The narrator, looking at Falk, seems to be mostly struck with his bodily magnificence, which he describes in mythological terms:

I saw the extraordinary breadth of the high cheek-bones, the perpendicular style of the features, the massive forehead, steep like a cliff. (200)

Hercules, I take it, was not an athlete. He was a strong man, susceptible to female charms and not afraid of dirt. (201)

He meant no offence, but his intercourse was characterized by that sort of frank disregard of susceptibilities a tall man, living in a world of dwarfs, would naturally assume, without in the least wishing to be unkind. (212–13)

As is the case with Conrad's other quasi-epic heroes, the narrative seems to deploy natural forces in a totally uninhibited manner which in any other context would immediately evoke the verdict of the 'pathetic fallacy'. When Falk comes on board to declare himself, he seems to have the very stars for witnesses:

raising my eyes, I beheld the glitter of a lofty sky above the Diana's mastheads. The multitude of stars gathered into clusters, in rows, in lines, in masses, in groups, shone all together, unanimously—and the few isolated ones, blazing by themselves in the midst of dark patches, seemed to be of a superior kind and of an inextinguishable nature. (215)

No wonder, then, that when the marriage is finally made possible, Falk accepts the news 'with calm gravity, as though he had all along trusted to the stars to fight for him in their courses' (238).[51]

---

[49] I have used the term 'evolutionary' to denote the phylogenetic aspects of the tale with some misgivings about the potentially reductive effect of this concept. 'Falk' has been read as a straightforward or even quasi-scientific Darwinian tale by Redmond O'Hanlon, 'Knife, *Falk* and Sexual Selection', *Essays in Criticism*, 31 (April 1981), 127–41; Walter E. Anderson, ''Falk': Conrad's Tale of Evolution', *Studies in Short Fiction* 25, no. 2 (Spring 1988), 101–8.

[50] The very name, 'Falk', may be a gesture towards the suggestion of a 'basic', 'authentic' mode of existence.

[51] Falk's 'atavistic' charm and its translation into a mythological frame of reference have been noted by more than one critic. Daniel R. Schwarz sees Falk as 'someone who

Survival, in its most naked and elemental form, is the single principle of conduct guiding this elemental being, who seems to be totally indifferent to 'the social organization of mankind' and to the cultural matrix of human existence (198). Entirely self-sufficient, a 'bloated monopolist to boot' (161), he represents humanity in its ostensibly 'natural state':[52]

He might have been the member of a herd, not of a society. Self-preservation was his only concern. Not selfishness, but mere self-preservation. Selfishness presupposes consciousness, choice, the presence of other men; but his instinct acted as though he were the last of mankind nursing that law like the only spark of a sacred fire. (198)

He wanted to live. He had always wanted to live. So we all do—but in us the instinct serves a complex conception, and in him this instinct existed alone. There is in such simple development a gigantic force, like the pathos of a child's naive and uncontrolled desire. (223-4)

If Hermann stands for a relatively late human species, whose 'anality' betokens the virtues of bourgeois capitalism, Falk appears to stand—both ontogenetically and phylogenetically— for an earlier phase of 'orality' in human development. His 'simple and elemental desire' (156) for the girl is described as a form of hunger;

He wanted the girl, and the utmost that can be said for him was that he wanted that particular girl alone. . . . He was a child. He was as frank as a child, too. He was hungry for the girl, terribly hungry, as he had been terribly hungry for food. Don't be shocked if I declare that in my belief it was the same need, the same pain, the same torture. We are in his case allowed to contemplate the foundation of all the emotions—that one joy which is to live, and the one sadness at the root of innumerable torments. (223-4)

has stripped himself of civilization's restraints and returned to man's temporal and emotional origins', and seems to endorse the narrator's use of 'magnifying contexts'— 'Ulyssean', 'Herculean', 'Olympean'— for the description of Falk and the niece; *Conrad: 'Almayer's Folly' to 'Under Western Eyes'* (London: Macmillan, 1980), 97, 101. Mario Curreli and Fausto Ciompi read the story as an ironic displacement, a bourgeois domestication of a mythical narrative. 'A Socio-Semiotic Reading of Conrad's "Falk"', *L'Epoque Conradienne* (1988), 35-45.

[52] 'Man's first feeling was that of his existence, his first concern was that of his preservation'. Jean-Jacques Rousseau, *A Discourse on Inequality* (1755), trans. Maurice Cranston (London: Penguin Books, 1984), 109.

Far from a tragic episode in his past, Falk's act of survival by cannibalism is symptomatic of the omnivorous orality of an elemental force. He is the very embodiment of desire. In his 'hunger' for the girl who, as we will presently see, seems to be made of a like substance, he feels 'incomplete'; his own body seems to be that of a 'centaur', a 'composite creature . . . man-boat' (162). His desire does not recognize the law of separation. It is a desire of incorporation, a manifest instance of what Freud has called the 'Oceanic' feeling.[53] The girl who is the object of Falk's omnivorous desire seems to be his female counterpart. Both are alluded to as pagan demi-gods, both are inarticulate, and both are perceived as irreducibly physical beings. It is not surprising that an unnamed editor, when approached about the publication of the story, rejected it because 'the girl never says anything' (author's note, p. viii). Indeed, it does not take an acute politically correct sensibility to resent the depiction of the nameless girl who not only remains dumb throughout the narrative, but is constantly described in terms of crude, even offensive physicality:

the first time I beheld her full length I surrendered to her proportions. They fix her in my mind, as great beauty, great intelligence, quickness of wit or kindness of heart might have made some other woman memorable. With her it was form and size. It was her physical personality that had this imposing charm. She might have been witty, intelligent, and kind to an exceptional degree. I don't know, and this is not to the point. All I know is that she was built on a magnificent scale. Built is the only word. She was constructed, she was erected, as it were, with regal lavishness. It staggered you to see this reckless expenditure of material upon a chit of a girl. She was youthful and also perfectly mature, as though she had been some fortunate immortal. She was heavy, too, perhaps, but that's nothing. It only added to that notion of permanence. She was barely nineteen. But such shoulders! Such round arms! Such a shadowing forth of mighty limbs. (151)

The girl was of the sort one necessarily casts eyes at in a sense. She made no noise, but she filled most satisfactorily a good bit of space. (183)[54]

---

[53] Referring to a letter written to him on 5 Dec. 1927 by Romain Rolland, Freud describes the 'oceanic' feeling as a sense of 'limitlessness and of a bond with the universe' (68).

[54] This is not too far from Shoemberg's leering, lip-smacking references to the niece as 'a fine lump of a girl' (194–5).

The narrator's insistent disclaimers of the very idea of sexual rivalry between Falk and himself are clearly incompatible with his overtly erotic descriptions of the girl. His sense of inadequacy, which is repeatedly brought up in the narrative, only seems to make her still more seductive for him.[55] When asked by Hermann whether he had not remarked that 'Falk had been casting eyes upon his niece', the narrator replies, 'No more than myself', an answer which he acknowledges to his audience is the 'literal truth'. But it is Hermann's reply which encapsulates the situation between the two men: 'But you, captain, are not the same kind of man' (183). An ostensible complimentary reference to the narrator's greater eligibility in Hermann's view, the answer highlights the lurking sense of inadequacy which underlies the narrator's perception of himself in relation to his rival:

How insignificant and contemptible I must appear, for the fellow to treat me like this—I reflected suddenly, writhing in silent agony. (177)

We had no quarrel. Natural forces are not quarrelsome. You can't quarrel with the wind. (200)

As the narrative proceeds, the narrator's unacknowledged but very real sense of rivalry with Falk gives way to a recognition of the other man's supremacy, and the initial note of crudity in his references to the girl evolves into a sense of wonder and humility before her bodily presence, which seems to tower above the scale of his own desire.

They were a complete couple. In her gray frock, palpitating with life, generous of form, Olympian and simple, she was indeed the siren to fascinate that dark navigator, this ruthless lover of the five senses. (239)[56]

What seems to emerge here is the relational pattern of what René Girard has called 'mimetic desire', a form of desire which is invariably 'triangular' in that it originates in and imitates the 'real

[55] Daniel Schwarz has rightly noted the self-deception of the retrospective speaker, and the discrepancy between his view of events and the view which is accessible to the reader. However, Schwarz relates the narrator's myopia only to the repression of his sexual rivalry with Falk and seems to accept the narrator's perception of himself as inadequate to his role (97–8).

[56] 'I saw the modest, sleek glory of the tawny head, and the full, grey shape of the girlish print frock she filled so perfectly, so satisfactorily, with the seduction of un-faltering curves—a very nymph of Diana the Huntress' (208).

or illusory desire' of a real or illusory other.[57] Girard posits a distinction between what he calls 'novelistic' and 'romantic' desire.[58] The romantic attitude insists on the autonomy of selfhood, its ability to generate its own spontaneous desire and its ultimate sovereignty. The novel, according to Girard, challenges the 'illusion of autonomy to which modern man is passionately devoted'.[59] Novelistic desire, as Girard conceives it, is always a borrowed desire. It is generated by an 'other', a mediator perceived as a rival for the same object. The object of mimetic desire is not chosen on its own inherent merits; its desirability is a function of the perceived desire of the other for it. The physical reality of the object is of little importance since it may be substituted at any time for any other object of the other's desire. Mimetic desire is 'always a desire to be Another'.[60] It is an attempt to appropriate the identity of an other who seems to have that plenitude which the hero lacks, a promise of self-sufficiency and autonomy which the hero cannot obtain unless, so he imagines, he becomes that rival mediator. 'The desiring subject wants to become his mediator; he wants to steal from the mediator his very being of "perfect knight" or "irresistible seducer".'[61]

It is no accident that the birth of a novel as the literary form coincides with the beginning of Modernity: the concept of mimetic or 'novelistic' desire is clearly related to the cultural parameters of Modernism—to its sense of belatedness, its disenchantment with culture, its valorization of the primitive as a form of authenticity no longer accessible, and its nostalgia for a 'pagan' form of vitality and plenitude. What we demand of literature, Trilling tells us, is 'the sentiment of being', synonymous with 'that 'strength' which, Schiller tells us, 'man brought with him from the state of savagery' and which he finds it so difficult to preserve in a highly developed culture. 'The sentiment of being is the sentiment of being strong. . . . [having] such energy as contrives that the centre shall hold, that the circumference of the self keep unbroken, that the

---

[57] René Girard, *Deceit, Desire and the Novel: Self and Other in Literary Structure*, trans. Yvonne Freccero (1961; Baltimore, Md: Johns Hopkins University Press, 1965), 105.

[58] The English translation of Girard's terms— 'romanesque' and 'romantique'—is somewhat frustrating, as the identical radical through which they are audibly related is lost.   [59] Girard, *Deceit, Desire and the Novel* 39.

[60] Ibid., 85–95, 83.   [61] Ibid., 54.

person be an integer, impenetrable, imperdurable, and autonomous in being if not in action.[62]

It is precisely this 'sentiment of being' or, in Girard's terms, the sense of plenitude, which the narrator feels lacking in himself. It is the same sense of inadequacy which moves him to shift his initial alliances. His earlier designations of Hermann and Falk notwithstanding, the narrator is clearly disgusted by Hermann's air of civic virtue and inclined to look up to Falk as a representative of some forgotten 'truth' of human nature:

[Hermann's] indignation and his personality together would have been enough to spoil the reality of the most authentic thing. When I looked at him I doubted the story—but the remembrance of Falk's words, looks, gestures, invested it not only with an air of reality but with the absolute truth of primitive passion. (223)

Oppressed by the sense of his own inadequacy, the narrator describes both Falk and the girl as earlier, more authentic beings, untouched by the aridity of modern times, close to nature and anterior to culture:

She could have stood for an allegoric statue of the Earth. I don't mean the worn-out earth of our possession, but a young Earth, a virginal planet undisturbed by the vision of a future teeming with the monstrous forms of life, clamorous with the cruel battles of hunger and thought. (152)

I think I saw then the obscure beginning, the seed germinating in the soil of an unconscious need, the first shoot of the tree bearing now for a mature mankind the flower and the fruit, the infinite gradation in shades and in flavour of our discriminating loves. (223–4)

Just as Falk seems to have been 'preserved for a witness to the mighty truth of an unerring and eternal principle' (235), she is perceived as his female counterpart: 'in her own way, and with her own profusion of sensuous charms she also seemed to illustrate the eternal truth of an unerring principle' (236). She too is 'a servant of that life that, in the midst of death, cries aloud to our senses . . . eminently fitted to interpret for him its feminine side' (236).

The narrator's voyeurism in relation to the girl is clearly related to his sense of himself as a latecomer, a mere epigone of manhood,

---

[62] *Sincerity and Authenticity*, 99.

and to his fear of this embodiment of femininity before which he feels entirely inadequate. His desire for the girl is mixed with a sense of lurking annihilation and loss of self: time and again, he refers to her as 'a siren' (239); talking of her glance, 'soft and diffuse as the moon beams upon a landscape', he says, 'you were drowned in it, and imagined yourself to appear blurred' (160). Indeed, it is his fear of drowning, of giving in to his desire, which leaves the narrator stranded on the arid shores of a passionless life: 'There may be tides in the affairs of men which taken at the flood . . . and so on. Personally I am still on the look-out for that important turn. I am, however, afraid that most of us are fated to flounder for ever in the dead water of a pool the shores of which are arid indeed' (169). Extrapolating from the Shakespearean complement of the quotation, one can only conclude that the narrator, failing to take his own tide 'at the flood' in fear of drowning, has condemned himself to a voyage of 'life . . . bound in shallows and in miseries' (*Julius Caesar*, IV, iii, 217). Falk, the 'dark navigator', the 'ruthless lover of the five senses' (239), is not afraid of drowning. It is this totality of desire which turns both him and the girl into a 'complete couple' (239). With the would-be rival stranded in the shallows of his mimetic desire, Falk and the girl are finally united, ready to die happily ever after.

As if in support of this construction, the Modernist sense of belatedness is enacted and reiterated through the narrative double framing. The frame narrative, which serves as a foil to the reality of the tale, makes repeated allusions to the same sense of belatedness. The story is told over dinner in a small river hostelry 'less than twenty [miles] from that shallow and dangerous puddle to which our coasting men give the grandiose name of the "German Ocean"', where the food is 'execrable' and 'all the feast [is] for the eyes' (145). The frame narrator talks of hunger, of the meat which is 'impossible to swallow', and of 'a strange mustiness in everything', which brings to mind 'the night of ages when the primeval man, evolving the first rudiments of cookery from his dim consciousness, scorched lumps of meat at a fire of sticks in the company of other good fellows; then, gorged and happy, sat him back among the gnawed bones to tell his artless tales of experience—the tales of hunger and hunt—and of women, perhaps!' (145–6).

The good fellows gathered for the occasion are similarly

occupied. They too eat and drink and tell their 'artless tales'. But just as their meat is musty, so too are the stories they tell as the crimson sunset fades away before their eyes: 'we agreed that the times were changed. . . . We talked of wrecks, of short rations and of heroism—or at least of what the newspapers would have called heroism at sea—a manifestation of virtues quite different from the heroism of primitive times' (146). The talk of hunger, of inedible meat, of a struggle for survival, will echo through the narrative, but their authenticity in Falk's case will make the frame recede into a pale imitation of the 'real thing', as their own tales of heroic adventure at sea seem to be drained of all power when compared to Falk's display of 'pitiless resolution, endurance, cunning and courage—all the qualities of classic heroism' (234).

But the text of self and culture is more complex than that. The opposition of self and culture , so neatly laid out in the story and so seductive in its clarity, may be both complemented and countered by another reading which challenges the conceptual opposition of Nature and Culture.[63] What is at stake in this reading, which I would call 'lateral' or 'relational', is the question of the 'natural state' of man which is the basic premise of the authenticity paradigm. Falk—a monopolist driven by desire and the instinct of survival—seems to be the embodiment of man in his natural state. The narrator—a self-deprecating man, conscious of his disadvantages against Falk's power and stature—is the representative of quite another order of human existence, which may, in fact, expose the concept of a 'natural state' of man, distinct from culture and opposed to it, as a colossal fallacy.

Subjectivity, the sense of selfhood, can only be generated in and through language. One of the earliest and best formulations of this inescapable symbiosis has been offered by Emile Benveniste, a

---

[63] Tony Tanner offers an extremely elegant reading of the story as a deconstruction of cultural oppositions such as sanity and unreason, nature and culture, savagery and civilization. Noting the relation of the narrative to 'the notional beginning and end of man' (24), he describes Falk as a 'de-socialized man' who finds himself in 'a completely de-categorized world', a 'reality unmediated through hitherto unquestioned taxonomies' (27–8). The breakdown of categories includes the individual human body, the social body ('corporate existence'), and language itself. Tony Tanner, '"Gnawed Bones" and "Artless Tales"—Eating and Narrative in Conrad', in *Joseph Conrad: A Commemoration*, ed. Norman Sherry (London: Macmillan, 1976), 17–36.

rarely acknowledged source of inspiration to Lacan and many of his contemporaries:

The pronoun I has no lexical reference. It refers to the act of individual discourse in which it is pronounced, and by this it designates the speaker. . . . The reality to which it refers is the reality of the discourse. It is in the instance of discourse in which I designates the speaker that the speaker proclaims himself as the 'subject'. And so it is literally true that the basis of subjectivity is in the exercise of language.[64]

Benveniste offers a relational conception of subjectivity, which acknowledges the discursive nature of the self but does not reduce it to an entirely fictitious construct. If inter-subjectivity precedes subjectivity, if discourse is a precondition of any notion of self-hood, the question of the 'natural state of man'—the concept of a being natural, solitary, unencumbered by social and cultural constraints—is in itself little more than a precarious cultural construct:

Language is in the nature of man, and he did not fabricate it. We are always inclined to that naive concept of a primordial period in which a complete man discovered another one, equally complete, and between the two of them language was worked out little by little. This is pure fiction. We can never get back to man separated from language and we shall never see him inventing it. We shall never get back to man reduced to himself and exercising his wits to conceive of the existence of another. It is a speaking man whom we find in the world, a man speaking to another man, and language provides the very definition of man. . . . It is in and through language that man constitutes himself as a *subject*.

Language alone establishes the concept of 'ego' in reality, in *its* reality which is that of the being. The 'subjectivity' we are discussing here is the capacity of the speaker to posit himself as 'subject.' It is defined . . . as the psychic unity that transcends the totality of the actual experiences it assembles and that makes the permanence of the consciousness. Now we hold that 'subjectivity,' whether it is placed in phenomenology or in psychology, as one may wish, is only the emergence in the being of a fundamental property of language. 'Ego' is he who *says* 'Ego.' That is where we see the foundation of 'subjectivity,' which is determined by the linguistic status of 'person.'[65]

[64] Emile Benveniste, 'Subjectivity in Language', in *Problems in General Linguistics*, vol. 1, trans. Mary E. Meek (1966; Coral Gables: University of Miami Press, 1971), 226.   [65] Benveniste, 'Subjectivity in Language', 223–5.

Let us now turn once again to 'Falk'. At the very beginning of his tale, the narrator makes an apparently idle comment on the differences between the German and the English terminology for the ranks of command, explaining his own preference for the latter: 'the alliteration is good, and there is something in *the nomenclature that gives us as a body the sense of corporate existence*: Apprentice, Mate, Master, in the ancient and honourable craft of the sea' (147, italics added). Indeed, it is precisely this view of the subject as part of some corporate existence which marks the narrator off from his rival.[66] Falk, the prototype of Rousseau's pre-social man (a 'member of a herd, not of a society', as the narrator puts it) vouchsafes no 'sense of recognition . . . to the organization of mankind'. The narrator cannot and does not wish to extricate himself from the communal bond, even when it is thrust on him by accident. Falk is motivated by 'mere self preservation' which is as unconscious and innocent as an animal's instinctual mode of being: 'Self-preservation was his only concern. Not selfishness, but mere self-preservation. Selfishness pre-supposes consciousness, choice, the presence of other men; but his instinct acted as though here were the last of mankind nursing that law like the only spark of a sacred fire' (198). The narrator who relates to Falk with a grudging sense of wonder as to a different, more 'authentic' or natural species is, in fact, more fully human and admirable.

The narrator's initial situation seems to be unresolvable. Having been appointed by the British Consul to take charge of a ship after the sudden death of her former captain, he is left with the legacy of his mad predecessor: 'some suspiciously unreceipted bills, a few dry-dock estimates hinting at bribery, and a quantity of vouchers for three years' extravagant expenditure; all these mixed up together in a dusty violin-case lined with ruby velvet' (153). There are no provisions on board, 'not an inch of spare rope or a

---

[66] Tanner also extricates his reading from a deconstructive whirlpool in describing the act of narration as part of the 'constituting process' of humanity: 'we must eat to live, but we must also narrate to love . . . telling is a crucial component of living, at least living with "a sense of corporate existence"' (35). I would argue, however, that Tanner's reading—rich and suggestive as it is—does not give due weight to the complex position of the narrator whom he relegates to the role of a mediator between Falk and Hermann, a 'necessary point of intersection' in that he is 'truly mundane' (21). The disembodiment of the narrator leaves no room for the interplay of culture and subjectivity which, I would argue, is central to the narrative.

yard of canvas' (154). The young captain gets no help from the other officers who are either incompetent or resentful of his appointment and leave him to cope alone with the illnesses of his crew, with the problem of obtaining cargo and fitting the ship for its homeward voyage. The theft of his own hard-earned savings, which he has kept for use as a last resort, leaves him overwhelmed by a sense of failure and defeat.

For a moment I felt myself about to go out of my mind with worry and desperation. Some allowance must be made for the feelings of a young man new to responsibility. I thought of my crew. Half of them were ill, and I really began to think that some of them would end by dying on board if I couldn't get them out to sea soon. . . . There were no pilots, no beacons, no buoys of any sort; but there was a very devil of a current for anybody to see, no end of shoal places . . . I didn't even know what my ship was capable of! I had never handled her in my life. A misunderstanding between a man and his ship, in a difficult river with no room to make it up, is bound to end in trouble for the man. . . . And that elderly seaman of mine, Gambril, had looked pretty ghastly when I went forward to dose him with quinine that morning. He would certainly die—not to speak of two or three others that seemed nearly as bad, and of the rest of them just ready to catch any tropical disease going. Horror, ruin, and everlasting remorse. And no help. None. (189)

It is at this point, when the 'corporate body' (of the ship, her captain, and her crew) is about to disintegrate, that the narrator should be evaluated against his apparently stronger rival. The story of Falk's steamer, the *Burgomaster Dahl* (appropriately christened and launched by the burgomaster of Falk's native town), serves as an illustration of what is at stake when, after a series of misfortunes, the corporate body, the 'organized life of the ship', comes to an end and the 'solidarity of the men' is gone (231). The disintegration of the social structure ends in utter regression to savagery, where 'the best [i.e. strongest] man should live', 'everybody for himself' and 'the ship open to all' (227). Cannibalism is the final and inevitable stage of this process. It is the ultimate failure of the ostensibly 'natural state of man'.

The alternative to this scenario is unwittingly figured by the narrator. Finding himself in an impossible situation not of his own making, he sets out to salvage that corporate mode of existence to which he has committed himself by vocation. In his desperate struggle to maintain the corporate body against the dissolution of the bonds of discipline and organization (228); in his willingness to use any means for the sake of the community with which he has been charged; in his unmitigated sense of responsibility for the fate of his ship, the narrator represents a communitarian ethos which is a viable alternative to the mode of existence of both his 'enemy' and his 'friend'. The ostensible supremacy of the magnificent, powerful monopolist over the narrator's younger self is put into question by the analogy of their respective moments of crisis.

Subjectivity, as we noted, is predicated on intersubjectivity: on discourse, on relations, on the symbolic order. In spite of his pagan magnificence, Falk is singularly inadequate. His omnivorous orality is complemented by a curious lack of language. The monopolist, the ultimate survivor, is totally inarticulate, conducting both his courtship and his business deals in silence, communicating with others by sighs, grunts, and nods (161, 166–7). It is the narrator who would not extricate himself from the social bond, who has to 'speak for' his magnificent rival (202), and who finally relays the story of his past.

It is in the narrative act that the discursive construction of subjectivity is acknowledged and played out: 'Man is in his actions and practice, as well as in his fictions, essentially a story-telling animal. . . . I can only answer the question "What am I to do?" if I can answer the prior question: 'Of what story or stories do I find myself a part?'' . . . Mythology, in its original sense, is at the heart of things.'[67] Storytelling is not only an epistemological aspect of human existence: it is, first and foremost, an ethical practice, a mode of self-definition and a source of subjective agency which takes intersubjectivity as its point of departure.[68] If the 'Modernist' sensibility is particularly vulnerable to the suggestions of belatedness and decay which the frame narrative so insistently makes, the alternative sensibility focuses on the transformation of the narrative act itself. By the end of the story the internal narrative blends into the frame narrative; the voice of the frame narrator is taken over by that of the internal narrator who now faces the reader within a situation of direct discourse. This

[67] Alasdair MacIntyre, *After Virtue* (1981; 2nd ed., London: Duckworth, 1985), 216.

[68] On the relationship between the communitarian ethos and the formative power of narrative see Alasdair MacIntyre's *After Virtue*, ch. 15.

dissolution of the mediating narrative frame turns the reader into a listener, a full member of the community of discourse.

   In his rather reticent author's note to the Doubleday Edition, Conrad wrote: 'What is the subject of "Falk"? I personally do not feel so very certain about it. He who reads must find out for himself' (*Typhoon and Other Stories*, p. vii, 1919). I believe that the subject of 'Falk' is no less than the question of modern subjectivity itself and the transition from a 'vertical' to a 'lateral' frame of reference, from the Origin to the Other.[69] If the story of Falk is an enactment of relentless desire, incorporating its object, driving itself through towards total consummation and death, the narrator's more humble version is a story of initiation into the Lacanian symbolic order and the symbolic castration it entails.[70] The narrative may be a wistful gesture towards authenticity, an impossible longing for a place beyond culture, which cannot be recovered within a linguistic order. But beyond this symptomatic sense of belatedness and loss there is a very real human accomplishment for the narrator, a hard-earned place within a community of action and discourse. Defeated, like all of us, in the quest of desire, his is a love well lost for the world.

   [69] I have dealt with this transition under the respective master tropes of synecdoche and metonymy in the section entitled 'The Failure of Metaphysics' in *Joseph Conrad and The Modern Temper*, 86–91.

   [70] Bernard C. Meyer (*Joseph Conrad: A Psychoanalytic Biography*, 1967) writes of an 'intense castration anxiety' which he relates to the voyeuristic aspects of Conrad's fiction (300). I would argue that rather than a form of pathology, this anxiety may be viewed in a Lacanian context, i.e. a symbolic castration which signifies the narrator's initiation into language and the symbolic order.

3
The Poetics of Cultural Depair

Irony, the self-surmounting of a subjectivity that has gone as far as it was possible to go, is the highest freedom that can be achieved in a world without God.[1]

THE EXACT NATURE of Conrad's political orientation is notoriously difficult to pinpoint. His 'political novels' (which novel is not?) are riddled with ideological ambivalence, and his private correspondence tends to refract the political and ideological orientation of the addressee (Cunninghame Graham and Ted Sanderson are good cases in point on both sides of the ideological map) rather than a coherent political stance. Having elsewhere related to Conrad as a 'disinherited conservative' or a conservative with nothing to conserve, I would now like to shift to a temperamental rather than political frame of reference, and suggest—borrowing Proudhon's diagnosis of Rousseau—that Conrad too was a man who 'had rigorously decided against society, while recognizing that there was no humanity outside of it'.[2] This loan is not a mere rhetorical accident: both the precursor of the Romantic movement and the French anarchist are relevant figures in our discussion of the form of cultural despair which marked the Romantic temper at the end of the eighteenth century and solidified into Modernism by the turn of the twentieth. To understand the close relationship between Conrad's sense of cultural despair and his ironic discursive strategies we need to go back, once again, to the Romantics.

It has by now become a matter of consensus that to define the Romantic movement in terms of shared categorical attributes is

---

[1] Georg Lukács, *The Theory of the Novel*, trans. Anna Bostock (London: Merlin Press, 1971), 92–3.

[2] *Système des Contradictions économiques* (Paris, 1923), vol. 1, 350; quoted in George Crowder's *Classical Anarchism: The Political Thought of Godwin, Proudhon, Bakunin, and Kropotkin* (Oxford: Clarendon Press, 1991), 25.

far less rewarding than to try and articulate the cultural unease, the questions with which the Romantics, in their diverse ways, had to grapple. In *Romanticism and Ideology* Morse Peckham suggests that 'the Romantics judged that something in European culture, something at the highest ideological level, was no longer appropriate, had become, indeed, harmful and destructive. Their emphasis upon the imagination, upon creativity, upon the artist and poet as prophet and priest, as unacknowledged legislators, was their way of recognizing that innovation was necessary, their way of defining their task as cultural transcendence'.[3] This project of cultural transcendence, a 'process of undermining the ideological superstructure of Western culture', has yielded, according to Peckham, the Romantic conception of the Self: 'a heuristic construct the function of which was to provide a justification for the innovative creation of value, for finding sources of one's own value in configurations not sanctified by existing social institutions and existing ideologies'.[4] While taking exception to 'Goethe's old wheeze about the classic being healthy and the Romantic being sick . . . [which] becomes clearer when we remember the equally famous and equally fatuous assertion by Freud that to question the value of life is already to be sick,'[5] Peckham himself resorts to a psychiatric analogy in his essay 'Romanticism and Behaviour' in which he equates the 'explanatory collapse' of a culture to the psychic breakdown of an individual.[6] The product of this explanatory collapse—an unresolvable sense of incoherence and loss of value—is a form of 'cultural vandalism', an 'all-encompassing negation of available high-level explanations and validations', a strategy through which the 'self' is experienced against the socio-cultural role.[7] Of the various behavioural patterns diagnosed by Peckham, the most interesting for the present discussion is Romantic irony—the discursive strategy of cultural vandalism.

For the 'romantic ironist' there is no terminus, no point at which the process of undoing is finally arrested in a complete, rounded-out statement:

---

[3] Morse Peckham, 'Cultural Transcendence: the Task of the Romantics' (1981), in *Romanticism and Ideology* (Greenwood, Fl.: Penkevill, 1985), 28.

[4] Ibid., 24, 30.   [5] Ibid., 22.

[6] Morse Peckham, 'Romanticism and Behavior' (1974), in *Collected Essays*, vol. 2 (Columbia: University of South Carolina Press, 1976), 3–31.   [7] Ibid., 23–4.

The romantic ironist shows his world and his selfhood perpetually in threat of dissolution. . . . For the romantic ironist the world is not simply fallen but in a perpetual state of fall*ing*, the condition of a gerund rather than a past participle.[8]

Like any other act of vandalism, cultural or literal, the bottomless sliding of Romantic irony has been perceived as deeply offensive and potentially dangerous. Hegel's critique of irony as 'annihilating scepticism, as irresponsible arbitrariness, as the apex of isolated subjectivity separating itself from the unifying substance',[9] is remarkably similar to the indignant protest addressed to Conrad's discursive strategies in *The Secret Agent*. From Irving Howe's early critique of the 'corrosive irony' of the novel to more recent critiques, readers of the novel have been troubled by its apparent lack of a positive terminus.[10] It is the same pervasive, unmitigated, ironic stance which underlies the narrative of 'An Outpost of Progress', 'An Anarchist', and 'The Informer', and which seems to undermine any structure of moral coherence and any possibility of ethical grounding. In the following discussion, I would argue that Conrad's ironic mode, both in *The Secret Agent* and in the shorter texts related to it, is not merely an aesthetic choice, a cognitive structure, or a disembodied philosophical position: it is both a symptom and a strategy of cultural despair, a mode of subjectivity having to do with questions of complicity and agency, guilt and responsibility. This ironic sliding does not have the distancing effect which would position the narrative voice above the sordid drama; it acts as a 'boomerang' discursive strategy which exposes rather than insulates the subject.

In 'Four Master Tropes', Kenneth Burke defines what he calls 'true' irony as a trope of acknowledged complicity.[11] Against 'Pharisaic' irony which arises 'as an aesthetic opposition to cultural philistinism, and in which the artist [considers] himself

---

[8] Frederick Garber, *Self, Text, and Romantic Irony: The Example of Byron* (Princeton, NJ: Princeton University Press, 1988), 310.

[9] Cited in Ernst Behler, *Irony and the Discourse of Modernity* (Seattle: University of Washington Press, 1990) 105.

[10] See Irving Howe, *Politics and the Novel* (New York: New Left Books, 1950); for a sampling of more recent evidence of this ethical unease see Paul B. Armstrong, 'The Politics of Irony in Reading Conrad', *Conradiana*, 26, no. 2–3 (Autumn 1994), 85–101; Mark A. Wollaeger, *Joseph Conrad and the Fictions of Skepticism* (Stanford, Ca: Stanford University Press, 1990), 23–4; 120–2; 145–8.

[11] *A Grammar of Motives* (New York: Prentice-Hall, 1952), Appendix D, 503–17.

outside of and *superior to* the role he [is] rejecting . . . (a sort of pamphleteering, or external attitude towards "the enemy")'. 'True' irony, according to Burke, is 'based upon a sense of fundamental kinship with the enemy, as one *needs* him, is *indebted* to him, is not merely outside him as an observer but contains him *within*, being consubstantial with him. . . . One sees it in Thomas Mann—and in what he once called, when applying the terms to another, "Judas psychology".'[12] This kind of ironic stance is very far from the here but for the grace of God go I attitude of an external observer/artist, thanking God or congratulating himself that he is not like other men. It is, on the contrary, an acknowledgement of complicity. 'Dialectic irony (or humility) here, we might even say, provides us with a kind of "technical equivalent for the doctrine of original sin." Folly and villainy are integral motives, necessary to wisdom or virtue.'[13] The proto-deconstructive sound of Burke's formulation, the recognition of an 'internal fatality', a consubstantiality of apparent opposites, or a principle of reversal operating from within, is highly significant, to my mind. In *Irony and the Discourse of Modernity*, Ernst Behler discusses the conceptual development of Romantic Irony which is 'inseparable from the evolution of the modern consciousness' and 'a decisive mark of literary modernity'.[14] Romantic irony, as perceived by Behler, is rather more than a rhetorical device: it is an intensely self-reflective mode of subjectivity, distinctly symptomatic of modernity, which constantly undermines and transcends itself. Irony is 'inseparable from the evolution of the modern consciousness', as Behler writes, because it is inextricably related to the 'self-critical awareness of our linguistic embeddedness [which] has . . . been a characteristic mark of Modernity since the romantic age and reached a new intensity with Nietzsche'.[15] From here to Derrida's recognition of our entrapment within the same structures, we would contest it is but one small step: 'we can pronounce not a single deconstructive proposition which has not already had to slip into the form, the logic, and the implicit postulations of precisely what it seeks to contest.' This entrap-

---

[12] *A Grammar of Motives*, 514.   [13] Ibid., 515.
[14] Behler, *Irony and the Discourse of Modernity*, 73.   [15] Ibid., 112.

ment, this bind of metaphysics requires, according to Derrida, 'a double play, a double gesticulation'.[16]

A double play, a double gesticulation, is precisely what we get in Conrad's work. The acute sense of cultural despair, combined with a refusal of utopian consolations or any other form of reconversion is played against an equally strong sense of moral outrage. Practising 'the art of being off-center', to use Jonathan Arac's adaptation of Benjamin's phrase, Conrad himself had refuted the charges of nihilism in an a tellingly ambiguous manner in his author's note to the novel. In reply to the claim that he has, in fact, duplicated in himself the violence he confronts by arguing that he has not committed a 'gratuitous outrage on the feelings of mankind'. Arac perceptively argues that this protest is subtly ironic, 'for Conrad is innocent not of outrage but only of "gratuitous outrage"; the outrage is necessary.'[17]

Hero and villain, hider and seeker, producer and audience, mirror each other as in the conclusion of Baudelaire's poem to the reader: 'Hypocrite lecteur—mon semblable—mon frère.' Reader and writer both see themselves in the work, but something nonetheless stands between them. If Conrad unites mankind in a 'fraternity' as Thorburn argues, this contestation of dueling brothers recalls Conrad's summary of 'fraternity' as 'the Cain–Abel business.' The Romanticism I find in Conrad, even the Wordsworth I find through Conrad, must include this violence.[18]

Far from the assumption of superior, contemptuous detachment, Conrad's ironic mode is a means of negotiating an ideological impasse. The loss of ethical anchorage, the 'doubt of the sovereign power enthroned in a fixed standard of conduct' has resulted in a sense of lost agency.[19]

The anchor may be gone, yet the anger remains. It is this sense of moral outrage and furious helplessness which lends some moral coherence to the narrative stance. It is the implicit authorial

---

[16] 'Structure, Sign, and Play in the Discourse of the Human Sciences' in *Writing and Difference*, trans. Alan Bass (Chicago: University of Chicago Press, 1978), 280–1. Behler relates Derrida's conception of differance directly to the ironic 'negativism' of Schlegel, Nietzsche, and Heidegger (105).

[17] Jonathan Arac, 'Romanticism, the Self and the City: *The Secret Agent* in Literary History', *Boundary* 2, 9, no. 1 (1980), 85.   [18] Ibid., 87–8.

[19] As Mark Wollaeger rightly observes, epistemological and moral scepticism are indeed closely related: 'Skepticism leads naturally to an anxiety about agency, and the problem of agency establishes a useful link between epistemological and moral skepticism in Conrad' (Wollaeger, *Joseph Conrad*, 120).

agreement with Stevie about a 'bad world for poor people' and with Winnie about the agents of law and order who are there 'so that them as have nothing shouldn't take anything from them who have' (*The Secret Agent*, 173). The same moral outrage breaks through the distant posture of the narrator in 'An Outpost of Progress', when the contemptuous indifference of the narrative voice gives way to the barely controlled fury of interjections like: 'everybody shows a respectful deference to certain sounds that he and his fellows can make. But about feelings people really know nothing. We talk with indignation or enthusiasm; we talk about oppression, cruelty, crime, devotion, self-sacrifice, virtue, and we know nothing real beyond the words. Nobody knows what suffering or sacrifice mean—except, perhaps the victims of the mysterious purpose of these illusions' (*Tales of Unrest*, 105–6). 'Progress was calling to Kayerts from the river. Progress and civilization and all the virtues. Society was calling to its accomplished child to come, to be taken care of, to be instructed, to be judged, to be condemned; it called him to return to that rubbish heap from which he had wandered away, so that justice could be done' (116). Romantic irony may well be, as Lukács defines it, 'the self recognition and, with it, the self-abolition of subjectivity,'[20] but the sense of moral outrage—pure, hot, and unambiguous—which energizes the corrosive irony of Conrad's narratives and turns it into a double-edged weapon, is paradoxically the strongest evidence of a subject position. This kind of energy must have its source in some form of ethically active subjectivity.

A true anarchist in a Derridean rather than an ideological sense, Conrad could not join what he perceived as dangerous political naïveté. The apocalyptic, utopian orientation which is evident in anarchism is one variety of the Romantic response to cultural despair, but Conrad was decidedly on the sceptical side of the Romantic tradition, the 'subtler Romanticism', to use Peckham's phrase, which 'recognized that the explanatory collapse which was the cultural trauma that precipitated Romanticism was the collapse of explanation itself'.[21] Though subject to the same sense of cultural despair which underlies anarchist thought, he was among those who could not reconvert or overlook the inescapable

---

[20] Lukács, *The Theory of the Novel*, 74.
[21] Peckham, 'Romanticism and Behavior', 30.

fictionality of explanatory cultural constructs. It is this anti-redemptive, anti-apocalyptic outlook—rather than bourgeois loyalties—which makes him so hostile to anarchism and other forms of utopian thought.[22] Conrad's way of negotiating the impasse was through a form of cultural vandalism performed from within the prison-house of language and against it, a bottomless ironic sliding, which would expose the failure of civilization without masking the writer's (and the reader's) own inevitable complicity in an unredeemable world.

'An Anarchist' (1906), subtitled 'A Desperate Tale', begins with an odd passage introducing the famous meat-extract manufacturing company, B.O.S. Ltd, and its advertising strategies:

B.O.S. Bos. You may have seen the three magic letters on the advertisement pages of magazines and newspapers. . . . They scatter pamphlets also, written in a sickly enthusiastic style and in several languages, giving statistics of slaughter and bloodshed enough to make a Turk turn faint. . . . Of course everybody knows the B.O.S. Ltd., with its unrivalled products: Vinobos, Jellybos, and the latest unequalled perfection, Tribos, whose nourishment is offered to you not only highly concentrated but already half digested. Such apparently is the love the Limited Company bears to its fellowmen—even as the love of the father and mother penguin for their hungry fledglings. (135)

The heavy sarcasm of this passage is interesting mainly for its symptomatic significance. It is directed at copy-writing which is the art of persuasion, the art of making you see, of making you feel—and ultimately, most important—of making you buy. Inevitably, the author's hostility towards the sister art is profoundly ambivalent: the better it is, the more insidious it becomes. The

---

[22] For a sampling of some recent views on Conrad's complex relation to anarchism, see Graham Holderness, 'Anarchism and Fiction', in H. Gustav Klaus (ed.), *The Rise of Socialist Fiction 1880–1914* (Brighton: Harvester Press, 1987); Jeremy Hawthorn, *Joseph Conrad: Narrative Technique and Ideological Commitment* (London: Edward Arnold, 1990); Paul Hollywood, 'Conrad and Anarchist Theories of Language', in *Contexts for Conrad*, ed. Keith Carabine, Owen Knowles, and Wieslaw Krajka (Boulder: East European Monographs; Maria Curie-Sklodowska University, Lublin; distributed by Columbia University Press, 1993), 243–64; Jennifer Shaddock, 'Hanging a Dog: The Politics of Naming in "An Anarchist"', *Conradiana*, 26, no. 1 (1994), 56–68; Carol Vanderveer Hamilton, 'Revolution from Within: Conrad's Natural Anarchists', *The Conradian*, 18, no. 2 (Autumn 1994), 31–48; Margaret Scanlon, 'Language and Terrorism in Conrad's "The Informer"', *Conradiana*, 27, no. 2 (Summer 1995), 115–22.

craft of rhetorical persuasion can become a dangerous weapon, a bomb perhaps, when enlisted in the service of ruthless powers. That ambivalence is compounded as the practice of that art not only offers the writer an opportunity of being truly effective, of 'making a difference'; it is also considerably more seductive in purely material terms. Like any other wordsmith, Conrad must have been painfully aware of this.

What we have in the introductory passage is an inverse mirror image of the rhetoric of advertising, the conversion of cant into satire. The surprisingly symbiotic relationship of these two discursive strategies is illuminated by Frederick Garber, who suggests in his study of Byron's irony that 'in both there is a structure in which surface utterance and depth intention stand at variance with each other. The language of cant disguises the depravity that initiates its version of the structure, while that language of rhetorical irony covers over the point of its barb. But it does not cover the point completely, and that makes for an essential difference between these curious cousins.'[23] Parody, then, is a form of 'implicating reflection', a mode of subversive discourse which abolishes distance and traps the commentator in a forced identification. The subject 'comes to see that the image in the glass is an implicating one, that the glass is indeed a mirror'.[24]

The narrator's position, however, is far from clear. His initial hostility and contempt for the company and the world in which it operates is modified by his subsequent qualifications, which confine his concern to advertising and the form of gullibility it feeds on. Having come to the island in pursuit of a rare butterfly for his collection, his own involvement with the story is presumably that of a chance spectator. Though a paying guest of the B.O.S. Company, he professes hostility towards Harry Gee, the manager of the cattle station, who considers the collection of butterflies 'the greatest absurdity in the world' as opposed to the B.O.S. Co. Ltd, which stands for 'the acme of nineteenth century's achievements' (137). However, listening to the manager's diatribe on anarchism, he chooses not to contest his own inclusion within the world threatened by the forces of anarchy:

[23] Frederick Garber, *Self, Text, and Romantic Irony: The Example of Byron* (Princeton, NJ, Princeton University Press, 1988), 273.   [24] Ibid., 296.

'That subversive sanguinary rot of doing away with all law and order in the world makes my blood boil. It's simply cutting the ground from under the feet of every decent, respectable, hard-working person. I tell you that the consciences of people who have them, like you or I, must be protected in some way; or else the first low scoundrel that came along would in every respect be just as good as myself'. . . . I nodded slightly and murmured that doubtless there was much subtle truth in his view. (144)

The friendship which develops between the butterfly-collector and the 'anarchist' leads to the convict's account. The man whose heart was wrung by 'the pity of mankind's cruel lot', who wept and cursed at the thought of the world as 'a dismal evil place where a multitude of poor wretches had to work and slave to the sole end that a few individuals should ride in carriages and live riotously in palaces', is yet another, only slightly more articulate version of Stevie. His outrage is the same helpless fury in the face of injustice and cruelty. A case of a 'warm heart and a weak head', according to the narrator's diagnosis.

But where does the story leave the narrator? The choice facing him seems to lie between the aestheticized, well-ordered, and dead world of the butterflies pinned down in their glass cases and the active world of capitalist enterprise and ruthless exploitation. Like the putative 'anarchist' who has been chained by the label to the 'penal settlement for condemned cattle' (137) and refuses his offer of escape, he too remains where he was. Like the 'anarchist', he is an amphibious creature, living half in and half out of the civilization epitomized by the ruthless efficiency of the meat-extract company, straddling both worlds but not at home in either of them. The only way out of this impasse is through an act of cultural vandalism directed against language itself. Looking back at the odd introductory passage, it becomes obvious that the narrator's aggressive sarcasm is a double-edged weapon, exposing both the role of language as an instrument of ideological manipulation and the inescapable accountability of the writer whose stock in trade it is. This double play is at the heart of 'The Informer', another 'anarchist' story written in 1906.

Conrad was, by his own testimony, a *homo duplex* in more than one sense, most notably, perhaps, in his ambivalent attitude towards writing. This ambivalence goes much deeper than the recognition of the instrumentality of rhetoric for various forms of oppression, as in the case of Kurtz, the arch-rhetorician of colonialism, or Peter Ivanovitch, the sham prophetic feminist, who represent the more obviously reprehensible aspects of ideological and linguistic manipulation. The other, more complex aspect of Conrad's suspicion of discourse is projected through Marlow of *Heart of Darkness*, whose attempts at a verbal mediation of his experience are constantly frustrated, and the narrator of *Under Western Eyes*, who prefaces his own narrative with 'words, as is well known, are the great foes of reality' (3). A craftsman who mistrusts his own tools, a writer deeply suspicious of rhetoric, Conrad directs his sense of cultural despair towards his own fictional surrogates.

The writer of fiction is always entangled with the question of truth. Engaged in the attempt to domesticate that which is formless, contingent, and unbounded, to plot and to narrativize it, a work of fiction invariably involves some 'aestheticization' of reality, a betrayal of its complexity and fullness for the sake of artistic containment. This attempt to impose the consolations of form on the irredeemable materiality of experience is precisely that mode of action which allows one to avoid the realm of choice and ethics. What, then, are the ethical implications of fiction-making? Is writing necessarily complicit with and subservient to the cultural system even as it claims to subvert it? Torn as he was between the ethical need to grapple with and act upon the real, and the aesthetic desire to endow it with form and significance, Conrad could not opt for silence. It is, I believe, arguable that his entire creative project is an attempt to engage in an essentially aesthetic production without an aestheticization of the real.[25]

The dilemma is forcefully present as the subtext of 'The

---

[25] In 'Conrad and Anarchist Theories of Language', Paul Hollywood illuminates the striking resemblance between Conrad's view, or rather views on the relationship of language and truth and the anarchist theory of language expounded in Henry Brewster's *Theories of Anarchy and Law* (1887). Both Conrad and Brewster seem to recognize the discursive construction of human subjectivity, but whereas the former celebrates the 'great lie or romance' without which life would have no value, Conrad resists such fictional consolations. In *Culture and Irony: Studies in Joseph Conrad's Major Novels*, Anthony Winner also notes the connection between Conrad's discursive strategies in *The Secret Agent* and the sense of cultural despair but argues that 'the irony . . . continually summons up a context of evaluation that we all share.' (Charlottesville: University Press of Virginia, 1988), 87.

Informer'. The frame narrator, the embodiment of the aestheticist outlook, is a man of leisure and means who spends his time between his precious collection of useless objects and the expensive, brilliantly lit restaurant. He describes himself as 'a quiet and peaceable product of civilization' (76), whose 'whole scheme of life' is based 'upon a suave and delicate discrimination of social and artistic values'. Violence and terror appear to him 'as unreal as giants, ogres, and seven-headed hydras . . . [in] legends and fairy-tales' (77): they are merely the characters of a text which he would not read, having no greater reality than the hunger of those less fortunate than himself. But the unimaginable text does force itself into his peaceful existence when he encounters the mysterious Mr X. Becoming uncomfortably aware that he would probably have been considered a prime target by the anarchists, he suddenly seems to hear 'above the festive bustle and clatter of the brilliant restaurant the mutter of a hungry and seditious multitude' (77). It is no wonder that he finds some reassurance in the knowledge that anarchist groups have no rigid hierarchical system of efficient organization (79–80).

The frame narrator's own life is the very epitome of order and organization. He is a collector of Chinese bronzes and porcelain, a man who knows no passion other than the passion for accumulating 'things which are rare, and must remain exquisite even if approaching to the monstrous' (76). His outlook is purely aesthetic as he values the precious items according to their rarity (i.e. monstrosity) rather than their usefulness or significance in a social context.[26] The only activity in which the pathological collector engages after the initial acquisition of his treasures is the (taxonomical) arrangement of his specimens and their preservation through a rigid system of insulation. It is a form of fetishism, an obsession involving both a withdrawal from life (as in the case of Stein, Conrad's most famous collector) and a constant attempt to introduce a fictional sense of order (hierarchy, method,

[26] For an alternative view of the collector's figure in the story, see Allan Hepburn's 'Collectors in Conrad's "The Informer",' *Studies in Short Fiction*, 29 no. 1 (Winter 1992), 103–12. Hepburn's discussion of the story revolves around Walter Benjamin's view of the true collector as a historian of culture, a view which I find rather difficult to reconcile with the blatant a-morality of the characters in the story. I am grateful to Reynold Humphries, who brought the article to my attention.

classification) into reality. One symptom of the collector's obsession is his fear of fire:

My treasures are disposed in three large rooms. . . . I allow no fires to be lighted, for fear of accidents, and a fire-proof door separates them from the rest of the house. (74)

The frame narrator seems to equate the danger of fire which might destroy his treasured collection with the threat of anarchy when, in response to Mr X's allegation that anarchist activities are condoned by the privileged classes, he protests 'Impossible! . . . We don't play with fire to that extent' (79). It is no accident that the revolutionary leaflet is called 'The Firebrand' (89).

The narrator's connection with Mr X is brought about through the mediation of a friend in Paris, himself a collector. The friend, however, collects acquaintances rather than bronzes or china.

My friend in Paris is a collector, too. . . . He collects acquaintances. It is delicate work. He brings to it the patience, the passion, the determination of a true collector of curiosities. His collection does not contain any royal personages. I don't think he considers them sufficiently rare and interesting; but, with that exception, he has met with and talked to everyone worth knowing on any conceivable ground. He observes them, listens to them, penetrates them, measures them, and puts the memory away in the galleries of his mind. He has schemed, plotted, and travelled all over Europe in order to add to his collection of distinguished personal acquaintances

As he is wealthy, well connected, and unprejudiced, his collection is pretty complete, including objects (or should I say subjects?) whose value is unappreciated by the vulgar, and often unknown to popular fame. Of those specimens my friend is naturally the most proud. (73)

The anonymous friend's passion is a form of collection which does not entail acquisition or possession; it does not depend upon the material resources of the collector nor does it entail considerations of future profit. It is therefore the quintessence of the collector's disinterested passion itself. The precise degree of this disinterestedness and its appalling implications become very clear when one realizes that this 'unprejudiced' collector does not care about the morality of his subjects/objects, that it is their very monstrosity which often makes them precious to him.

At the opposite end of the scale we find Sevrin, the police informer, and Horne, the leader of the anarchist group, the only two characters in the story who act with conviction and faith, who are not 'amateurs of emotion', opportunists, or poseurs. It is significant that both of them are artist figures and both are dead by the time the story is told. Horne, a Blakean character, 'an engraver and etcher of genius', is the guiding spirit of the anarchist group, a man whose passionate belief in the need for social revolution is kindled by grief for his dead wife and child. Sevrin, on the other side of the ideological struggle, is a 'converted atheist', whose 'ardent humanitarianism' had led him to anarchism and back to the defence of the social order. He too is a writer, but his diary, 'a record of the most damnatory kind', is a production unfit for the entertainment and consumption of the leisured classes (100). Sevrin is described as an actor. He is, in fact, acting out the role of an anarchist, but his conscious masquerade is the enactment of a deep conviction and a total, almost religious commitment to the cause he has chosen to serve. Unlike the girl, 'our young Lady Amateur' (84), who is an unconscious actor, whose involvement with the anarchists is a hollow pose, a gesture of supreme narcissistic vanity, and who knows 'little of anything except of words' (86), Sevrin is an actor 'in desperate earnest' (93), both in love and in his ideological struggle. Sevrin is also described as a fanatical priest, a monk, or a 'converted atheist' (85, 100), who wears the leather case with the secret of his mission like a 'scapular' on his breast (95). The recurrent religious allusions are not merely a reflection on his severely ascetic appearance or the religious intensity of his dedication. Like a true priest in the act of communion, Sevrin, who believes in the 'absolute value of conventional signs' (93), is trying to 'suit the action to the word', to bring together the symbolic and the real.

The figure of Sevrin, the 'informer' in Mr X's account, is simultaneously that of an actor, a priest, and a writer—he is the only character who refuses to accept the purely conventional, arbitrary nature of human discourse. But the artist who tries to achieve that religious fusion of the symbolic and the real in his art cannot survive in a modern secular world. Like Stevie in *The Secret Agent*, another mad artist, Sevrin is foredoomed. Surrounded by a textual network of aesthetes and collectors, a world of empty gestures and hollow words, he will eventually turn into yet another specimen in someone's collection of human rarities. It is, perhaps, one of the most masterful and cruel ironic strokes of this self-proclaimed 'ironic tale' that the one actor who has acted out of faith is defeated through the 'theatrical expedient' devised by Mr X (86). It is appropriate that his actor's face is lit, or haloed, minutes before his martyrdom, by a 'gas-jet . . . near his head' (91). He is, unlike the frame narrator, clearly one of those who are not afraid of fire, who would, in the words of another Conradian figure, 'burn rather than rot'.

Mr X, the main narrator of the story, is a man of both worlds, at home in the polished, decadent surroundings of the frame narrator and in the underground realm of the anarchists. The man described as 'the greatest rebel (revolté) of modern times', a 'revolutionary writer' and 'the active inspirer of secret societies, the mysterious unknown Number One of desperate conspiracies' (73–4), is also 'an enlightened connoisseur of bronzes and china' (74), a fashionable and elegant *bon vivant* who frequents the same good restaurant as the frame narrator, indistinguishable from the other members of the privileged classes. Appalled by the resemblance between himself and this infamous rebel the frame narrator observes:

He was alive and European; he had the manner of good society, wore a coat and hat like mine, and had pretty near the same taste in cooking. It was too frightful to think of. (76)

When asked about the incongruity of his praxis, the incompatibility of his own luxurious life and his preaching of revolt and violence to the starving proletariat of Europe, Mr X remains unmoved:

'Do I feed on their toil and own their heart's blood? Am I a speculator or a capitalist? Did I steal my fortune from the starving people? No!. . . . What I have acquired has come to me through my writings; not from the millions of pamphlets distributed gratis to the hungry and the oppressed, but from the hundreds of thousands of copies sold to the well-fed bourgeois. You know that my writings were at one time the rage, the fashion—the thing to read with wonder and horror, to turn your eyes up at my pathos . . . or else, to laugh in ecstasies at my wit.' (77–8)

The disturbing ambiguity of this character, whose voice takes over the entire narrative, becomes the pivot of the text. Mr X, it is claimed, had 'laid bare the rottenness of the most venerable institutions' with his 'savage irony'; he 'has scalped every venerated head, and has mangled at the stake of his wit every received opinion and every recognized principle of conduct and policy'; he has written 'flaming red revolutionary pamphlets' which used to 'overwhelm the powers of every Continental police like a plague of crimson gadflies' (74). And yet, he has turned this very same literature into literal capital, which he uses liberally for the same pleasures enjoyed by the enemy, the 'idle and selfish class' he would ostensibly overthrow.

There is a distinct element of bathos in the description of X's own celebrated rhetoric and the lethal effects attributed to it. The man who is called a 'firebrand' exhibits 'the least possible amount of warmth and animation' (76). His literary—rather than literal—bombs are as effective as the 'bombe glacée' on his plate (82). The victims of his 'venomous pen stabs' (76), his 'savage irony', and his fierce wit are apparently in good health and as prosperous as ever. How should one relate to the discourse of this man? Does rhetorical effectiveness depend on sincerity? Is there a real difference between false and true rhetoric? Can the same words have 'real meaning' when addressed to one reader and a false one when addressed to another? The question of rhetoric is persistently brought up and deconstructed by the narrative. It is not only the personal integrity of a fictional character which is at stake here: it is the question of the relationship between discourse and praxis, the symbolic and the real, aesthetics and ethics, which the narrative has to resolve.

I would suggest that Mr X may be seen as an authorial figuration. He is a failed author (an author *manqué*) in that he has turned the real—the suffering, the action, the revolt of his fellow-men—into an aesthetic product for the consumption of his declared enemies. It is he, rather than Sevrin, who is the real informer, who sets off the tragic action and then converts it into hard currency and sits back to enjoy its aesthetic effects. He is the survivor who returns with a tale for the pleasure of the listener, the reader, the bourgeois collector. This problematic character embodies the essential dilemma of the writer: the betrayal of real action in the world of ethics through an aestheticization of reality, the enclosure of art as an autonomous sphere at the expense of its own power.

Where, then, does the implied or real author stand in this world of actors, informers, and collectors? Should the writing of fiction necessarily be relegated to the world of aesthetics? Is the writer invariably guilty of a betrayal of reality? If he is, can he claim any moral authority? Mark Conroy, who follows the 'de-legitimating process' which 'implicates the narrative itself', has argued that 'The Secret Agent's bleak scenario undercuts the viability of literature as an institution. After all, if there is no legitimate ruling order, no cohesive audience, and no moral authority in this world—and for this text to be successful, that world must be convincing—then there is not much of a role for literature as an institution to play. At such a juncture, the legitimation of literature becomes purely aesthetic, a question of style.'[27] My own view is that aestheticism is precisely what Conrad rejects in his 'anarchist' works through the deployment of irony which does not allow either the author or the reader the luxury of being mere observers of the bleak scenario.

In his *Theory of the Avant-Garde* Peter Burger defines aesthetic radicalism as that form of art which breaks with the 'Institution' of art or literature in bourgeois society. The avant-garde, according to Burger, turns against the neutralization of art and its autonomous detachment from the praxis of life. It refuses to be contained within the institution of art and 'purified' of anything but aesthetics. The avant-gardists recognize that aesthetic autonomy is bought at the expense of social critique, and their work exposes the 'nexus between autonomy and the absence of any consequences'.[28] I would suggest that 'The Informer' can be read as just such an avant-garde gesture. The ambiguity of the authorial figure in the story is clearly related to the issues which Conrad was to treat shortly afterwards in *The Secret Agent*. Beyond their common subject-matter, the apparent chronological continuity (the intertextual bonding through the appearance of the mad professor in both the short story and the novel), these two works are similarly problematic in their refusal of a clear-cut affirmative stance and in the pervasive irony which destabilizes and subverts every possible construction of an authoritative, authorial 'message'. The novel and the short story are tropo-

[27] *Modernism and Authority: Strategies of Legitimation in Flaubert and Conrad* (Baltimore: Johns Hopkins University Press, 1985), 159.
[28] Peter Burger, *Theory of the Avant-Garde* (first published in 1974), trans. Michael Shaw (Minneapolis: University of Minnesota Press, 1984), 22.

logically related in their equation of literary and literal bombs, as in the suggestive resemblance and symbiosis between characters who are ostensibly on opposite sides of the social arena (Heat and Verloc, Mr X and the frame narrator).

In an earlier discussion of the novel I have suggested the term 'anarchist poetics' for the peculiar textual strategy deployed by Conrad in this disturbing work.[29] Viewing anarchism as a form of cultural despair, I suggested that Conrad's stance was not that of an established arch-conservative, but that of a disinherited one, a conservative who has lost faith in the ability—or, indeed, the will—of social institutions and political organization to create a better world. The catachretic strategies employed by the text, its violation of rhetorical normativity, its brutal exposure of the gap between signifieds and signifiers and of any symbolic representation are modes of cultural dissent, a refusal to become implicated in the sham rhetoric of the powerful. The persistent ('corrosive' as critics have often defined it) irony of the narrative is of the frustrating variety defined by Booth as 'unstable, infinite, irony' or 'endless negativity':[30] it is a structure of meaning which constantly demands to be restructured, a set of endless subversions and aporias. This ironic modality practised by the narrator and embodied in the figure of the assistant commissioner is, I have suggested, another way out of the 'slimy aquarium'. Being a mode of perception which is invariably split, it allows the separation of the subject participant from the subject observer. If one cannot escape the symbolic order and its representations, one can at least be conscious of one's inescapable complicity.

The ironic narrator in 'The Informer' is not the frame narrator, who fails to understand 'where the joke comes in' (and who is, in fact, the butt of this 'ironic tale'), but Mr X who straddles both worlds, who enjoys both the sensual luxuries of the bourgeois aesthetes and the moral luxury of holding their world in contempt. Mr X practices anarchism as a 'trade', and capitalizes on his revolutionary writings, using them as hard currency within an economic system of exchange. He can, however, appreciate the

---

[29] See Daphna Erdinast-Vulcan, '"Sudden Holes in Space and Time": Conrad's Anarchist Aesthetics in *The Secret Agent*', in *Conrad's Cities: A Festschrift for Hans van Marle*, ed. Gene M. Moore (Amsterdam andAtlanta, Ga.: Rodopi, 1992), 207–22.

[30] Wayne C. Booth, *A Rhetoric of Irony* (Chicago: University of Chicago Press, 1974).

difference between 'trade' and 'mission' and realizes that the latter is just what Sevrin, the police informer, had died for. As the story unfolds, the attribution of roles becomes more problematic. The frame narrator loses his initial position and turns into a bewildered listener or reader as X takes over the narrative. Sevrin, the putative informer, becomes a priest or an actor. But an actor is both an agent of deception (when he assumes the role of another) and the performer of an action. He can be either the agent who turns away from reality (through his play-acting) or the one who engages with it through action. Sevrin, it appears, belongs to the latter category: he is an actor 'in desperate earnest'.

X, the authorial figure, is also an actor or a stage-director who devises the 'theatrical expedient' in order to trap Sevrin. He is the real informer both in a very literal sense (the character who imparts the information) and in the borrowed sense, as it is he who betrays the real for the aesthetic. His contempt for the young 'Lady Amateur' whose commitment to his cause is yet another hollow gesture, does not stand in the way of his aesthetic appreciation of her 'consummate art', her imitation of passion which is 'better than the very thing itself' (85). He expresses contempt for the rich consumers of his writings whose 'own life [is] all a matter of pose and gesture' and who are 'unable to realize the power and danger of a real movement and of words that have no sham meaning' (78). And yet, he is all too ready to call himself a 'demagogue' as he carries these 'amateurs of emotion' with him and, not incidentally, feeds well on their need for rhetorical stimulation (78). He allows and enjoys the neutralization of his social critique as it turns into an object of art. Is he a real revolutionary who disguises himself as an aesthete or the most decadent of aesthetes who poses as a rebel? Isn't he also a collaborator with the bourgeois aestheticist collectors who fetishize his revolutionary art of literary bombs and thereby defuse it? The unresolved ambiguity of this authorial figure is what turns the story into an 'ironic tale'. Irony is one mode of discourse which facilitates the traffic between ethics and aesthetics, in that it splits the subject into a participant/actor on the one hand and an observer/informer on the other. When the writer perceives his own complicity in the aesthetic ordering (and falsification) of reality, when the drive towards form is constantly checked by an awareness of the precariousness of form, the

dynamics of art become infinitely more complex. It is this fundamentally schizophrenic character of writing which turns every
good story into an 'ironic tale' and every author or reader into a
Homo duplex.

4
The Romantic Paradox

'HE IS ROMANTIC—romantic . . . And that is very bad—very bad. . . . Very good, too' (*Lord Jim*, 216). Stein's cryptic diagnosis of Jim encapsulates one of the best commentaries on the 'Romantic temper', on the author himself, and on the problem of subjectivity in his work. Conrad's troubled relationship with the cultural legacy of Romanticism has been the subject of several studies, following the same itinerary as that of changing cultural and historical views of the Romantic tradition itself.[1] Of the many possible angles of this relationship, I will focus on the conception of the self, the 'key innovation of the Romantic Programme':

Romanticism became a cultural program and the source of cumulative cultural change because it rested upon a shared belief in a new term for action, the 'self,' and upon the relation of that term to the culture. . . . In the last decades of the eighteenth century the 'self' had emerged, at least for a narrow cultural elite, as the term that could justify the creation of innovative cultural products.[2]

---

[1] For the earliest discussions of Conrad's relationship with the Romantic tradition see Ian Watt, *Conrad in the Nineteenth Century* (London: Chalto & Windus, 1980); David Thorburn, *Conrad's Romanticism* (New Haven: Yale University Press, 1974); Elsa Nettels, *James and Conrad* (Athens: University of Georgia Press, 1977); Michael Jones, *Conrad's Heroism: A Paradise Lost* (Ann Arbor: University of Michigan Press, 1985). These readings, while offering valuable insights, still fall within the 'organicist' view of Romanticism. A more recent and most valuable contribution to this ongoing discussion is William Bonney's essay 'Conrad's Romanticism Reconsidered', *Conradiana*, 27 no. 3 (1995), 189–222. Bonney offers a dense, learned, often strident critique of the Romantic-organicist interpretations of Conrad's work (most notably Ian Watt's and David Thorburn's) and views Conrad's work as uncompromisingly subversive of explanatory postures and doctrinal resolutions: 'Instead of compensatory absolutes, Conrad's universe features various narrative perspectives incorporating geographically and culturally diverse perceptions that offer, in place of comprehensive assertions, only recalcitrant fragments . . . a form of scepticism which elicits the Romantic innovation of the "self" . . . as a "heuristic construct"' (195).

[2] John H. Gagnon, 'Success = Failure/Failure = Success', in *Romanticism and Culture*, ed. H. W. Matalene (Columbia, SC: Camden, 1984), 98.

It is, I would argue, the same conception of the self, anterior to and differentiated from culture or civilization, which underlies both the pathos of a lost authenticity and the total empowerment of the creative imagination. According to Gagnon, the physical and mental journeying so typical of the Romantics, the willed option of social, cultural, and spatial dislocation, are gestures of 'deviation' designed to maintain the split between self and other.

The mountains, the deserts, the sea, the tropical island were places in which one could free oneself from the other. If such journeys involved profound cultural disorientation so much the better since the powers of the self, indeed its very existence, could be found in its ability to survive dislocation. The innovative cultural products that were constructed from experiences of isolation were themselves another form of evidence for the primacy of the self.

The central category of value which was to be forged in the romantic journey was the self. The journey, the product, the performance (including the anti-roles) were devoted to creating and maintaining the self.

Seen in this light, Conrad's own willed exile seems to have been one of these Romantic lifelong gestures. But the 'Romantic programme', at least in its naïve form, was no longer simply available for a writer who is, as Gagnon rightly observes, 'a bridging figure between the late romantics and the early moderns', afflicted by more than a suspicion 'that the self cannot escape the other'.[3] The dynamics of subjectivity in Conrad's work are closely related to his ambivalent relationship with Romanticism as a cultural mode of being and with the genre of Romance as a mode of writing. But before we look at this troubled relationship, let us consider for a moment the apparently straightforward derivation of the cultural label from the generic one. Etymology, we should remember, is not a guarantee of filiation.

In a seminal essay entitled 'The Internalization of the Quest Romance', Harold Bloom argues that 'Freud's embryonic theory of romance contains within it the potential for an adequate account of romanticism'; 'English Romanticism legitimately can be called . . . a revival of romance. More than a revival, it is an internalization of romance, particularly of the quest variety, an

---

[3] Ibid., 100, 106, 102.

internalization made for more than therapeutic purposes, because made in the humanizing hope that approaches apocalyptic intensity.'[4] The poetic revolution of Romanticism is marked, according to Bloom, 'by the evanescence of any subject but subjectivity', and the internalization of the quest romance is rather more than a figural shift: it is a change of conscience of a truly 'Copernican' magnitude.[5] Romanticism, Bloom argues, has internalized, aestheticized, and distilled this quest in its movement from the battlefield to the realm of consciousness, from the heroic knight to the visionary poet who 'takes the patterns of quest romance and transposes them into his own imaginary life'.[6] But even from the prophetic heights of visionary Romanticism the dangers attendant on this paradigm shift from Nature to Imagination are all too apparent, and Bloom seems to be somewhat ill at ease with his own aestheticized view: 'The movement of the quest romance, before its internalization by the High Romantics, was from nature to redeemed nature, the sanction of redemption being the gift of some external spiritual authority, sometimes magical. The Romantic movement is from nature to the imagination's freedom (sometimes a reluctant freedom), and the imagination's freedom is frequently purgatorial, redemptive in direction but destructive of the social self.'[7]

A more qualified view of the romantic self has been offered by Geoffrey Hartman.[8] While keeping to the 'redemptive' orientation of the romance quest, Hartman acknowledges the compensatory, 'remedial' element in the Romantic conception of an all-inclusive consciousness and a return to a 'second naivete' against the 'corrosive power of analysis and self-consciousness'. 'The attempt to think mythically is itself part of a crucial defense against the self-conscious intellect. . . . Whether myth-making is still possible,

---

[4] Harold Bloom, 'The Internalization of the Quest Romance' (1969), reprinted in *Romanticism and Consciousness: Essays in Criticism* (New York: Norton, 1970), 4, 5.
[5] Ibid., 8.
[6] Harold Bloom, *The Ringers in the Tower: Studies in Romantic Tradition* (Chicago: University of Chicago Press, 1971), chs. 1–2. See also Goeffery Hartman's 'False Themes and Gentle Minds', in *Beyond Formalism* (New Haven: Yale University Press, 1970), 283–97.   [7] Ibid., 5–6.
[8] Geoffrey Hartman, 'Romanticism and Anti-Self-Consciousness', first published in *Centennial Review*, 6 (1962), 553–65; reprinted in *Beyond Formalism* (New Haven: Yale University Press, 1970); and in *Romanticism*, ed. Cynthia Chase, Longman Critical Readers (London: Longman, 1993), 43–54.

whether the mind can find an unselfconscious medium for itself or maintain something of the interacting unity of self and life, is a central concern of the Romantic poets'; 'The Romantic "I" emerges nostalgically when certainty and simplicity of self are lost'; The 'aggrandizement of art' is a symptom of anxiety, when the 'burden of selfhood' and the problem of self-consciousness achieve an unprecedented urgency against the loss of religious consolations. 'Subjectivity—even solipsism—becomes the subject of poems which *qua* poetry seek to transmute it.'[9]

The full reversal of the 'redemptive' view of Romanticism was accomplished by Paul de Man's diagnosis of this tradition as implicated in 'a conflict between a conception of the self seen in its authentically temporal predicament and a defensive strategy that tries to hide from this negative self-knowledge.'[10] The precarious nature of the this defensive strategy was all too clear to the Romantics themselves: 'Poetic language can do nothing but originate anew over and over again: it is always constitutive, able to posit regardless of presence but, by the same token, unable to give a foundation to what it posits except as an intent of consciousness.'[11] De Man's deconstruction of Romantic rhetoric has been followed by a whole generation of Poststructuralist, anti-organicist readings in keeping with the cultural climate of the late 1970s and the early 1980s.[12]

A particularly illuminating treatment of the 'dark side' of Romanticism was offered by Tilottama Rajan, who studies Romanticism as 'a literature than stands on the edge of Modernism, in a universe already recognized as discontinuous rather than organic'.[13] Rajan's critique is directed against 'traditional critics such as Abrams and Frye' who 'assimilate Romanticism to romance and thus endorse the period's most idealistic statements

<hr/>

[9] Ibid., 45, 46, 48, 49.

[10] Paul de Man, 'The Rhetoric of Temporality' (1969); reprinted in *Blindness and Insight: Essays on the Rhetoric of Contemporary Criticism* (London: Routledge, 1983), 208.

[11] Paul de Man, 'The Intentional Structure of the Romantic Image' in *Romanticism and Consciousness*, ed. Harold Bloom (New York: Norton, 1970), 69.

[12] For a good sampling of such readings see Arden Reed's *Romanticism and Language* (London: Methuen, 1984). For a lucid and useful survey of the critical/theoretical itinerary in relation to Romanticism see Aidan Day, *Romanticism*, The New Critical Idiom (London: Routledge, 1996).

[13] *Dark Interpreter: The Discourse of Romanticism* (Ithaca and London: Cornell University Press,1980), 15.

about the power of art'.[14] Going back to the relation of genre and the cultural climate, Rajan points to the obverse of Bloom's redemptive aesthetics:

Art, as the power to invent, is paradigmatic of man's capacity to take existence itself into the mind and rewrite it according to the images of desire. Indeed the historical and etymological connection of the term 'Romanticism' with 'romance' points to a view of literature as an idealizing rather than a mimetic activity, a mode of consciousness that envisions the unreal and the possible across the barrier of the actual. Yet implicit in this belief that the mind can create the unreal must be a doubt as to the reality of a mental creation.[15]

The Romantics' claim to a mythopoetic power and their visionary drive, the 'apparently utopian narrative of Romantic desire', are questioned and probed by the Romantics themselves:

Schiller, in his distinction of sentimental from naive poetry, is one of the first theorists to concede that there may exist, alongside the art which creates a golden work a second, non-ideal art in which the distance between human consciousness and plenitude is the structuring principle. . . . Schiller, in revealing the compensatory structure of idealization, and indeed of symbolization itself, discloses the dividedness of Romantic vision, which involves an insight into the very emptiness it seeks to negate. . . . In Schiller's theory we have for the first time a questioning of the naive aesthetics on which modern or organicist interpretations of Romantic poetry as the union of consciousness and nature base themselves. The sentimental sight is an intentional sight: it recognizes the separateness of imagination from actuality.[16]

The apparent rehabilitation of Romance in the second half of the eighteenth century functions as 'a metonymy for the idealizing power of aesthetic illusion in general' and 'marks a major shift in pre-Romantic aesthetics toward the affirmation of poetic discourse as something that transcends temporality'. It is all the more significant, then, that it is precisely this form which is

---

[14] Frye, Rajan claims, 'uses Romanticism as a way of explaining the philosophical underpinnings of romance [a movement from an original innocence through a nightmare world to an idyllic world recovered in the future], and thus implies that romance can provide us with a way of understanding Romanticism'. Abrams similarly relies on the archetypal romance journey from night to day in his analysis of post-Kantian idealism as 'a spiralling journey through self-consciousness to psychic reintegration', 40–1.   [15] Ibid., 13

[16] Ibid., 21, 30–1.

systematically ironized and deconstructed (in Keats's work, for instance) by the intrusion of realistic or grotesque elements and by the distancing of the narrative voice. The emotional indeterminacy so typical of these ostensibly rehabilitated romances (or anti-romances) is symptomatic of the 'radical homelessness of a poetic voice that is unable to make habitable the empty space that follows the expulsion of illusions', and the equally radical 'heteronomy in the self and its enterprises disclosed by the movement beyond the sphere of illusion [which] cannot be covered up or healed, but only mediated'.[17]

It is at this point that we should turn back to Conrad, whose treatment of the 'Romantic temper' is of particular significance in *Lord Jim, Chance, Victory, The Rescue* (subtitled *A Romance of the Shallows*), and *The Arrow of Gold*.[18] These novels are generically marked by a profusion of signals which set up a 'Romance' frame of reading, but their ostensible conformity to the conventions of the genre is extremely precarious: the generic signals are systematically subverted and eventually pre-empted by a corrosive undercurrent of irony, exposing and challenging the naïveté of the very genre to which the narrative pretends to conform. The subversion of generic conventions, along with the evidence of Conrad's reiterated faith in 'the truth which alone is the justification of fiction',[19] his scorn for all forms of escape, and his notorious incompetence in dealing with love might justify the view that Conrad was, in fact, deeply hostile to the genre and retained much of its paraphernalia only to undermine it more effectively.[20] In a letter to a friend, Conrad described the novel entitled *Romance* as 'something of no importance'; a 'purely aesthetic' exercise; an attempt to produce 'something which was very much in vogue with the public at that moment',[21] a summary dismissal which could apply to the genre itself.

Why did Conrad choose to go back, time and again, to a genre he regarded as trivial? Was it a compromise of authorial integrity

---

[17] Ibid., 23, 100, 102, 141.

[18] I have dealt with these novels as instances of 'The Failure of Textuality' in *Joseph Conrad and the Modern Temper* (Oxford: Oxford University Press, 1991).

[19] Author's note to *Under Western Eyes*.

[20] Elsa Nettles, *James and Conrad* (Athens: University of Georgia Press, 1977), 131–3.

[21] A Letter to Kazimierz Waliszewski, 8 Nov. 1903. *Conrad's Polish Background*, ed. Z. Najder, trans. Halina Carroll (London: Oxford University Press, 1964), 236.

for the promise of greater financial solvency which the genre seemed to hold? Conrad's own testimony seems to indicate that it was. But serving Mammon at the expense of God proved to be far more difficult than one would imagine, even in Conrad's perennially straitened circumstances. These problematic works which pretend to be popular romances present some serious questions regarding the fundamental premises of the genre. The complexity of the relationship is further compounded in view of Conrad's insistence that the 'romantic feeling of reality' was an 'inborn faculty' with him.[22] I believe that the ambiguity and complexity of Conrad's attitude to the Romantic tradition is symptomatic of the unresolvable ideological tension and the ambivalence which lies at the core of Romanticism itself.

The generic contract entailed in the Romance implies a teleological orientation; a homecoming which, however deferred, is ultimately accomplished; a quest which, however convoluted, is ultimately rewarded; an implicit and fundamental promise of resolution which has remained unchanged throughout the various mutations of the genre, and may well be one of the major reasons for its amazing cultural durability and popularity. As we have seen, however, the Romantic temper is not really reducible to this or any other benevolent formulation. When taken far enough, the Romantic glorification of the creative artistic imagination and the insistence on its autonomy and sovereignty ultimately recoils upon itself, as it questions the very existence of objective reality and thus invalidates the truth-claims of art. It is, then, not the promised homecoming but rather the initial homelessness which generates the quest in the first place.

Romanticism at its most profound, says Hartman, shares the Modernist 'horror of seduction'; it 'reveals the depth of the enchantment in which we live. We dream, we wake on the cold hillside, and our sole self pursues the dream once more. In the beginning was the dream, and the task of disenchantment never ends.'[23] The same ideological tension inherent in the Romantic outlook reflects the central dynamics of Conrad's work. Conrad's preoccupation with the relation of life to art, truth to fiction, and reality to the dream, which is the thematic core of the works under

---

[22] In the author's note to *Within the Tides*, p. vii.
[23] Hartman, 'Romanticism and Anti-Self-Consciousness', 50.

discussion, articulates the Romantic paradox. The deliberate choice of the Romance as a 'prototext' in the works cited above, and the no less deliberate subversion of this generic identity are symptomatic of the writer's oscillation between a 'metaphysics of presence'—an affirmation of the power of the word to create and sustain a world—and a 'metaphysics of absence' which recognizes its own fictitious nature.

Once upon a time there was a magician king. He had been over-thrown by a ruthless brother and lived secluded on a charmed island with his beautiful daughter. One day a prince was ship-wrecked in a storm off the shores of the island. He saw the beautiful daughter and fell in love with her. The daughter, who had never seen the face of any man but her father, also fell in love with the prince. But the magician wanted to test their love before he let them marry. He made the prince work hard in order to try him. The prince passed his trial and married the daughter. The magician was reinstated. They all lived happily ever after. This crude rendering of the plot of *The Tempest* is one subtext of Conrad's 'A Smile of Fortune'. The ingredients are all there: an exotic enchanted island, a man who had been cast out by a society dominated by his brutish brother, a beautiful daughter living with her father in utter seclusion, and a young man who comes ashore after a stormy night at sea. But Conrad's story does not end happily. His prince fails his test. He chooses the potatoes rather than the daughter.

The relationship between Conrad's story and Shakespeare's play is not merely a parodic inversion. The epigraph for the volume in which the story was included is a quotation from Arthur Symons: 'Life is a tragic folly / Let us laugh and be jolly / Away with melancholy / Bring me a branch of holly / life is a tragic folly.' This playful epigraph, with its strong Shakespearean notes, pro-vides a clue to the generic ambiguity which is built into the story, and which can be accounted for in the very same terms. The dramatic conflict in the story is ultimately a conflict of mutually exclusive constructions, neither of which is finally validated as the 'truth', even after the narrator's final choice. The young captain, who wavers between these two constructions throughout the story, finally determines its end by opting for one of them. The reader's dilemma is less easily resolved, as there is nothing in the tale itself which would justify the young Captain's eventual choice and resolve the hermeneutic tension. It is the reader who must decide whether to become a sharer of the narrator's vision or to challenge it by opting for the other construction.

The two alternatives are presented right at the beginning of the story. The narrator's destination is 'a fertile and beautiful island of the tropics. The more enthusiastic of its inhabitants delight in describing it as the "Pearl of the Ocean". Well, let us call it the "Pearl". It's a good name. A pearl distilling much sweetness upon the world.' The first perception of the island seems to bear a promise of enchantment: 'I became entranced by this blue, pinnacled apparition, almost transparent against the light of the sky . . . and I wondered half seriously whether it was a good omen, whether what should meet me in that island would be as luckily exceptional as this beautiful, dreamlike vision. . . . But horrid thoughts of business interfered with my enjoyment' (3–4). The incompatibility of enchantment and business is thus established at the very outset. Jacobus's visit seems to bring out this implicit opposition:

What did this call mean? Was is the sign of some dark design against my commercial innocence? Ah! These commercial interests—spoiling the finest life under the sun. Why must the sea be used for trade—and for war as well? Why kill and traffic on it, pursuing selfish aims of no great importance after all? It would have been so much nicer just to sail about with here and there a port and a bit of land to stretch one's legs on, buy a few books and get a change of cooking for a while. But, living in a world more or less homicidal and desperately mercantile, it was plainly my duty to make the best of its opportunities. (6)

Having to choose between enchantment and commerce, the young captain narrator feels duty-bound to pursue the business opportunities he perceives. The truism that 'man is the creature and the victim of lost opportunities' (15), which occurs to him some time later, does not seem to be applicable to his case, as 'opportunity' is initially perceived to be an economic term, just as the concept of 'fortune' is. After making his final choice between commerce and enchantment, he will realize that 'it was as if a supreme opportunity had been missed' (77). These two constructions are related, of course, to the figure of Jacobus and to the biblical story which is the other subtext, or proto-text as I would rather call it, of Conrad's tale. The biblical Jacob is problematic in the same sense that his namesake in the story is. He is a trickster who disguises himself as his elder brother Esau, in order to obtain the blessing conferred on the first-born son. Jacobus in the story follows in the footsteps of his biblical ancestor: he too makes use (albeit unknowingly) of his brother's name in order to gain first access to the captain's cabin. The brother is described in both stories as a brutish, inarticulate creature (25–9).[24] The biblical Jacob pays for his own act of deception when he becomes the victim of a similar ploy. After having slaved for seven years for the sake of Rachel, he is tricked into marrying the wrong woman by Laban's clever substitution of his elder daughter for her sister on the wedding night. Refusing to accept the substitution of Leah for Rachel, the promised bride, he slaves for another seven years in order to marry his beloved (Genesis 29). The biblical story of the ordeals of perseverance and love is echoed—albeit with a touch of bathos—in the story of Jacobus and his love for the circus lady.

Who then is the Jacobus in our story? Is he the lover or the trickster? The devoted father magician who is trying to provide for his daughter's happiness or the cunning procurer, who is willing to use his daughter as a bait in order to exchange her honour for financial gains in a commercial transaction? It is not by accident that deception takes the form of substitution, the exchange of the 'right' person for the wrong one. It is the idea of interchange-ability which makes commerce possible: we trade one commodity for another when we perceive them as interchangeable or exchangeable, when we can substitute the one for the other. The choice that one has to make, along with the narrator, revolves around the concept of substitution when applied to human relationships. Can human relations be predicated on an economic matrix? Are human beings interchangeable and exchangeable?

The answer to this question is given at the very beginning of the story, when the narrator meets the skipper of the *Hilda*, who had lost the figurehead of his ship. 'The *Hilda* had unaccountably lost her figurehead in the bay of Bengal, and her captain was greatly affected by this. He and the ship had been getting on in years together and the old gentleman imagined this strange loss even to be the fore-runner of his own early dissolution' (10–11). The old

---

[24] See Genesis 27, 29.

man, who seems to have retained an 'angelic' and 'boyish' appearance, accosts the narrator at the funeral with the story of his lost
figurehead, 'a woman in a blue tunic edged with gold, the face
perhaps not so very, very pretty, but her bare arms beautifully
shaped and extended as if she were swimming' (18–19). The
younger man finds this grief for a little wooden figure ludicrous,
and suggests that 'surely another figure of a woman could be
procured', only to find himself severely reproved.

The old boy flushed pink under his clear tan as if I had proposed something improper. One could replace masts, I was told, or a lost rudder —
any working part of a ship; but where was the use of sticking up a new
figurehead? What satisfaction? How could one care for it? It was easy to
see that I had never been shipmates with a figurehead for over twenty
years. 'A new figurehead!' he scolded in unquenchable indignation. 'Why!
I've been a widower now for eight-and-twenty years come next May and I
would just as soon think of getting a new wife.' (19)

Oddly enough, the young man is contemptuously equated at this
point with Jacobus, who had apparently offered to 'procure'
another figurehead for the bereaved old man. The contemptible
verb is later reiterated by the narrator himself when he tries to
account to himself for the fascination of Jacobus's daughter, and
for his willingness to give up the society of the respectable family
of S— for her company. 'Though vexed with my forgetfulness (it
would be rather awkward to explain) I couldn't help thinking that
it had *procured* me a more amusing evening. And besides—business. The sacred business—' (50, my emphasis). The young man
has to make a choice. He has to define his relationship with
Jacobus and his daughter in terms of either commerce or romance.
The opposition between the two is irreconcilable, as the notion of
substitution, which is the underlying principle of the one, is
unacceptable in the other. There is no substitute for the beloved
figurehead or the beloved woman. It is not for nothing that the
girl's worst visions take the form of a business deal between her
would-be suitor and her father.

Having been placed in Jacobus's 'custody' as the narrator puts
it, his initial construction of the situation takes on the parameters
of romance. When the charterers' clerk makes vague allusions to
Jacobus's character and to certain offences of which he was guilty,
the young man responds with derision. 'He resembled an old

maid. A commercial old maid shocked by some impropriety. Was it a commercial impropriety? Commercial impropriety is a serious matter, for it aims at one's pocket' (14–15).[25] The narrator later finds out that Jacobus's 'impropriety' was not of a commercial nature; it was the social offence of following his passion and bearing responsibility for it. The narrator dissociates himself from the respectable bourgeoisie of the island, the old French families, descendants of the old colonialists. These people marry off their 'ineffectual young man' to a 'woman nearly twice his age, comparatively well off', forget to pay their debts, and yet despise Jacobus for having formed his unsuitable connection and, much worse, for having taken responsibility for his actions. Their disapproval does not extend to the other Jacobus, the wealthy, influential, and 'respectable bachelor', who brutally abuses his illegitimate son. 'There had never been open scandal in that connection. His life had been quite regular' (34). Not surprisingly, the ethos of that old decadent bourgeoisie which comprises the 'respectable' element in the island is closely linked to a commercial frame of reference. The elder brother of the young man who was married off to the tyrannical but wealthy old woman talks of 'facilitating' matters by 'disposing of' the girl (57). Our narrator, enraged by the hypocrisy of these people who have sentenced the girl to moral solitude, chooses to give them up (58, 65).

The narrator's initial suspicion of Jacobus dissolves under the magic of the walled garden in which the girl sits enclosed and isolated. He seems to opt for romance when he chooses to view Alice and her father as 'a lonely pair of castaways, on a desert island; the girl sheltering in the house as if it were a cavern in a cliff, and Jacobus going out to pick up a living for both on the beach—exactly like two shipwrecked people who always hope for some rescuer to bring them back at last into touch with the rest of mankind' (39; see also 40, 59). Obviously, it is himself that the narrator casts in the role of the rescuer. Moving further into the realm of Romance, the narrator's descriptions of the girl appear to draw on the idiom of fairy tales. The magnificent walled garden with its 'smooth green lawns' and 'the gorgeous maze

---

[25] The very same man, the prudish charterers' clerk, is later revealed as commercially dishonest in his dealings with the captain, when he knowingly withholds the information regarding the shortage of loading-bags, and protects his own interests with an obvious lie (39–40).

of flower-beds' is lying in 'brilliantly coloured solitude, drowsing in a warm, voluptuous silence'. The girl is as still as 'a figure in a tapestry' (42–3); The sad story of her life takes on a larger, almost cosmic significance, lending her the dignity of a tragic figure: 'the garden was one mass of gloom, like a cemetery of flowers buried in the darkness, and she, in the chair, seemed to muse mournfully over the extinction of light and colour. Only whiffs of heavy scent passed like wandering, fragrant souls of that departed multitude of blossoms' (53).

However, even when the narrator seems to be committed to the ethos of the Romance, he never fully succumbs to it. His allusions to his own role as the rescuer are invariably qualified by conditionals: 'I talked in a subdued tone. To a listener it would have sounded like the murmur of a pleading lover' (53–4); 'She was like a spell-bound creature ... I felt myself growing attached to her by the bond of an irrealizable desire, for I kept my head—quite' (59). The generic signals which establish the story as a romance are brutally subverted on the point of realiza- tion. Sleeping Beauty finally awakens to the voice of the self- appointed rescuer, but her awakening triggers an unexpected response from her lover.

To watch the change in the girl was like watching a miracle—the gradual but swift relaxation of her tense glance, of her stiffened muscles, of every fibre of her body. That black, fixed stare into which I had read a tragic meaning more than once, in which I had found a sombre seduction, was perfectly empty now, void of all consciousness whatever, and not even aware any longer of my presence; It has become a little sleepy, in the Jacobus fashion. . . . I felt as though I had been cheated in some rather complicated deal into which I had entered against my better judgement, Yes, cheated without any regard for, at least, the forms of decency. (68)

The narrator's desire for the girl was real only so long as it was 'irrealizable' (sic, 59), just as the idiom of romance and fairy tale is predicated on the self-proclaimed fictionality of the genre. The paradox is embedded in the very definition of the romance: we, the readers, are prepared to accept the miraculous and the fantastic elements of the genre, precisely because we know it does not pretend to be real.

The unravelling of the fairy tale is aptly concluded with an inversion of *Cinderella*. The lost slipper, left on the veranda by the girl in her flight, becomes the issue of the muted struggle between the narrator and Jacobus.

In the absolute stillness of the house we stared at the high-heeled slipper. . . . We stared. It lay overturned. After what seemed a very long time to me, Jacobus hitched his chair forward, stooped with extended arm and picked it up. It looked a slender thing in his big thick hands. . . . I sat down, keeping my eyes on the fascinating object. Jacobus turned his daughter's shoe over and over in his cushioned paws. . . . He went on looking at the shoe which he held now crushed in the middle, the worn point of the toe and the high heel protruding on each side of the heavy fist. (72–3)

But the narrator refuses to recognize the slipper. He retracts the allusion to the fairy tale, thereby retracting his commitment to the girl. 'It was not really a slipper, but a low shoe of blue, glazed kid, rubbed and shabby. It had straps to go over the instep, but the girl only thrust her feet in, after her slovenly manner' (72). It is this denial of the literary meaning of the slipper which makes it possible for the narrator to make the 'potato deal' with Jacobus, to re-enter the world of commerce.

The bourgeois ethos which the narrator has formerly scorned now becomes the standard on which he acts. 'My mortification was extreme. The scandal would be horrible: that was unavoidable' (71). The only way to avert the scandal is obviously to trade with the father, to barter his commitment to the girl for the price of the potatoes. 'I did not want an open scandal, but I thought that outward decency may be bought too dearly at times. I included Jacobus, myself, the whole population of the island, in the same contemptuous disgust as though we had been partners in some ignoble transaction' (74). But he does go through with this ignoble transaction, breaking his promise to the girl, and adopting the ethos of the real world in exchange for that of romance. He seems to be fully aware that in doing so he has banished himself from the enchanted garden, and exchanged the fragrance of its blossoms for the odour of rotting potatoes.

My bargain with all its remotest associations, mental and visual—the garden of flowers and scents, the girl with her provoking contempt and her tragic loneliness of a hopeless castaway—was everlastingly dangled before my eyes, for thousands of miles along the open sea. And as if by a satanic refinement of irony it was accompanied by a most awful smell.

Whiffs from decaying potatoes pursued me on the poop, they mingled with my thoughts, with my food, poisoned my very dreams. They made an atmosphere of corruption for the ship. (82)

The narrator's voluntary expulsion of himself from the walled garden and the enchanted island is followed by an initiation into the world of commercial prosperity. 'That night I dreamt of a pile of gold in the form of a grave in which a girl was buried, and woke up callous with greed' (84); 'The demon of lucre had taken possession of me' (85). The friendly letter from the 'right' Jacobus, the wealthy merchant, to the owners of the ship, seals his fate. The narrator's last vision of the island, 'diaphanous and blue' as he first saw it, recalls the initial terms of the conflict. 'The unsubstantial, clear marvel of it as if evoked by the art of a beautiful and pure magic. . . . Was this the fortune this vaporous and rare apparition had held for me?' (74). Having made his choice between two incompatible constructions of the experience, and having acted on his choice, the narrator emerges with a 'weary conviction of the emptiness of all things under heaven', feeling that 'everything in our life is common, short, and empty' (79). Having grabbed the commercial opportunity and made his fortune, he has become the creature and the victim of the unacknowledged opportunity and the rejected fortune.

Our revels now are ended. All we are left with is the realization that reality may be a mere story that we cast ourselves into; that the only liberty given to us is that of choosing between alternative texts. 'A Smile of Fortune' ends with a rude awakening on the cold hillside, a sense of disenchantment hanging over both narrator and reader. It is Prospero who seems to have the last word; we are, indeed, the stuff that dreams are made of. Our reality is what we choose to dream up; our truth is the fiction we choose to live by.

One of the most interesting, if rather scandalous, theoretical formulations of the relation between culture and subjectivity has been offered by René Girard in *Deceit, Desire and the Novel*.[26] Girard posits a distinction between what he calls 'romantic' and 'novelistic' or 'mimetic' desire.[27] The romantic attitude insists on

[26] René Girard, *Deceit, Desire and the Novel: Self and Other in Literary Structure*, trans. Yvonne Freccero (1961; Baltimore, Md: Johns Hopkins University Press, 1965).

[27] The French terms 'romantique' and 'romanesque' bring out the contradiction rather more powerfully, having the same radical and different endings.

the autonomy of selfhood, its ability to generate its own spontaneous desire, its ultimate sovereignty. The novel, Girard argues, challenges the 'illusion of autonomy to which modern man is passionately devoted'. Novelistic desire, as Girard says, is always a borrowed desire. It is generated by an 'other', a mediator perceived as a rival for the same object. It is a 'mimetic' desire in that it imitates the supposed desire of that other. It is invariably 'triangular' in that it originates in another 'real or illusory desire'.[28]

The desiring subject wants to become his mediator; he wants to steal from the mediator his very being of 'perfect knight' or 'irresistible seducer'. The object of mimetic desire is not chosen on its own inherent merits; its desirability is a function of the perceived desire of the other for it. The physical reality of the object is of little importance since it may be substituted at any time for any other object of the other's desire.[29]

Now this is an extremely disturbing theory if one takes its phenomenological implications far enough. I would like, however, to set aside those immense issues, and concentrate on the short story at hand, which seems to be such a perfect case in point. 'Freya of the Seven Isles' follows the time-honoured formula of the melodramatic romance: two handsome, fair lovers, a pathetic father at the mercy of a dark, raving villain, a faithful maid, and a trusted friend and confidant who remains behind to tell the tale. But in spite of the perfect conventionality of the cast, the set-up, and the plot, this melodramatic romance refuses to behave as it should. The story, like Conrad's longer putative romances, defies the generic conventions of the genre not only in terms of its plot but in a much more profound and disturbing way. The symmetrical arrangement of damsel and knight, knight and rival, confidant and faithful maid, is unbalanced by the intrusion of a form of desire alien to the very spirit of the genre. What we seem to have here is not a romance but an anti-romance: a story of mimetic rather than romantic desire, which involves not only the stock characters of the melodramatic cast—the fair, blue-eyed lovers and the dark raving villain—but, much more importantly, the narrator himself.

There are 'three guests in the house' (163), and Freya, we are

---

[28] Girard, *Deceit, Desire and the Novel*, 39, 105.   [29] Ibid., 54.

told, is 'vanquished in her struggle with three men's absurdities' (238). She thinks of these men as one: 'Men were absurd in many ways: lovably like Jasper, impractically like her father, odiously like that grotesquely supine creature in the chair' (193); 'The absurdities of three men were forcing this anxiety upon her: Jasper's impetuosity, her father's fears, Heemskirk's infatuation' (187). But the third man is not her father. It is the narrator who, as we shall see, not only tells the story but actually tries to become one of its characters as well. It seems to me that what we have here is a series of triangular relationships, as Girard would call them. These triangles are superimposed on each other, creating a kaleidoscope of opposing but symmetrical desires which inevitably crashes, leaving behind a mass of broken, colourful fragments of glass.

The smaller and least interesting triangle is the relationship of Freya and Jasper. But where is the third party to this ostensibly romantic relationship? Girard's theory suggests an interesting answer:

In sexual desire, the presence of a rival is not needed in order to term the desire triangular. The beloved is divided into both subject and object in the lover's eyes. . . . The division produces a triangle whose three corners are occupied by the lover, the beloved, and the body of this beloved. . . . To imitate one's lover's desire is to desire *oneself*, thanks to that lover's desire. This particular form of double mediation is called 'coquetry'.

The coquette does not wish to surrender her precious self to the desire which she arouses, but were she not to provoke it, she would not feel so precious. . . . Thus we have a vicious circle of double mediation. (105–6)

The 'the third party in that fascinating game' (156), to use the narrator's own words, is Freya's body as represented by the brig, the point of convergence for these parallel lines of desire: for Jasper, the boat is totally merged with the woman he loves.

there was nothing unnatural in Jasper Allen treating her like a lover. . . . He clothed her in many coats of the very best white paint. . . . A narrow gilt moulding defined her elegant sheer as she sat on the water. . . . His feelings for the brig and for the girl were as insolubly united in his heart as you may use two precious metals together in one crucible. (157–8)

Jasper frets at the delay in the proposed elopement, but is 'consoled' by the brig which is 'pervaded by the spirit of Freya' (167). 'Dependent on things as all men are, Jasper loved his vessel—the house of his dreams. He lent to her something of Freya's soul. Her deck was the foothold of their love. The possession of his brig appeased his passion in a soothing certitude of happiness already possessed' (210; see also 218). The Freudian symbolism in this passage speaks for itself. It is not surprising that when Jasper loses the boat, he cannot go back to the woman. For Freya, in love with her own self, nourished by desire which she stimulates by denial, the brig is a mirror. She is 'not the sort of girl that gets carried off' (190). Refusing to elope with Jasper Allen, she says: 'It will be no man who will carry me off—it will be the brig, your brig—our brig. . . . I love the beauty!' (190). It is, of course, her own beauty she is in love with. It appears then, that our star-crossed lovers are not the victims of cruel fate, for Jasper is a fool, and Freya is a coquette. They are defeated by their own vanity and folly.

The second triangle of mimetic desire is Freya's relationship with Heemskirk, the obnoxious villain of the piece. Heemskirk's 'mediator' is, of course, Jasper Allen. Their rivalry is explicit and loaded with gestures of rather crude symbolic significance. Heemskirk amuses himself by knocking down Jasper's beacons (172, 185).[30] When their boats meet for the final and crucial confrontation, they are both described as the embodiments of their respective owners. The *Neptune*, 'belching out' smoke from her 'short black funnel' (208), is a 'short, squat' gunboat 'with her stumpy dark spars naked like dead trees, raised against the luminous sky of that resplendent night' (211). The *Bonito*, 'with her fine lines and her white sails' looks 'vaporous and sylph-like in the moonlight' (211). Both vessels are headed east (208). Both men desire the woman who watches out for them as she sits there, on the east veranda (234). But Freya, far from the traditional heroine of the genre, is not the innocent victim of the villain's lust. Her use of the piano, her 'upright grand', as an instrument of sexual communication, is curiously undiscriminating.[31]

Jasper Allen told me that early of a morning on the deck of the *Bonito* (his wonderfully fast and pretty brig) he could hear Freya playing her scales quite distinctly. But the fellow always anchored foolishly close to the point, as I told him more than once. (151)

---

[30] Freya is also likened to an 'unerring beacon' (168).

[31] It is worth noting that Freya's piano, an 'upright grand' had been freighted to the island by the narrator (151).

Freya would sit down to the piano and play fierce Wagner music in the flicker of blinding flashes, with thunderbolts falling all round, enough to make your hair stand on end. (152)

Freya's playing for her lover is natural enough. But the same music is heard again soon afterwards in entirely different circumstances. Freya, left alone with Heemskirk in the evening, plays the same 'fierce piece of music' for him, in an attempt to silence his amorous overtures (194). The same music is played yet again the following morning. Heemskirk secretly watches Freya as she gets up barefoot in her dressing-gown to watch her lover's boat sail away:

And Freya knew that he was watching her. She knew. She had seen the door move as she came out of the passage. She was aware of his eyes being on her, with scornful bitterness, with triumphant contempt. 'You are there,' she thought, levelling the long glasses. 'Oh, well, look on then!' . . . In that attitude of supreme cry she stood still glowing with the consciousness of Jasper's adoration going out to her figure held in the field of his glass away there, and warmed, too, by the feeling of evil passion, the burning covetous eyes of the other, fastened on her back. In the fervour of her love, in the caprice of her mind, and with that mysterious knowledge of masculine nature women seem to be born to, she thought: 'You are looking on—you will—you must! Then you shall see something.' (204)

And then she sends out passionate kisses to the man at sea, who 'dips the ensign' of his brig in response. Not content with that, she returns to her room, leaving the door open to watch the response of the voyeur.

She was excited, she tingled all over, she had tasted blood!. . . . [She] dashed at the piano, which had stood open all night, and made the rosewood monster growl savagely in an irritated bass. She struck chords as if firing shots after that straddling broad figure . . . and then she pursued him with the same thing she had played the evening before—a modern, fierce piece of love music which had been tried more than once against the thunderstorms of the group. She accentuated its rhythm with triumphant malice. (205–6)

The piece of fierce love music is, of course, the same Wagner music Freya had once played for her lover in the thunderstorm, and the previous evening for Heemskirk himself. This tragic coquette uses the same sounds to nourish Jasper's hopeless desire, to provoke Heemskirk's lust and finally to punish the

latter for the voyeurism which she has consciously and deliberately provoked.

The third and most interesting triangle involves the narrator
himself. The narrator, another seaman and voyageur, presents
himself as an old family friend, a trusted confidant of the lovers.
But this, as we shall see, is a far cry from his actual role in the story.
The narrator's initial description of Freya is highly symptomatic:

there's no use concealing the fact that what one remembered really was
[Nelson or Nielsen's] daughter. . . . Freya Nelson (or Nielsen) was the
kind of girl one remembers. The oval of her face was perfect; and within
that fascinating frame the most happy disposition of line and feature . . .
[and so on and so forth]. I will not compare her eyes to violets, because
the real shade of their colour was peculiar, not so dark and more lustrous.
. . . I never did see the long, dark eyelashes lowered—I dare say Jasper
Allen did, being a privileged person—but I have no doubt that the
expression must have been charming in a complex way. She could—
Jasper told me once with a touchingly imbecile exultation—sit on her
hair. I dare say, I dare say. It was not for me to behold these wonders; I
was content to admire.

And then follows a description with distinct erotic suggestions of
Freya's glossy 'wealth of hair', her 'round, solid arms with the fine
wrists', etc., etc. (149–50), alternating with the narrator's disclaimers of familiarity: 'Was it the magic of her face, of her voice,
of her glances . . . ? I am no man to discuss such mysteries' (158).
Clearly, the narrator is not content with being a mere friendly
spectator in the drama.

The narrator seems to be present on every occasion of the
lovers' meetings. 'One day I remember I watched with Freya on
the verandah the brig approaching the point from the northward. I
suppose Jasper made the girl out with his long glass.'[32] Jasper
performs one of his feats of daring in order to approach his
beloved as close and as fast as he can, the narrator draws his
breath, and Freya swears.

Then, looking at me with a little heightened colour—not much—she
remarked, 'I forgot you were there,' and laughed. To be sure, to be sure.
When Jasper was in sight she was not likely to remember that anybody
else in the world was there. In my concern at this mad trick I couldn't

[32] The narrator, too, watches Freya from afar with his 'glasses' when he tows Jasper
out of Nelson's cove (164).

help appealing to her sympathetic common sense. 'Isn't he a fool?' I said with feeling. 'Perfect idiot,' she agreed warmly.[33]

Freya then decides to teach her lover a lesson and deprive him of her company for 'a whole hour', and the narrator remains on the veranda to welcome Jasper: 'the funny thing was that the fellow actually suffered. I could see it. . . . And the next still funnier thing was that the girl calmly walked out of her room in less then ten minutes. And then I left' (152–3).

The narrator is presumably there to help the lovers along, but his actions have precisely the opposite effect. His sessions with Nelson or Nielsen, the pathetic 'comedy father' as he calls him, are oddly similar to the old man's sessions with Heemskirk himself. He too compulsively brings up the subject of Freya's relationship with Jasper, betraying the secret of the lovers whose trusted friend he is supposed to be.

And then I left. I mean to say that I went away to seek old Nelson (or Nielsen) . . . with the kind purpose of engaging him in conversation lest he should start roaming about and intrude unwittingly where he was not wanted just then. (153)

But what happens to this 'kind purpose'?

while I was trying to entertain him with a very funny and somewhat scandalous adventure . . . he exclaimed suddenly: 'What the devil does he want to turn up here for!' Clearly he had not heard a word of the anecdote. And this annoyed me, because the anecdote was really good. I stared at him. 'Come, come!' I cried. 'Don't you know what Jasper Allen is turning up here for?' It was the first allusion I had ever made to the true state of affairs between Jasper and his daughter. (155)

Like Heemskirk, the narrator capitalizes on his standing with the dreaded 'authorities' to gain access to Freya's father. Old Nelson or Nielsen 'had a certain regard for my judgment, and a certain respect, not for my moral qualities, however, but for the good terms I was supposed to be on with the Dutch "authorities"'. (155). Even as the narrator assures the old man about Heemskirk, he seems to cultivate Nelson or Nielsen's fears in his own subtle way. 'Getting up a scare about Heemskirk now! Heemskirk! . . . Really, one hadn't the patience—. . . . For, pray,

---

[33] This is the usual line of conversation between Freya and the narrator: 'It was our joke to speak of Jasper abusively' (162).

who was Heemskirk? You shall see at once how unreasonable this dread of Heemskirk. . . . Certainly, his nature was malevolent enough' (159). '[Nelson] let the beggar treat him with heavy contempt, devour his daughter with his eyes, and drink the best part of his little stock of wine. I saw something of this, and on one occasion I tried to pass a remark on the subject. . . . I was going to tell him that the fellow was after his girl' (160–1). In his role as Freya's confidant, the narrator offers to tow Jasper's boat out in the morning in order to 'get him away at the earliest possible moment' (164), ostensibly to forestall a confrontation between the rivals, but in fact leaving the ground clear for Heemskirk. It is quite appropriate that if Jasper, the 'knight', is the owner of a brig, and Heemskirk, the villain, is captain of a gunboat, the narrator should be the owner of a tugboat . . .

Like Heemskirk, the narrator has the habit of 'appropriating' Freya's person in his thoughts. 'My eyes alone could detect a faint shadow in the radiance of her personality' (162). He often watches the lovers in the same voyeuristic manner: 'On this sofa she and Jasper sat as close together as is possible in this imperfect world where neither can a body be in two places at once nor yet two bodies can be in one place at the same time. . . . On this foliage-embowered verandah, and at this late hour of the afternoon, he bent down a little, and possessing himself of Freya's hands, was kissing them one after the other' (183). In his role as Jasper's confidant, the narrator usually takes the position of mature common sense and caution. He repeatedly scolds Jasper for his impetuousness, his recklessness, and his total belief in his luck. But when this advice would be most needed, the narrator sounds a different note. When Jasper tells him that he has taken on the notorious Schultz with the wonderful voice and the 'awkward habit of stealing the stores of every ship he has ever been in' as mate of the brig, he expects the narrator to be true to form and warn him of his folly:

'Now, I am a lunatic—am I not? Mad, of course. Come on! Lay it thick. Let yourself go. I can see you get excited.' He so evidently expected me to scold that I took special pleasure in exaggerating the calmness of my attitude. . . . 'He will do. . . . Apart from this little weakness, let me tell you that Schultz is a smarter sailor than many who never took a drop of drink in their lives, and perhaps no worse morally that some men you and I know who have never stolen the value of a penny. He may not be a desirable person to have on board one's ship, but since you have no choice he may be made to do, I believe. The important thing is to understand his psychology. Don't give him any money till you have done with him.' (169)

The narrator goes so far as to recommend Schultz as a 'first rate' seaman (171). This, of course, is the worst possible advice, for the man with the 'voice fit to talk to the angels' (170) will eventually bring about Jasper's ruin.

What then is the narrator's role in the story? Is he the faithful confidant or another would-be knight, subtle and insidious, and therefore much more dangerous that Heemskirk with his outright brutish villainy? There is a point in the story in which the narrator seems to be offered a choice between these two alternatives. He can become what he pretends to be, if he changes the course of his desire. The meeting with Freya's maid, the 'comedy *camerista*', as he calls her, is an opportunity for him to choose the role of the 'faithful attendant' who will eventually be paired off with the 'lady in waiting' to compound the symmetry of the happy ending, with wedding bells ringing for both couples. There is certainly enough feeling between these two to make such a choice possible:

we have often exchanged nods and smiles—and a few words, too. She was a pretty creature. And once I had watched her approvingly make funny and expressive grimaces behind Heemskirk's back. I understood (from Jasper) that she was in the secret, like a comedy *camerista*. She was to accompany Freya on her irregular way to matrimony and 'ever after' happiness'. [The quotation marks are in the source!] Why should she be roaming by night near the cove—unless on some love affair of her own—I asked myself. But there was nobody suitable within the Seven Isles group, as far as I knew. It flashed upon me that it was myself she had been lying in wait for. . . . I advanced another pace, and how I felt is nobody's business. (178)

But this scene is followed by the narrator's sudden departure. The romance set-up does not materialize. It seems as if the narrator has given up his position, privileged enough as a confidant, but limited for someone who would like another role in the story, making way for Heemskirk to step in. The story continues in the narrator's absence, but the viewpoint now is entirely omniscient, including—for the first time—full access to the thoughts and feelings of the villain himself, whose view of Freya is oddly similar to that of the narrator.

Standing behind her, he devoured her with his eyes, from the golden crown of her rigidly motionless head to the heels of her shoes, the line of her shapely shoulders, the curves of her fine figure swaying a little before the keyboard. She had on a light dress; the sleeves stopped short at the elbows in an edging of lace. A satin ribbon encircled her waist. (195)

Freya's 'big, violet eyes' are now seen through Heemskirk's eyes, but the choice of language is that of the absent narrator (196). Heemskirk's sessions with Freya and with her father are also reminiscent of the narrator's supposedly well-intentioned ones earlier in the story: 'Heemskirk sat down by the old chap, and by the sort of talk which he knew was best calculated for the purposed, reduced him before long to a state of concealed and perspiring nervousness. It was a horrid talk of "authorities".' Heemskirk too bursts out with the thought of Jasper's 'flirting' with Freya, and, as in the conversation with the narrator, old Nelson protects himself by denying the very possibility of reciprocity on Freya's part (181). A curious symmetry, that!

In the narrator's earlier conversation with Freya, the mention of Heemskirk's name, which the narrator 'somehow or other' brings up, elicits a burst of hysterical laughter from Freya:

Her eyes flashed at me a sort of frightened merriment, and suddenly she exploded into a clear burst of laughter. 'Ha, ha, ha!' I echoed it heartily but not with the same charming tone: 'Ha, ha, ha! . . . Isn't he grotesque? Ha, ha ha!'
'He looks,' I spluttered, 'he looks—Ha, ha ha!—amongst you three . . . like an unhappy black beetle. Ha, ha ha!' She gave out another ringing peal, ran off into her own room, and slammed the door behind her, leaving me profoundly astounded. (174–5)

Freya's reaction in her session with Heemskirk is an echo of her earlier response to the narrator: 'She laughed outright, a clear, nervous laugh in which Heemskirk joined suddenly with a harsh "Ha, ha ha!"' (192). This curious identity of the narrator and the villain seals the last triangle in Conrad's kaleidoscope of mimetic desires. Mimetic desire is 'always a desire to be Another' (Girard, *Deceit*, 83). It is an attempt to appropriate the identity of an other who seems to have that plenitude which the hero lacks, a promise of self-sufficiency and autonomy which the hero cannot obtain unless, so he imagines, he becomes that rival mediator. 'Freya of the Seven Isles' might have been conceived initially as yet another popular romance. It has turned out to be an anti-romance, the story of a narrator who will do anything to become a character in his own story.

5
Addressing the Woman

It's queer how out of touch with truth women are. They live in a world of their own, and there had never been anything like it, and never can be. It's too beautiful altogether, and if they were to set it up it would go to pieces before the first sunset. Some confounded fact we men have been living contentedly with ever since the day of creation would start up and knock the whole thing over (*Heart of Darkness*, 59).

Did I mention the girl? Oh, she is out of it—completely. They—the women I mean—are out of it—should be out of it. We must help them to stay in that beautiful world of their own lest ours gets worse. Oh, she had to be out of it. You should have heard the disinterred body of Mr. Kurtz saying, 'My Intended.' You would have perceived directly then how completely she was out of it (*Heart of Darkness*, 115).

WOMEN, FOR CONRAD, are notoriously 'out of it'. Whether ornamentally passive and destined to victimization or ominously elemental and potentially destructive, the Woman—capitalized, singularized, depersonalized like a force of nature—never attains the full status of a character in the fiction. She becomes, in a sense, a metaphysical principle, the principle of the Feminine. It is difficult (and probably unnecessary) to evaluate the extent of conscious authorial control or even awareness of this aesthetic strategy, which may be construed as a form of evasion, misogynist exclusion, or denial; but there can be little doubt that there is a complex mechanism of self-subversion and exposure at work in some of Conrad's most seemingly sexist texts. As Andrew Roberts argues, 'much of Conrad's fiction is strongly marked by the presence of patriarchal and sexist ideology but . . . it also provides the basis for a strong feminist critique. . . . The spirit of scepticism, the epistemological uncertainty, and the destabilizing effect of the narrative technique involve the texts in processes of self-questioning as well as making them highly responsive to the interpretation and critique of their readers.'[1] As with any other obsession, repression, or denial, this complex issue can be negotiated in terms of a boomerang action.

While it is impossible to provide even a partial fair-minded sampling of critical responses to this issue, it is interesting to note that the positions taken by readers concerned with the 'Woman Question' run parallel to those on the question of colonialism and race in Conrad's work: from a view of the text as entirely caught up in a patriarchal frame of reference or as a straightforward expression of misogyny, to a view of the text as a process of self-questioning and an exposure of patriarchal ideology and discourse.[2] These parallels are obviously significant, not least because both issues centre on force fields of culture and subjectivity in which author and reader are just as fully implicated as the fictional narrator or the protagonists.

But women are 'out of it' not only as fictional characters: they are 'out of it' as readers as well. The best of Conrad's work creates, as Nina Pelican Straus so astutely observes, an exclusive masculine circle of narrators, characters, listeners, and readers. The woman reader, like the female characters, is out of it.[3] But this particular exclusion seems to give way around 1912 to a different, equally ambiguous sensibility, when Conrad makes a conscious decision to break the circle of exclusion and address his work to women readers. At this moment of transition it becomes quite clear that the author's obsession with the Woman Question is closely and problematically related to the dynamics of writing and to the inscription of subjectivity in fiction.

[1] 'Introduction' to *Conrad and Gender*, ed. Andrew Michael Roberts, *The Conradian* (Amsterdam: Rodopi, 1993), p. viii. See also Roberts' 'Action, Passivity, and Gender in Chance', in *Conrad and Gender*, 89–104.

[2] These two issues are, in fact, interestingly conflated in Benitta Parry, *Conrad and Imperialism: Ideological Boundaries and Visionary Frontiers* (London: Macmillan, 1983); Padmini Mongia 'Empire, Narrative and the Feminine in *Lord Jim* and *Heart of Darkness*,' in *Contexts for Conrad*, ed. Keith Carabine, Owen Knowles, Wieslaw Krajka (Boulder: East European Monographs, Maria Curie-Sklodowska University, Lublin; distributed by Columbia University Press, 1993); Padmini Mongia, '"Ghosts of the Gothic": Spectral Women and Colonized Spaces in *Lord Jim*', in *Conrad and Gender*, ed. Andrew Roberts, *The Conradian* (Amsterdam: Rodopi, 1993), 1–16; Rebecca Stott, 'The Woman in Black: Race and Gender in The Secret Agent', in *Conrad and Gender*, 39–58.

[3] Nina Pelican Straus, 'The Exclusion of the Intended from Secret Sharing', *Novel*, 20 (1987), 123–37; reprinted in *Conrad's Heart of Darkness, Nostromo, The Secret Agent*, New Casebook Series, ed. Elaine Jordan (London: Macmillan, 1996), 48–66.

'The Planter of Malata' (1914) was written in the beginning of the phase which was to become known as that of Conrad's artistic 'decline'. Notable exceptions such as *The Shadow-Line* notwithstanding, there seems to be a virtual critical unanimity concerning the overall poorer quality of the works produced by Conrad during this last phase of his work. The reasons for this decline and the relative merits of the later works have been debated by critics at length, but the one question that seems to have been neglected relates to the extent to which Conrad himself was conscious of the artistic impoverishment of his work. Given his invariable dissatisfaction with his work even at its very best, and the frequent onsets of depression which plagued him throughout his writing life, one cannot hope to find any evidence of such new awareness in his personal letters. I would suggest, however, that there is much to indicate that Conrad was indeed, at least subliminally, conscious of and anxious about his own artistic loss of ground. I believe that the evidence is to be found in the subtext of the fictional work itself, and particularly in 'The Planter of Malata', which may be studied as an unconscious self-reflexive parable on Conrad's own art, a projection of his subconscious anxiety about his conscious artistic choices.

There can be little doubt about the personal significance of the story for its author: Conrad's ongoing obsession with this short piece even at a distance of seven years, the biographical material which found its way into it and the various transformations it has undergone, as well as the dynamics of the story itself, can undoubtedly provide (and indeed have provided) ample material for a psychological analysis. But the point of departure for the present discussion is psycho-textual rather than psychoanalytic: the view of the pathology which is clearly at work in the text is directed at the dynamics of writing and at the struggle within the creative unconscious. The tragedy of Conrad's decline lies in the fact that he was apparently unaware of the metafictional aspects of his own work, or unable to act upon the moral of his own story.

Like many of Conrad's later works, 'The Planter of Malata' is generically schizophrenic: it is ostensibly a romance which involves a damsel and a knight, a quest for a missing lover, an exotic island and other obvious generic markers. However, Conrad's treatment of the genre is clearly problematic: the quest is undertaken by a woman whose integrity is questioned at the very outset, the missing lover is never recovered, and the protagonist is driven to self-annihilation at the end of the quest. Questions of selfhood, identity, and gender relations are treated in a manner which seems to undermine the traditional premises of the genre.[4] The structure of the story is also problematic: Renouard's viewpoint is technically framed by that of the all-knowing Editor who introduces and concludes the tale. But the epilogue is extremely thin: there is no sense of the story being rounded off, there is a peculiar imbalance, a diminishing of the framing perspective. I will deal with the symptomatic significance of this lop-sided framing as yet another aspect of the creative pathology which, I believe, is at work here. Moving from the tale and its frame to the metafictional aspects of this work, I will touch upon the broader significance of the story: why was it so important for Conrad who seemed to recognize its deficiencies and yet devoted several pages of apologia to it in his author's note to *Within the Tides*? How is the story related to Conrad's later work? How is it related to *Chance*, which preceded it and which has an obvious (albeit parodistic and self-conscious) affinity to the romance?

The two major characters in the story, Geoffrey Renouard and Felicia Moorsom, are presented, at the very outset, as utterly incompatible. They are, in fact, the two opposite poles on a scale of human possibilities. He is initially described as super-masculine: a 'lean, lounging, active man' with a 'fine bronzed face' (3), an 'explorer' (24), a 'man of definite conquering tasks, the familiar of wide horizons' (35), a 'pioneer', and a 'leading man' (42) whose current enterprise is a 'five-years' programme of scientific adventure, of work, of danger and endurance' (6); who has earned the fascinating notoriety of a man who 'did his work' and 'never counted the cost' (42–3). In short, a strong silent man, an early prototype of the Clint Eastwood variety.

Felicia Moorsom belongs to an entirely different world. She 'has been playing the London hostess to tip-top people ever since she put her hair up' (15), had ' hosts of distinguished friends' and was expected to make a 'brilliant marriage with somebody very rich and of high position, have a house in London and in the country and entertain . . . splendidly' (45, 44). Her world, as described by

---

[4] I have dealt with this 'generic schizophrenia' in Conrad's novels in *Joseph Conrad and the Modern Temper* (Oxford: Oxford University Press, 1991), 139–200.

the all-knowing Editor, is dominated by the 'two big F's': Fashion
and Finance. There is no real exchange between these two
characters. Renouard is half-aware and initially mistrustful of
her essential though unconscious falsehood, of the role she has
written for herself in the glorified pseudo-romantic quest she has
undertaken. He is contemptuous of the absent man who has had a
foot in the two big F's, and adds yet another F to the Editor's list:
'A Fool', he calls him (17–18). He recognizes the intellectual
debauchery of the Professor (who entertains his provincial hosts
with lengthy discussions of the 'Impermanency of the Measur-
able') as merely another facet of this world of F's: it is mere 'Froth
and Foam' (45). And yet, he refuses to see that Miss Moorsom,
who seems to him like a 'tragic Venus arising before him' (36), is
herself a creature of Foam and Froth, of Fashion and Finance. Her
very name, appropriately beginning with an F, is a lie: it is Falsehood rather than Felicity that she holds for him.

   This rather crude juxtaposition of masculine integrity versus
feminine falsehood is, in fact, in keeping with the underlying
assumptions of Conrad's work through most of his writing life.
In her study of paradigmatic critical readings of *Heart of Darkness* and the collaboration/collusion of traditional, patriarchal,
critical readings of Conrad's work with the patriarchal ideology of
the text, Nina Pelican Straus suggests that 'Marlow presents a
world distinctly split into male and female realms—the first
harbouring the possibility of "truth" and the second dedicated
to the maintenance of delusion. "Truth", then, is directed at and
intended for men only'; 'Heroic maleness is defined precisely in
adverse relation to delusional femininity.'[5] But it is not Marlow
alone who excludes women from the shared secret truths of the
masculine realm. As Pelican Straus argues, the text's 'insistence on
a male circle of readers' (by the deliberate use of a frame which
includes readers as listeners) contextualizes this exclusion and
extends it to the relationship between Conrad and his male
readers as well. The heroic consciousness that Conrad presents
is part of a masculinist tradition from which the feminist reader is
necessarily excluded.

   Renouard's initial integrity gradually dissolves as he surrenders

---

[5] Nina Pelican Straus, 'The Exclusion of the Intended from Secret Sharing', 50, 57.

himself to Felicia's frame of reference, which assimilates, emascu-
lates, and finally kills him. The protagonist's fate is prefigured, in
an obvious and rather heavy-handed manner, in a dream:

He lay on his bed, sighing profoundly in the dark, and suddenly beheld
his very own self, carrying a small bizarre lamp, reflected in a long mirror
inside a room in an empty and unfurnished palace. . . . He lost himself
utterly—he found his way again. . . . At last the lamp went out, and he
stumbled against some object which, when he stooped for it, he found to
be very cold and heavy to lift. The sickly white light of dawn showed him
the head of a statue. Its marble hair was done in the bold lines of a
helmet, on its lips the chisel had left a faint smile, and it resembled Miss
Moorsom. While he was staring at it fixedly, the head began to grow light
in his fingers, to diminish and crumble to pieces, and at last turned into a
handful of dust, which was blown away by a puff of wind. (31)

His subsequent interpretation of the dream is quite interesting,
not least because, in spite of its apparent obviousness, it is so
utterly wrong:

The lamp, of course, he connected with the search for a man. But on
closer examination he perceived that the reflection of himself in the
mirror was not really the true Renouard, but someone else whose face
he could not remember. . . . The marble head with Miss Moorsom's face!
Well! What other face could he have dreamed of? (32)

The dreamer is the object, rather than the subject of the dream. It
is not he but the woman who sets out on a quest for a man. The
identification of the marble head as that of Felicia Moorsom does
seem to be validated by the recurrent allusions of the narrative to
her hair in the very terms of the dream, but a few pages later,
Renouard's own profile is also described as resembling a Minerva's
head, such 'as may be seen amongst the bronzes of classical
museums, pure under a crested helmet' (38, see also 75).[6] As
his infatuation with Miss Moorsom builds up, Renouard increas-
ingly grows to resemble her until, at the moment when he has to
make a choice between truth and lies, they are described as 'a well-
matched couple, animated yet statuesque in their calmness and in
their pallor' (50). Their physical resemblance is a measure of his
metamorphosis which accelerates until he becomes a mere reflec-

---

[6] Renouard is irresistibly drawn to that 'mass of arranged hair . . . incandescent,
chiselled and fluid, with the daring suggestion of a helmet of burnished copper and the
flowing lines of molten metal' (10).

tion of her will, and it is his own personality, rather than her marble likeness, which will eventually crumble and 'turn to dead dust' (65).

Felicia's project is described from Renouard's perspective as a romance with all the generic ingredients of frustrated love, a quest for the lost lover and a beautiful lady with two 'attendant grey-heads' (30). The visitors seem to him like people 'under a spell' (8). Even as he realizes that it is 'the spell of a dead romance' (56) he wishes to substitute himself for the absent man to whom he refers as 'Prince Charming' (22). Feeling that he too has fallen under a spell, he seems to fear 'disenchantment rather than sortilege' (30; see also 48). Renouard's willingness to enter Miss Moorsom's false romance, to step into the role of the object of the quest, is the 'moral poison of falsehood' which causes the disintegration of his old self (65). The face he sees in the mirror of the dream is not that of the 'true Renouard' because, in his desire to replace the missing lover, he has exchanged his old self for the dead man, the creature of her false romantic discourse.

The question of selfhood is embedded in the very rhetoric of the text: the linguistic boundaries between the various men in the story are extremely tenuous, and the merging of identities is potentially operative from first moment of contact. The Editor tells Renouard that Felicia and her entourage are 'out looking for a man' (17). The same indeterminate reference recurs in Renouard's interpretation of his dream, when he connects the lamp with 'the search for a man' (32). The absence of the definite article is not incidental: any man willing to become the construct of Felicia's romance will be, by definition, the object of the quest.[7]

When the Editor finally discovers the whereabouts of the missing man, he bursts into the Dunsters' living-room shouting: 'Found!' and then again, 'I tell you he is found.' Seconds later, he catches sight of Renouard and, indicating him, continues: 'he's

---

[7] There are numerous other proleptic indications of the interchangeability of the two men: the allusion to the absent man's correspondence and, immediately afterwards, to Renouard's estrangement from his own family for whom he has 'a profound and remorseful affection' (26); the reference to Renouard as an 'explorer' and then to the possibility that the absent man may be 'prospecting the back of beyond' (24); The description of Renouard's hallucination (71, 74), which foreshadows the assistant's fall into the ravine. The Professor's allusion to the absent man as a 'complicated simpleton' (39), and the speculation that he might have 'become morally disintegrated' (40) are equally applicable to Renouard himself.

the very man we want. . . . You are the very man, Renouard' (50).
The ambiguity of the personal pronoun 'he' is significant. The
Editor simply means that Renouard will lead them to his assistant
who is the man they have been looking for. Assuming the role of
the missing lover who has never been anything but her creature,
Renouard compounds his former lie with another when he says 'I
have him there' (51).[8] One can, perhaps, understand why the story
was initially named 'The Assistant', after the absent man, as it
were. It is indeed the story of an absent man, but that man is the
protagonist, a man who exchanges his selfhood for a glorious
fictional construct.

At an earlier point in the story Renouard seems to be offered a
choice of selves. There are a number of vague allusions to Felicia's
dead brother, who had been to the same school with him and had
also been 'inclined to action' (11, 46). The old Professor, who
recognizes the false sentimentality behind his daughter's quest,
seems to have 'never forgiven his daughter for not dying instead
of his son' (46). It is that choice between the dead son, a man of
action, and the living daughter, a woman of lies, that Renouard is
forced to make. It is a choice between his former 'masculine',
'true' self and the exhausted, passive creature of the false
romance woven by Felicia. Felicia's frame of reference, the
mode of romance which she imposes on her quest, is presented
as distinctly 'feminine'. She has

> moved, breathed, existed, and even triumphed in the mere smother and
> froth of life—the brilliant froth. There thoughts, sentiments, opinions,
> feelings, actions too, are nothing but agitation in empty space—to amuse
> life—a sort of superior debauchery, exciting and fatiguing, meaning
> nothing, leading nowhere. . . . [except a] dangerous trifling with roman-
> tic images. No woman can stand that mode of life in which women rule,
> and remain a perfectly genuine, simple human being. (41)[9]

---

[8] The confusion of personal pronoun references continues during the passage to
Malata. 'The professor's sister leaned over towards Renouard. Through all these days
at sea *the man's—the found man's*—existence had not been alluded to on board the
schooner' (58, italics added). The text seems to be conscious of the possible confusion
of identities; hence the need for the paranthetical clarification which 'corrects' the
grammatical ambiguity.

[9] The elderly aunt who accompanies the maiden on her romantic quest, described as
a 'wax flower under glass', there are no 'traces of the dust of life's battles on her
anywhere' (44), is represented as the apotheosis of this 'feminine' world of artifice. She
is fascinated by 'the sentiment and romance of the situation' (58), but her conception

As we shall see in the last section of this chapter, the misogynist association of gender and genre is not incidental.

Throughout their brief acquaintance there seems to be a struggle between the man and the woman over the question of truth. Her repeated assertions 'I have an instinct for truth' (43); 'I stand for truth here' (48); 'It's I who stand for truth here' (75); 'Here I stand for truth itself' (78) are all part of her supreme lie. When finally confronted with the truth, she is 'not fit to hear it': she reverts to French, the language of false gentility, to reject him: '"Assez! J'ai horreur de tout cela"' (78). Renouard's moral disintegration begins immediately after their first meeting when he withholds the truth of his assistant's death from his friend. It gathers momentum through a series of lies which he tells in order to sustain this first deception, and his moral surrender is complete when he joins in her fiction and becomes her creature, when he too discards the truth in exchange for that deception which would prolong her quest: 'What was truth to him in the face of that great passion?' (56).

But lying, as any reader of Conrad would know, is tantamount to dying. Seeking to prolong his concealment of the other man's death, Renouard swims over to Malata at night, to prepare his servants for the arrival of the group. When he jumps 'over the knights' heads' off his schooner, he is already a dead man whose 'ghostly white torso' is all but an empty shell (60). His subsequent exhaustion, the longing for peace and rest, is another echo of the call of death.

On this swim back he felt the mournful fatigue of all that length of traversed road, which brought him no nearer to his desire. It was as if his love had sapped the invisible supports of his strength. There came a moment when it seemed to him that he must have swum beyond the confines of life. He had a sensation of eternity close at hand, demanding no effort—offering its peace. (62)

The sense of exhaustion, this yearning for peace and rest, remain with him to the end of the story. He is subsequently described as 'vanquished' at Felicia's feet, his hands are 'listless', he converses

---

of the romance is as hollow as her personality and her exclusion of anything but appearances. She likes Renouard only in his evening clothes when he looks like 'the son of a duke' (44), and as for 'poor Arthur' the object of the quest, 'having never seen him otherwise than in his town clothes she had no idea what he would look like' (63).

'languidly' (65), and feels 'that he must rest his forehead on her feet and burst into tears' (66; see also 73, 78, 79, 80). When not lying down, Renouard wanders about his estate 'like a frightened soul' (69), and the persistent references to ghosts haunting the plantation (66–71) reinforce the vision of the living man who has turned into the ghost of the dead one. When Renouard tells Felicia of her lover's death he says: 'He is dead. His very ghost shall be done with presently' (79), and then, confirming his own meta-morphosis: 'To me you can never make reparation. . . . I shall haunt you' (82). On leaving the island, the Professor cryptically thanks Renouard for 'being what he is' (81). This is, of course, highly ironic, for Renouard has long ceased to be what he was. He has become the creature of the woman's romantic fiction and the ghost of a man who might have been his opposite.

The artistic failure of the story is due to a large extent to the failure of the initial framing strategy. The story is narrated by a distant, apparently extra-diegetic, omniscient voice. The perspec-tive, however, shifts from that of the all-knowing Editor, with which the story opens, to Renouard's (8–9) which is sustained until the departure of the boys (part xi), and then reverts to the Editor, who goes out to the island to investigate his friend's disappearance. This structural framing is determined both by the need to present Renouard as perceived by the world before his meeting with the woman and by the need for an account of his end. But the structural frame is also accompanied by a change in the quality of the narrating voice. The all-knowing Editor is a cynic who has no illusions about the society over which he presides in his role as 'the press'. In telling the story he uses the stock phrases of his trade with explicit and implicit quotation marks, fully aware of and amused by these provincial social mechanisms which he serves. He labels the characters as they would be tagged in his own society columns, referring to Old Dunster as 'the eminent colonial statesman' (3); to Renouard as the 'local celebrity . . . the explorer, whose indomitable energy, etc.' (15); and to himself, with more than a touch of irony, as 'the only apostle of letters in the hemisphere, the solitary patron of culture, the Slave of the Lamp' (49).

When the perspective shifts from the Editor to Renouard, the quality of the voice changes. Renouard rejects the discourse of the

Editor: Felicia's tale seems to be 'robbed . . . of all glamour by the prosaic personality of the narrator' (22). Thus, when Renouard's voice takes over, the narrative tone changes from the urbane scepticism of the Editor to a pseudo-poetic discourse, an indiscriminate outpouring of lovers' sentimentality, crude enough to sound like a parody of itself:

her approach woke up in his brain the image of love's infinite grace and the sense of the inexpressible joy that lives in beauty. (10)

She was a misty and fair creature, fitted for invisible music, for the shadows of love, for the murmurs of water. . . . There was a sparkle in the clear lucidity of her eyes; and when she turned them on him they seemed to give a new meaning to life. He would say to himself that another man would have found long before the happy release of madness, his wits burnt to cinders in that radiance. But no such luck for him. (35)

There is, unfortunately, much more of the same. Felicia is described as 'a magic painting of charm, fascination, and desire, glowing mysteriously on the dark background' (47), 'a shining dream woman uttering words of wistful inquiry' (59). The sight of her hair, 'that resplendent vision of woman's glory', has the 'power to flutter his heart like a reminder of the mortality of his frame' (41).[10]

It is important to note here that the narrative throughout the story does not dissociate itself from the discourse of the protagonist. Even when the perspective shifts back to the Editor, there is no substantial correction of the previous narrative rhetoric. The epilogue does open on a note of irony, when the Editor finds himself dissatisfied with the sentimental tale of 'how Miss Moorsom—the fashionable and clever beauty—found her betrothed in Malata only to see him die in her arms', and decides to learn 'more than the rest of the world' (84). But the scepticism of the all-knowing Editor wavers and is ultimately suspended and muted before the 'black cloud', the 'mysterious silence' which casts its shadow over Malata. One cannot help feeling that the framing strategy might have redeemed the story, if the two

---

[10] Willam Freedman, whose reading of the story is predicated on a paradoxical identification of Felicia Moorsom with 'the Truth', notes the Medusan aspects of Felicia's hair which 'represent a fused, almost redundant threat to masculine self-possession and the (writerly) power of speech, retrievable only with the aversion of the gaze' (Freedman, work in progress).

attitudes—the gushing sentimentality of the protagonist and the initial scepticism of the Editor—had been more evenly balanced. As it is, however, the potentially sobering function of the Editor is never realized. Defined as a man whose profession is 'to know everything', the 'all-knowing journalist' (8; see also 10, 11, 13) does not find out what has really happened to Renouard, and the tale ends in silence.

The Editor does, however, make one comment which may be a reflection on the whole story, or, indeed, on the entire phase in Conrad's subsequent career. Talking of the Professor who has 'made philosophy pay' and has done most of his philosophical writing 'with his tongue in his cheek' (and, not incidentally, turned into a great social 'swell', the 'fashionable philosopher of the age'), the Editor tells Renouard that 'the only really honest writing is to be found in newspapers and nowhere else' (15). Coming from the self-appointed 'apostle of letters' who is all too aware of the fictions of journalistic reporting (particularly the 'social paragraphs' he writes), this view of non-journalism (including, of course, the art of fiction) as dishonest is highly problematic.[11] The failure of the framing strategy is symptomatic of the failure of the author to extricate himself from the very same trap. Conrad writes about a character who loses his 'masculine self' when he is assimilated into the false 'feminine discourse' of romance, the very same discourse which Conrad himself had always held in contempt, but which was to become the idiom of his work in the years which followed.

Conrad's author's notes, written for the Doubleday Sun Dial Edition of his Works in 1920, are, with a few notable exceptions, what one might expect from a well-established and successful writer: bland projections of the author's public persona, conversational in tone and remarkably conventional in their content. Conrad's author's note to *Within the Tides* (almost entirely devoted to 'The Planter of Malata', a single story out of a volume containing four) is different and more interesting in that it is written on a distinct note of discomfort: 'I am glad I have attempted the story . . . but

---

[11] It is the old paradox of the liar: should we believe the man who says that all men in his country are liars? If he is telling the truth, then he must be an honest man rather than a liar; but he cannot be an honest man since he has lied by calling himself a liar.

I am not so inordinately pleased with the result as not to be able to forgive a patient reader who may find it somewhat disappointing' (p. xi). It seems that even at a seven-year distance, the story is still profoundly disturbing for the author: he appears to recognize its weaknesses and yet refuses to let go of it. This elaborate and peculiar apologia for the story is both a direct reply to critical charges and a muffled, not quite coherent, attempt at an artistic manifesto, embracing and at the same time disclaiming an ill-defined 'romanticism', denying and at the same time suggesting an affinity between the author and his characters.

The nature of the knowledge, suggestions or hints used in my imaginative work has depended directly on the conditions of my active life. It depended more on contacts, and very slight contacts at that, than on actual experience; because my life as a matter of fact was far from being adventurous in itself. Even now when I look back on it with a certain regret (who would not regret his youth) and positive affection, its colouring wears the sober hue of hard work and exacting calls of duty, things which in themselves are not much charged with a feeling of romance. If these things appeal strongly to me even in retrospect it is, I suppose, because *the romantic feeling of reality was in me an inborn faculty. This in itself may be a curse* but when disciplined by a sense of personal responsibility and a recognition of the hard facts of existence shared with the rest of mankind becomes but a point of view from which the very shadows of life appear endowed with an internal glow. And *such romanticism is not a sin. It is none the worse for the knowledge of truth.* It only tries to make the best of it, hard as it may be; and in this hardness discovers a certain aspect of beauty. I am speaking of romanticism in relation to life, not of romanticism in relation to imaginative literature, which, in its early days, was associated simply with mediaeval subjects, or, an any rate, with subjects sought for in a remote past. My subjects are not mediaeval and I have a very natural right to them because my past is very much my own. (pp. vii–viii; italics added)

The ambivalence of the note regarding the ethos of what Conrad calls 'romanticism' is obviously related to romance as a genre rather than to the artistic frame of mind that we have come to call by that name.[12] Conrad writes of the 'romantic feeling of reality' which is a 'curse' unless disciplined by a recognition of

---

[12] For a more elaborate discussion of the relationship between the artistic movement and the genre from which it has derived its name, see *Joseph Conrad and the Modern Temper*, 139–56.

communal reality and a 'knowledge of truth', yet in defending that ill-defined 'disciplined' romanticism which is 'not a sin', he seems to imply that other types of romanticism may well be open to the charge of sinfulness. 'Romanticism in relation to imaginative literature' is associated with the medieval romances, which Conrad seems to dismiss in his author's note. However, when his own tormented protagonist realizes that he has implicated himself in a false romance, he seems to regret the passing of the medieval, original, and genuine version of this outlook:

I don't mean that you are like the men and women of the time of armours, castles, and great deeds. Oh, No! They stood on the naked soil, had traditions to be faithful to, had their feet on this earth of passions and death which is not a hothouse. They would have been too plebeian to you since they had to lead, to suffer with, to understand the commonest humanity. No, you are merely of the topmost layer, the mere pure froth and bubble on the inscrutable depths which some day will toss you out of existence. . . . it is your soul that is made of foam. (76–7)

What Conrad apparently objects to is the aestheticization of truth, a withdrawal from the world rather than engagement with it through fiction. It is not surprising that he has had to grapple with the romance in this manner: the history of the genre is indeed a 'history of decadence'. It reflects a gradual loss of authenticity, a process of trivialization which has eventually turned the modern mutations of the genre into fictions of pure aesthetic escapism.[13]

But the implications of extreme aestheticism seem to have been lost on the ageing author who describes the story as 'a piece of writing the primary intention of which was mainly aesthetic; an essay in description and narrative around a given psychological situation' (p. ix). This is a peculiar echo of a letter he wrote twenty years earlier, when he felt the need to disown *Romance*, an embarrassingly inferior novel produced in collaboration with Ford Madox Ford:

There are certain things that are difficult to explain, especially after they have happened. I consider *Romance* as something of no importance. I collaborated on it at a time when it was impossible for me to do anything else. It was easy to relate a few events without being otherwise involved in the subject. The idea was purely aesthetic: to depict in an appropriate way

[13] Gillian Beer, *The Romance* (London: Methuen, 1970), 1. Beer's exposition of the genre, its evolution and its problematic is highly relevant to the present discussion.

certain scenes and certain situations. Also it did not displease us to be able to show that we could do something which was very much in vogue with the public at that moment.[14]

The younger Conrad, who was yet to write his greatest works, was apparently more willing to admit this artistic lapse of good faith. The elderly author of 'The Planter of Malata' is considerably less candid with his readers and perhaps with himself as well. The substitution of aesthetics for ethics, of beauty for truth, is not unlike the fall of the protagonist who enters the falsely aestheticized romance of Felicia Moorsom, discards his conceptions of duty and truth and thereby surrenders his 'masculine' self.

The acknowledged relationship between the artist's biography and the artistic subject-matter is also not quite clear. Conrad's strange claim on his 'natural right' to his subjects (strange, because no one would have dreamed of denying it) is supported by an enigmatic reference to his own past. He implies that the story is derived from his own 'active life', but immediately goes on to deny the biographical connection. His subsequent concession that the weakness of the story (a 'regrettable defect', as he calls it) may lie in the confession scene is also given a distinct personal note:

I resemble Geoffrey Renouard in so far that when once engaged in an adventure I cannot bear the idea of turning back. The moment had arrived for these people [i.e. the two characters in the story] to disclose themselves. They had to do it. To render a crucial point of feelings in terms of human speech is really an impossible task. Written words can only form a sort of translation. And if that translation happens, from want of skill or from over-anxiety, to be too literal, the people caught in the toils of passion, instead of disclosing themselves, which would be an art, are made to give themselves away, which is neither art nor life. Nor yet truth! At any rate, not the whole truth; for it is truth robbed of all its necessary and sympathetic reservations and qualifications which give it its fair form, its just proportions, its semblance of human fellowship. (pp. x–xi)

This too seems to beg some serious questions. What is the difference between disclosing oneself and giving oneself away? What is the position of art between truth and fiction? Has the author of *Heart of Darkness* become an advocate for that artistic formulation which

---

[14] A letter written to Kazimierz Waliszewski on 8 Nov. 1903. In Zdzislaw Najder, *Conrad's Polish Background* (London: Oxford University Press, 1964) 236.

endows truth with 'fair form', 'just proportions', and with a *'semblance* of human fellowship'?

In his psychoanalytic biography of Conrad, Bernard Meyer has come up with some interesting clues linking the unrequited love of the fictional protagonist to Conrad's own frustrated courtship of Eugénie Renouf in Mauritius in the autumn of 1888. Like Felicia Moorsom, Miss Renouf was already engaged to another man and turned down Conrad's proposal of marriage. This voyage back from Australia was to be Conrad's last as a ship's captain. When instructed by the charterers of the *Otago* to return to Mauritus later, Conrad resigned his command and returned to England as a passenger via the Suez Canal.[15] The resemblance of the names Renouf and Renouard is, of course, extremely interesting, primarily, as Meyer points out, for the reversal of the masculine and feminine roles. Conrad, it seems, has named his fictional protagonist after the woman who had rejected him. I would argue, however, that this reversal is not merely a defence mechanism as diagnosed by Meyer: it is closely related, as we shall presently see, to the emasculation of Renouard in the course of the story, and to the subsequent metaphoric emasculation which the author had dreaded.

Another interesting biographical document noted by Meyer is the parlour game of questions and answers recorded in the Renouf family 'Album de Confidences': the questions were posed in French. Conrad's answers were given in English:

Par quels moyens cherchez-vous a plaire [in what ways do you try do be liked]? By making myself scarce. . . . Ou habite la personne qui occupe votre pensée [where does the person who occupies your thoughts live]? A castle in Spain. . . . Que désirez-vous être [what would you like to be]? Should like not to be. . . . Quelle est votre plus grande distraction [what is your favourite pastime]? Chasing wild geese. . . . Que détestez-vous le plus [what do you dislike the most]? False pretences.[16]

Meyer is mainly interested in the reversal of this linguistic exchange during the confession scene, when Renouard speaks to Felicia in English and she reverts to French for the ultimate rejection. I believe that the playful replies of the young Korzeniowski, as Conrad was then called, are no less noteworthy for their bear-

[15] Bernard C. Meyer, *Joseph Conrad: A Psychoanalytic Biography* (Princeton, NJ: Princeton University Press, 1967), 73.   [16] Ibid., 72.

ing on the question of selfhood and being—or rather, non-being—in relation to the protagonist as well as his author. Both the fictional character and the living author seem to associate Eros with Thanatos, the love of a woman with the annihilation of the masculine self. However, the focus of this study is not the psycho-biographical subtext of the story, but its significance as a reflection of the creative unconscious. Here too, there is a close analogy between the author and his character, who resemble each other not in the glorified and acknowledged 'no turning back', but in their surrender to an ostensibly 'feminine' discourse, their conversion to an aestheticized conception of life and art, and their complicity in that variety of romanticism which Conrad himself implicitly condemns as a sin. It is this metaphoric translation of the character's failure that we now turn to.

'The Planter of Malata' was written in 1913, shortly after *Chance*. The great success of the novel, which is a self-conscious romance (with sections entitled 'The Damsel', 'The Knight'), established Conrad as a popular and commercially successful writer. He did finally, to borrow the words of the cynical all-knowing Editor, 'make literature pay'. Conrad himself defined *Chance* as a 'girl-novel' and ascribed the novel's commercial success to the 'steady run of references to women in general all along'.[17] In a letter to the Sunday magazine of the *New York Herald* which serialized the novel in America, Conrad wrote: 'it gives me great pleasure when I find that womankind appreciates my work, and in writing the story for the N.Y.H. I aimed at treating my subject in a way which would interest women.'[18] There seems to have been a connection in his mind between 'writing for women' and the romance as a genre.[19]

[17] Quoted by Zdzislaw Najder, in *Joseph Conrad: A Chronicle*, trans, Halina Carroll-Najder (Cambridge: Cambridge University Press, 1983), 390.
[18] *The Collected Letters of Joseph Conrad*, ed. Frederic Karl and Laurence Davies, vol. 4: 1908–1911 (Cambridge: Cambridge University Press, 1990), 531–2. For an interesting treatment of this shift of sensibility see Laurence Davies, 'Conrad, *Chance*, and Women Readers', in *Conrad and Gender*, ed. Andrew Roberts, *The Conradian* (Amsterdam: Rodopi, 1993), 75–88.
[19] The relationship between gender and genre in Conrad's work has been discussed by Padmini Mongia, in ' "Ghosts of the Gothic": Spectral Woman and Colonized Spaces in *Lord Jim*', in *Conrad and Gender*, ed. Andrew Roberts, *The Conradian* (Amsterdam: Rodopi, 1993), 1–16; Scott McRacken, ' "A hard and absolute condition of existence": Reading Masculinity in Lord Jim', in *Conrad and Gender*, ed. Andrew Roberts, *The Conradian* (Amsterdam: Rodopi, 1993), 17–38. Both readers see Patusan as a 'feminized' space which marks a generic transition.

The commercial success of the novel was followed by what is commonly referred to as Conrad's 'decline'. If *Chance* is a self-conscious, highly ironic romance, most of the later works— *Victory*, *The Arrow of Gold*, *The Rover*, the unfinished *Suspense*, and to some extent *The Rescue* (completed, after twenty years of suspension, during this last phase)—have already lost the edge of irony which redeems this novel. These problematic novels are interesting mainly for the generic schizophrenia which they too seem to display: the generic markers of the romance are all there—a damsel in distress, a chivalric male who comes to the rescue, love and adventure in remote exotic settings—but the male protagonists are oddly unequal to their respective tasks, and the romance framework invariably crumbles.

In his pioneering study of Conrad's work, Thomas Moser has outlined the problematic trajectory of the author's creative life, and argued that the decline in the artistic quality of the later work was due to the choice of an 'uncongenial subject', i.e. love, for the central theme of this phase.[20] I would like to take the argument one step further and suggest that the choice of the genre of romance, which Conrad had apparently relegated to the realm of women, unleashed the writer's own pathological fear of losing his 'masculine' self and his deeply rooted misogyny, which is nowhere more conspicuous than when he sets out to 'write for women'. In a letter written shortly before the completion of *Chance*, the author wrote: 'The wretched Conrad has written a long (and stupid) novel. . . . It is *disgusting* even to talk about it; just imagine what writing it was like! It's made me disgusted with myself, with paper, with ink—with everything. And there are still forty or so pages to scrawl out! When I think of it, the pen falls from my hand.'[21] To misquote Freud, a pen may occasionally be just a pen, but the shadow of the protagonist—a man who has lost his energy, his integrity, and his 'masculine' voice by surrendering to the fictional construct of a woman—does seem to hover behind the back of the author who, while writing a novel designed to

[20] Thomas Moser, *Joseph Conrad: Achievement and Decline* (1957; rpt. Hamden, Conn.: Archon, 1966), 14. The view of women readers as indiscriminate consumers of the debased romance is reflected in the treatment of Miss Moorsom, the creature of this 'mode of life which women rule' where all feeling and thought dwindle into 'dangerous trifling with romantic images' (41).

[21] A letter to a fellow writer, Henri Ghéon, written on 22 Nov. 1911. *Collected Letters*, 4, 510.

please 'womankind', worries about the loss of the pen/phallus, the metaphoric emasculation to which he was about to surrender himself.

This complex interaction of the authorial consciousness with that of the protagonist explains the fact that the debased romantic discourse of the character is neither repudiated nor contained by an authorial voice. The ontological gap between the character and his author diminishes when one realizes that the living man was, just like his fictional protagonist, made of the 'stuff that dreams [and stories] are made of'. Renouard has let himself be seduced and sucked into the false 'women's romance' woven by Felicia Moorsom. His entrapment within this fictitious mode of existence leads to his death, not in the medieval sense of erotic fulfilment but in a stark, literal sense. He loses his voice, adopts the crudely sentimental discourse of the 'feminine' plot, and thereafter dies. The ageing author seems to have experienced a fate similar to that of his protagonist on a different level, when he discarded what he must have conceived of as his 'true' artistic voice and surrendered to the 'curse' of romance. He chose to write 'for' women, to write (as his misogyny would make him see it) *like* a woman, and thereafter began to lie, to write precisely that type of fiction which he despised, but believed would appeal to women.

This 'surrender' must have been subconsciously perceived as suicidal by the author, who was at least partly aware that 'making literature pay' was going to demand a high price in artistic integrity. This might explain the subliminal warning he has written for himself but was apparently unable to decode, his subsequent obsession with this inferior story and his need to justify his choices in the peculiar author's note. The misogynist association of the world of women readers with the debased romance and with the promise of greater financial reward and popular success would seem to place Conrad as yet another victim of the big F's: Fashion, and Finance, Foolishness and False Felicity.

There is a story waiting to be told . . . a theory of modernity: an interpretation of modernity on the verge of a shift in paradigms. . . . the hegemony of a vision-based, vision-centered episteme is weakened, and an experimental space is opened up, where it may be possible for people to practice and institute a new postmodern paradigm for knowledge, truth, and reality, based and centered instead on the norms of a communicatively formed rationality that are implicit in our speaking and listening.[22]

Conrad's 'The Tale'(1917), written near the end of a writing career which began with the imperative 'to make you see', may well be this story of shifting paradigms, a story which turns away from the scopic regime of modernity towards an alternative mode of being-in-the-world. It is yet another strange story which somehow does not get off the ground, which does not quite 'work', but which—I would argue—can be read as a significant psycho-cultural text. Written in 1916 during the Great War, narrated by an anonymous officer in the midst of an unnamed war, and revolving on an episode which took place in the course of yet another unnamed war, the story is propelled over and out of its textual contours. It is, perhaps, this *mise en abîme*, the echo-chamber effect, which brought the story too close to the bone for an ageing author who had invested a lifetime of work in the inscription of masculine subjectivity.

The narrative begins with what is ostensibly a bedroom scene: a man and a woman, obviously lovers, alone in a darkened room. But the lovers' exchange is curiously passionless, devoid of erotic suggestion, almost lifeless. The thin trickle of energy between the reclining woman and the seated man seems to be generated by a subtle antagonism on both sides. It is the woman who finally has, in the peculiar words of the narrative, the 'courage' to make a sound. It is she who demands of her lover, with 'a hint of a loved woman's capricious will', the offering of a tale (157). Recalling the 'simple and professional tales' he used to tell her before the war, she persists in the face of his reticence, for which he obliquely accounts (in a chillingly 'dead' tone of voice) as having to do with the ongoing war. 'But now, you see, the war is going on' (158).

Why should this war, taking place at an unspecified distance away from the lovers, impede the telling of tales? The exchange which follows does little to clarify the nature of either the impediment or the lovers' relationship. His five days' leave are matched by the leave she has taken from what she describes, after a momentary hesitation, as her 'duties'. Their differences over the

[22] David Michael Levin, 'Decline and Fall: Ocularcentrism in Heidegger's Reading of the History of Metaphysics', in *Modernity and the Hegemony of Vision*, ed. David Michael Levin (Berkeley: University of California Press, 1993), 192.

notion of 'duties' are also remarkably obscure. While she expresses her horror of the word, he talks of that 'infinity of absolution' contained within it. The precise nature of the sin which can be absolved by an invocation of 'duty' remains, at this point, unclear.[23]

Another point of subtle contention between the lovers is the distinction between their own world, to which they refer as 'this world', and the 'other world' where the tale took place. Her request for a tale 'not of this world' is not a utopian invocation of a better or heavenly world (159). It is, then, an 'other world' in a sense which she does not specify. For the narrator too, it is an other world, much like the earth, 'a world of sea and continents and islands' (160–1), but different in that the actors within it— the Commanding Officer and a Northman—are to be nameless. The namelessness of characters and places; the a-temporality of the tale; the narrator's use of the third person pronoun to designate himself through most of the tale—are highly symptomatic.[24] Dissociating the present from the past, separating himself from the younger self who had been the protagonist of the tale, insisting that his tale took place 'elsewhere', the narrator protests too much. The Latin term for 'elsewhere' is 'alibi'.

This other world, which has in it 'more than meets the eye', the narrator tells his mistress, is a world which has to be constantly watched, 'watched by acute minds and also by actual sharp eyes. They had to be very sharp indeed' (163). The ubiquity of subsequent references to sight and vision in the text is anything but subtle: the narrator describes his war mission (referring to himself in the third person) as having been 'sent out . . . to see what he could see. Just that' (165). The generic definition of the tale itself seems to be predicated on the question of visibility: the woman's

[23] The ambiguity of 'The Tale', exceptional even on the Conradian scale, has been noted by Jeremy Hawthorn, who argues that the story dramatizes 'the elusiveness and inaccessibility of the truth behind the surface appearances of the world. And by presenting the reader with tantalizingly opaque and ambiguous surface appearances and "seeming" in the work itself it forces us to become aware of the potentiality in us for the same sort of neurotic reaching after certainty that we witness in the commanding officer'. See Hawthorn, *Joseph Conrad: Narrative Technique and Ideological Commitment* (London: Edward Arnold, 1990), 267–8.

[24] Jakob Lothe, in *Conrad's Narrative Method* (Oxford: Oxford University Press, 1989), 77n., sees both the fairly-tale opening of the officer's account and the namelessness of the characters as 'distancing devices which supplement [the officer's] use of the third person singular'.

expressed anticipation of a 'comic story' is countered by a peculiar qualification on his part: 'Yes. In a way. In a very grim way.' Comedy, for him is only 'a matter of the visual angle' (162). Indeed, it is the 'visual angle' which determines the course of events. The centrality of vision, sight, and light in the text has been noted by Jakob Lothe, who relates the commander's 'inability to see' to epistemological uncertainty, but does not go beyond the suggestion that there might be

some interesting affinities between the narrative and thematic structure of [Conrad's] fiction and central issues posed in the history of epistemology. . . . As in epistemology, one of the main questions asked by 'The Tale' is the very general one of whether knowledge can be related to some class of truth, or indeed whether knowledge is possible at all. As epistemology is related to a general scepticism as regards knowledge, so the thematic tenor of the commander's uncertainty and suspicion in 'The Tale' is related to the pervasive scepticism of Conrad's fiction.[25]

I would argue that 'The Tale' does considerably more than dramatize a state of epistemological uncertainty: it is, in fact, a subversion of the most fundamental Platonic paradigm, the cultural episteme which conflates light, visibility, knowledge, and truth; which equates knowledge with instrumental mastery; which is so central to Modernity itself. Much has been written of the scopic regime of the modern era, the 'vigorous privileging of vision', that 'probing, penetrating, searching' outlook which had turned the world into an object of exploration and enabled the scientific revolution of Modernity:

The activist reevaluation of curiosity and the legitimation of probing vision were especially evident in the new confidence in the technical enhancement of the eye. Broadly speaking, the innovations of the early modern era took two forms: the extension of the range and power of our

---

[25] Jakob Lothe, *Conrad's Narrative Method,* 84. J. Hillis Miller, who notes the ubiquity of references to vision in Conrad's fiction and specifically in *Heart of Darkness,* also remains strictly within the epistemic boundaries of the same paradigm, arguing that 'All Conrad's work turns on this double paradox, first the paradox of the two sense of seeing, seeing as physical vision and seeing as seeing though, as penetrating to or unveiling the hidden invisible truth, and second the paradox of seeing the darkness in terms of the light'. J. Hillis Miller, '*Heart of Darkness* Revisited', in *Conrad's Heart of Darkness,* ed. Ross C. Murfin (New York: St Martin's Press, 1989), 37. It is hard to see just where the alleged paradox lies: is there a fundamental contradiction between sight and insight?

ocular apparatus and the improvement of our ability to disseminate the results in visually accessible ways.[26]

But the borderlines between epistemology and ethics are not clearly distinguishable. The ocularcentric paradigm has also, it is argued, turned the world into a visual field and the body into an object of observation. The externality of sight 'allows the observer to avoid direct engagement with the object of his gaze . . . [and] the constitutive link between subject and object is suppressed or forgotten'.[27] However, as Hans Jonas reminds us, the implications of this scopic regime for the psychic economy of the species cannot be unequivocally beneficial:

The gain is the concept of objectivity, of the thing as it is in itself as distinct from the thing as it affects me, and from this distinction arises the whole idea of theoria and theoretical truth. Furthermore, this image is handed over to imagination, which can deal with it in complete detachment from the actual presence of the original object: this detach-ability of the image . . . of 'essence' from 'existence', is at the bottom of abstraction and therefore of all free thought.[28]

The loss, Jonas argues, consists in 'the elimination of the causal connection from the visual account', and the concomitant loss of the original encounter with reality through the experience of touch:

Touch is the true test of reality: I can dispel every suspicion of illusion by grasping the doubtful object and trying its reality in terms of the resis-tance it offers to my efforts to displace it. Differently expressed, external reality is disclosed in the same act with the disclosure of my own reality. . . . In feeling my own reality by some sort of effort I make, I feel the reality of the world. And I make an effort in the encounter with something other than myself.[29]

Distance, abstraction, disembodiment of perception, objectifi-cation of the world—these are not merely cognitive effects. They are, more importantly for our own concerns, the constituents of

---

[26] Martin Jay, *Downcast Eyes: The Denigration of Vision in Twentieth-Century French Thought* (Berkeley: University of California Press, 1993), 65.

[27] Ibid., 25.

[28] Hans Jonas, 'The Nobility of Sight: A Study in the Phenomenology of the Senses', in *The Phenomenon of Life: Toward a Philosophical Biology* (New York: Harper and Row, 1966), 135–56; reprinted in *The Philosophy of the Body*, ed. Stuart F. Spicker (Chicago: Quadrangle, 1970), 312–32. [29] Ibid., 324.

human relations as well. The scopic regime which has dominated the modern epistemological order, according to Foucault, has yielded Bentham's Panopticon, the perfect architectural embodiment of the power relations which underlie the socio-political regime of the age. With its observation tower, with its constant searching light, with the utter visibility of its inmates in their cells and the utter invisibility of the observing eye, the Panopticon is 'a machine for creating and sustaining a power relation independent of the person who exercises it'; 'a machine for dissociating the see/being seen dyad'.[30] This 'seeing machine', as Foucault calls it, 'automatizes and disindividualizes power' which has its principle 'not so much in a person as in a certain concerted distribution of bodies, surfaces, lights, gazes'.[31] There is no physical confrontation, no touch, no listening or telling involved in the contact. The supremacy of the invisible observer is decided in advance and perpetuated as the observed is reduced to an object of speculation. 'For Modernity, vision has become supervision.'[32]

It is the very same ocular paradigm which structures the Commanding Officer's outlook in 'The Tale'. His obsession with the need to see what he can see, with the necessity for sharp eyes, sharp indeed, his passion for what he calls 'Truth'—the symptoms of the scopic regime are all there. They are, moreover, clearly related to the need for control and mastery, which has been identified with a particularly masculine libidinal economy: 'The will, the male power, imposes its own thought and wish on others, and makes that military eye which controls boys as it controls men'.[33] The ruling episteme in this all-masculine, military world is thoroughly ocularcentric. It is no wonder that the narrator's preface to his tale begins with the assurance that 'all the long guns' in the tale will be 'as dumb as so many telescopes' (162). The peculiar analogy between these two phallic objects cannot be missed. It is the same 'probing, penetrating, searching' quality of

---

[30] Foucault, *Discipline and Punish: The Birth of the Prison*, trans. Alan Sheridan (New York: Pantheon, 1977), 201, 202. See also 'The Eye of Power,' in *Power/Knowledge: Selected Interviews and Other Writings 1972–1977*, trans. Colin Gordon et al. (New York: Pantheon, 1980).   [31] *Discipline and Punish*, 207, 202.

[32] Thomas R. Flynn, 'Foucault and the Eclipse of Vision' in *Modernity and the Hegemony of Vision*, ed. David Michael Levin (Berkeley: University of California Press, 1993), 281.

[33] Ralph Waldo Emerson, 'Education', in *The Portable Emerson*, ed. Mark Van Doran (New York: Viking), 269.

active vision, so central to the scientific revolution and to the early geographical explorations of early modernity, which becomes a metaphoric vehicle for mastery and domination.[34] Would it be entirely inappropriate to remind ourselves at this point that shortly before the story was written, when Conrad's son Borys joined the army and was gazetted second lieutenant, his proud father had made him a present of 'a pair of field glasses'?[35]

The narrator's declared 'passion for the truth' and 'horror of deceit' (205; see also 173, 184, 195) establishes a significant textual relationship between 'The Tale' and *Heart of Darkness*:

At night the Commanding Officer could let his thoughts get away—I won't tell you where. Somewhere where there was no choice but between truth and death. ('The Tale', 167–8)

The Commanding Officer was one of those men who are made morally and almost physically uncomfortable by the mere thought of having to beat down a lie. He shrank from the act in scorn and disgust, which was invincible because more temperamental than moral. (192–3)

This odd conflation of epistemology with temperamental idiosyncrasy, which undermines the very foundation of any epistemological quest, sounds like an echo of Marlow's expressed abhorrence of lies:

You know I hate, detest, and can't bear a lie, not because I am straighter than the rest of us, but simply because it appalls me. There is a taint of death, a flavour of mortality in lies—which is exactly what I hate and detest in the world—what I want to forget. It makes me miserable and sick, like [sic] biting something rotten would do. Temperament, I suppose. (*Heart of Darkness*, 82)

'Truth or death.' The same postulate. The same need for log-books and maps, for clarity of vision in the heart of darkness or in the blinding fog. But Marlow, the better man, will eventually opt for a lie. The Commanding Officer's passion for the Truth will

---

[34] In 'The Woman in Black: Race and Gender in *The Secret Agent*', Rebecca Stott rightly points to the disruption of the 'all-seeing gaze of the imperial trope' and the 'position of mastery of seer over seen' in Conrad's *Heart of Darkness* through the feminized landscape which resists meaning (44), in *Conrad and Gender*, ed. Andrew Roberts, *The Conradian* (Amsterdam: Rodopi, 1993), 39–58.

[35] Zdzislaw Najder, *Joseph Conrad: A Chronicle*, trans. Halina Carrol-Najder (Cambridge: Cambridge University Press, 1983), 409.

ultimately lead him into an act of murderous deception. His mastery of maps and logbooks (186, 191) is more than an instrument for survival in this context. Using his advantage over the Northman, who has lost all sense of direction, he will actively manoeuvre the other into a deadly route. The officer's obsession with the need to see, his description of the 'deceitful' mist and the 'dead luminosity of the fog', generate and build up a sense of visual tension which is not dissipated when the officer does finally see 'what he could see'. But his account of 'the object' seems to make a deliberate detour around it, to avoid the need to name or describe it:

I may tell you at once that the object was not dangerous in itself. No use in describing it. It may have been nothing more remarkable than, say, a barrel of a certain shape and colour. But it was significant. (169)

This unnamed object which, once perceived, is 'turned away from with apparent indifference' is taken as evidence 'of the activity of certain neutrals', which 'had in many cases taken the form of replenishing the stores of certain submarines at sea'. The careful adjectival modulations of this proposition are further qualified by the bland statement that 'this was generally believed, if not absolutely known' (170). These initial tentative speculations gradually congeal into the 'conclusion' that 'it was left there most likely by accident, complicated possibly by some unforeseen necessity; such, perhaps, as the sudden need to get away quickly from the spot, or something of that kind' (171). From an unspecified object of no apparent significance, the literal floating signifier, to borrow Vivienne Rundle's apt tag, is summarily converted into hard evidence: 'well, it's evidence. That's what this is. Evidence of what we were pretty certain of before. And plain, too' (172).[36] Oddly, the narrator who refuses to describe or name the object, but seems to be uncomfortably impelled to qualify his retrospective account of this ocular proof, makes no reference to the hasty judgement of his

[36] Rundle, however, reads the story as a parable on reading and is mostly concerned with the Commanding Officer's refusal to 'acknowledge the arbitrary nature of the signifier' and his subsequent "failure as a reader"'. Vivienne Rundle, '"The Tale" and the Ethics of Interpretation', *The Conradian*, 17, no. 1 (Autumn 1992), 17–36, at 24. I would suggest that, our Poststructuralist academic training notwithstanding, we all tend to live by a fairly straightforward assumption concerning the signifiers around us, which might turn us into incompetent readers, but not—hopefully—into mass murderers.

younger self. It is at this point that 'a wall of fog' advances upon
the officer's ship and envelops her:

Great convolutions of vapour flew over, swirling about masts and funnel,
which looked as if they were beginning to melt. Then they vanished. The
ship was stopped, all sounds ceased, and the very fog became motionless,
growing denser and as if solid in its amazing dumb immobility. The men
at their stations lost sight of each other. Footsteps sounded stealthily;
rare voices, impersonal and remote, died out without resonance. A blind
white stillness took possession of the world. (174–5)

The ultimate trial of truth is to take place in the midst of this
blind, white stillness. The 'Northman', suspected of being that
'neutral' who *might* have been the owner of the unnamed object
which *might* have been a container for enemy provisions—regardless of the fact that, by the narrator's own admission, there are no
real grounds for the inference, 'no flaw in the logbook story'
(193), and 'no shadow of reason' for suspicion, let alone certainty
of his complicity (194)—is ordered to set out into the blind fog.
Following the officer's instructions, he wrecks the ship against a
deadly ledge of rock. He has, it seems, spoken the truth, at least as
far as his own disorientation (203–4). The 'supreme trial' is a
reversal of the initial Truth-or-Death equation set forth by the
officer. It is Truth, or the obsession with absolute knowledge,
which leads to death.

'That course would lead the Northman straight on a deadly ledge of
rock. And the Commanding Officer gave it to him. He steamed out—ran
on it—and went down. So he had spoken the truth. He did not know
where he was. But it proves nothing. Nothing either way. It may have been
the only truth in all his story. And yet . . . He seems to have been driven
out by a menacing stare—nothing more.'
     He abandoned all pretence. 'Yes, *I gave that course to him*. It seemed to
me a supreme test.' (203–4)

At the moment of acknowledged responsibility the narrator
discards the third-person narrative mode and shifts to the first
person. Significantly, the only other point where such a transition
takes place is related to an oblique reference to love, which he
hastily withdraws at the very beginning of his tale. Talking of that
'other world' where the episode took place, he adds, 'and since I
could find in the universe only what was deeply rooted in the fibres
of my being there was love in it too.' However, his immediate

exclusion of that subject from his tale ('but we won't talk of that') and the woman's ready acquiescence mark a difference between their own enclave of existence (precarious and ghostly as the relationship appears to be) and the tale which cannot accommodate love (161). These two narratorial slips, like the fault-lines which crack open the distancing third-person, and the insistently a-temporal and a-spatial narrative, are the points at which the alibi is broken and the story unravels. It is the shift to the first-person narrative that turns the story into a double-edged sword in the hands of the officer.

Going back to the initial scene, we can now understand some of its obscurities. The entire episode seems to be perceived through a semi-opaque pane: the 'crepuscular light dying out slowly in a great square gleam without colour'; the 'shadowy couch' with 'the shadowy suggestion of a reclining woman', the 'sombre' figure of the man sitting on a chair nearby who can 'only see the faint oval of her face . . . her pale hands . . . too weary to move' (155–6). The ostensible love scene is oddly, insistently, reminiscent of a drowning scene. It is, in fact, a visual echo of the drowning which concludes the tale. The lovers' lifelessness—their lethargic attitude, the weariness which colours their exchange, their silence and immobility ('The officer bent forward towards the couch where no movement betrayed the presence of a living person' (203)—is an enactment of death by drowning. Their careful separation of 'their world' from that 'elsewhere' where the narrated events took place appears to have failed.[37]

Even as he insists on the need to see, even as he reiterates the fear and conviction that 'some day you will die from something you have not seen' (165), the officer describes the coming of the blinding night as a form of 'relief': 'there are circumstances when the sunlight may grow as odious to one as falsehood itself. Night is all right' (167). In an analogous manner, a whole set of oppositions which are visually structured is undermined by the workings of the tale. We have already noted the unnamed object which serves as an 'ocular proof' of the crime which, for all we know, has never been committed. The object which, the officer hints,

---

[37] The lexical echoes of the frame in the tale, or vice versa, have been noted by readers of the story (See Gaetano D'Elia, 'Let Us Make Tales, Not Love: Conrad's "The Tale"', The Conradian, 12, no. 1 [May 1987], 50–8). The significance of this echo-chamber effect has, I believe, been overlooked.

may be a container ('a barrel, say') embodies the conceptual distinction between 'appearance' and 'reality', a conception of truth as that which is to be discovered behind or inside the visual surface. The deconstruction of this opposition, the de-substantiation of the 'kernel beneath the shell', is carried further by additional allusions to containers—'packages, barrels, tins, copper tubes—what not' (200)—rather than to their contents. The most firmly entrenched structuring episteme that privileges the kernel over the shell is no longer valid.

But epistemology cannot be easily separated from ethics. As William W. Bonney observes, there is a close connection between the quest for absolute vision and the exercise of brute power in the story: 'As a figurative means of discussing experience in an implicitly moralistic manner, the commander insistently uses a vocabulary derived from exercise of the visual sense. . . . Consequently he becomes entrapped hopelessly within his own lexicon.' His inability to 'accept an epistemologically flawed world', becomes a 'pathological fixation' which 'causes him to employ gross military power to try to force the world into sharp definition'. Bonney's moving description of the final scene in this 'achromatic story, dominated by twilight, shadows, mist', offers more significant insights:

As light fades, all physical appearances are negated, and the mistress vanishes into an exclusively auditory dimension, becoming only 'the voice from the couch'. Devoid of telescopes, logbook, maps, guns, and even a visual impression of his listener, the commander's entire world is reduced into an immediate verbal performance.[38]

I would offer a somewhat different reading of the erotic conflict which, I believe, is primarily an epistemic conflict. The conjunction of the narrator's desire for a visible truth and his need for mastery and control is culturally symptomatic:

The will to power is very strong in vision. There is a very strong tendency in vision to grasp and fixate, to reify and totalize, a tendency to dominate, secure, and control, which eventually, because it was so extensively promoted, assumed a certain uncontested hegemony over our culture and its philosophical discourse, establishing, in keeping with the instrumental

---

[38] William W. Bonney, *Thorns and Arabesques: Contexts for Conrad's Fiction* (Baltimore: Johns Hopkins University Press, 1980) 211, 213.

rationality of our culture and the technological character of our society, an ocularcentric metaphysics of presence.[39]

Modernism has challenged the scopic regime of Modernity. The Modernist 'aesthetics of uncertainty', launched by Bergson's frontal attack on ocularcentrism, demolished the received visual order, challenged the fetishization of sight, and reinstated 'the right of the body against the tyranny of the eye'.[40] The ethics of narration, the subversion of the Enlightenment structuring episteme which conflates light and truth, vision and knowledge, underlies the relation of 'The Tale' to *Heart of Darkness*. Clearly not one of those 'simple and professional' stories which the officer had told his mistress in the past, nor one of those seamen's yarns with their 'direct simplicity, the whole meaning of which lies within the shell of a cracked nut', the tale is much closer to Marlow's narrative in *Heart of Darkness*. It is an episode whose significance is produced in the act of telling, at the surface, 'as a glow brings out a haze, in the likeness of one of those misty halos that sometimes are made visible by the spectral illumination of moonshine' (*Heart of Darkness*, 48).

This brings us back to the subtle undercurrent of antagonism or even hostility between the lovers. Conrad does tend to resort to female analogues when his male characters struggle to 'orient themselves toward the dark, elusive otherness that is their experience of the phenomenal world'. But the reason why these 'epistemic questers' are 'typically not good lovers', as Bonney speculates, is not necessarily a simple form of misogyny but a deeper conflict of ethical paradigms.[41] Conrad's troubled attitude to the 'Woman Question' is not reducible to a mere personal pathology.[42] It ought to be read, as Robert Hampson rightly suggests, in the context of the 'erotophobic nature of Victorian patriarchy'.[43] A major aspect of this erotophobia is the conflict between the masculine economy of the probing gaze and the feminine economy of the listening ear.

---

[39] David Michael Levin, 'Decline and Fall: Ocularcentrism in Heidegger's Reading of the History of Meaphysics', in *Modernity and the Hegemony of Vision*, ed. David Michael Levin, 212.   [40] Martin Jay, *Downcast Eyes*, 159–61, 192.

[41] Bonney, *Thorns and Arabesques*, 214.

[42] In his psychobiographical study of Conrad's work Bernard C. Meyer cites the story as a sample of the author's misogyny which, he argues, becomes less restrained during the last decade of his life. *Joseph Conrad: A Psychoanalytic Biography*, 237–8.

[43] *Joseph Conrad: Betayal and Identity* (London: St Martin's Press, 1992), 28.

It is significant that at the outset of their exchange the officer's mistress should protest against his abstract invocation of 'duty' and its 'infinity of absolution' as a form of escape from his responsibility for the lives of men lost because of his 'passion for truth'. It is equally significant that the storytelling is triggered by the demand of the beloved woman: feminine psychic economy does not privilege the gaze to the same extent, and the challenge to patriarchal hegemony is often related to a critique of the masculine scopic regime and the shift to an auditory, communicational paradigm. French feminism often couches its claims to a 'woman's language' (*parler femme, écriture feminine*) in anti-ocular terms, 'pitting the temporal rhythms of the body against the mortifying spatialization of the eye', insisting on 'a language of proximity rather than distance, a language close to the senses of touch and taste than sight'.[44] The complicity of ocularcentrism and phallogocentrism has been most explicitly articulated in the work of Luce Irigaray:

Investment in the look is not as privileged in women as in men. More than any other sense, the eye objectifies and it masters. It sets at a distance, and maintains a distance. In our culture the predominance of the look over smell, taste, touch and hearing has brought about an impoverishment of bodily relations.[45]

The predominance of the visual, and of the discrimination and individuation of form, is particularly foreign to female eroticism. Woman takes pleasure more from touching than from looking, and her entry into a dominant scopic economy signifies, again, her consignment to passivity: she is to be the beautiful object of contemplation.[46]

During one of the brief exchanges which break up the narration, the listening woman responds to the officer's account of his suffering at the thought of deception, and he acknowledges her sympathy with an oblique comment: '"everything should be

---

[44] Martin Jay, *Downcast Eyes*, 528, 529.

[45] Luce Irigaray, interview in *Les femmes, la pornographie et l'erotisme*, ed. Marie Françoise Hans and Gilles Lapouge (Paris, 1978), quoted in Martin Jay, *Downcast Eyes*, 493. Irigary's seminal work, *The Speculum of the Other Woman*, is an exposure of the 'optics of Truth' in Western philosophy and its complicity with patriarchal hegemony; the *Speculum of the Other Woman* (1974), trans. G. C. Gill (Ithaca, NY: Cornell University Press, 1985).

[46] *This Sex Which Is Not One*, trans. Catherine Porter (1977; Ithaca: Cornell University Press, 1985), 25–6.

open in love and war. Open as the day, since both are the call of an
ideal which it is so easy, so terribly easy, to degrade in the name of
Victory"' (173–4). The analogy between love and war is trite
enough to overlook, but its literalization in this context is rather
disturbing. There is, as he reminds her, a war going on even as the
tale is being told. It is not clear whether this is the same war he
tells about: the temporal and spatial matrix of the tale is deliberately blurred, obscuring the borderlines between the narration and
the narrative. The horror of war cannot be contained within the
narrated episode: they spill over and contaminate the frame itself.
It is the woman who asks the Commanding Officer to tell his tale,
it is she who listens, it is she who attempts to touch the man. But
her attempts at making emotional contact are repelled. Following
what he refers to as the 'supreme test', the officer is left to wonder
whether his act had been one of 'stern retribution' or 'murder';
whether the corpses he had added to those which 'litter the bed of
the unreadable sea' are those of men 'completely innocent' or
'basely guilty' (204). There is no doubt, however, that even if the
Northman had indeed been guilty of providing the enemy with
food, he would not have deserved the sentence of death by drowning to which the officer has condemned him. Not even the notion of
'duty' and its 'infinity of absolution' to which the narrator clings at
the outset can redeem the guilt incurred in the act of quasi-divine
judgement. It is at this point that the tale ends and the officer's
mistress, knowing 'his passion for truth, his horror of deceit, his
humanity' attempts to touch him. It is at this point that he
'disengages' himself (note the military verb) and leaves the
room. Love and war, it seems, are not easily equated after all: if
war is predicated on the scopic paradigm, on the desire for
mastery, on the need to make the other totally visible, the ethos
of love is made up of listening in the dark; of the responsive touch;
and of the answering caress.

Coda: Re-enter the Reader

A theory of the author, or of the absence of the author, cannot withstand the practice of reading, for there is not an absolute *cogito* of which individual authors are the subalternant manifestations, but authors, many authors, and the differences (in gender, history, class, ethnology, in the nature of scientific, philosophical, and literary authorship, in the degree or authorship itself) that exist between authors—within authorship—defy reduction to any universalizing aesthetic.

Yet the promulgation of a textual theory can no more elude the question of the author than contain it. As we have seen, the essential problem posed by the author is that whilst authorial subjectivity is theoretically unassimilable, it cannot be practically circumvented. The processes of intention, influence and revision, the interfertility of life and work, autobiography and the autobiographical, author-functions, signature-effects, the proper name in general, the authority and creativity of the critic, all these are points at which the question of the author exerts its pressure on the textual enclosure.[1]

CONRAD'S WORK HAS never really lent itself to de-authorizing criticism, and has only rarely been subjected to wholly intrinsic and textualist readings. As we have seen, however, the question of authorial subjectivity is no longer a simple premise, but the constitutive question of the text. The recognition and identification of the authorial voice in the text no longer stabilizes the meaning of the text but, as Bette London writes, it does 'lend a peculiar poignancy to the gap between presumed authorial desire and textual effect'.[2] It is this gap that my own reading has attempted to address, to address, rather than fill in. Most poignant of all, perhaps, is the conviction that the philosophical death of the capitalized Author has not absolved the biographical author— historically and culturally situated, as vulnerable and mortal as the rest of us—from the onus of ethical responsibility. If anything,

---

[1] Sean Burke, *The Death and Return of the Author* (Edinburgh: Edinburgh University Press, 1992), 173.

[2] Bette Lynn London, *The Appropriated Voice; Narrative Authority in Conrad, Forster, and Woolf* (Ann Arbor: University of Michigan Press, 1990), 10.

that responsibility has become the ballast which counters the 'moral weightlessness' generated by the exilic leap.[3] Conrad's work is a lifetime project invested in countering just that—to use the words of a fellow exile—unbearable lightness of being.

Having begun this study from the perspective of Romanticism, it is inevitable that we should find ourselves in the territory, or no man's land of Postmodernism. The various aspects of this study can all be viewed through a Postmodernist prism: The concept of 'heterobiography' which I have used as an *ad-hoc* designation of permeable boundary lines; the 'logic of fratricide' which supplants the logic of sameness and self-identity; the 'pathos of authenticity' which emerges from the loss of origins and destinations; the 'poetics of cultural despair' which position writing as a Trojan Horse; the 'romantic paradox' which underlies the circularity of desire and subjectivity; and the foredoomed desire to bolster up the borderlines of masculinity in the attempt to 'address the woman'. The very same questions which energize Conrad's fiction during the first two decades of the century have only begun to surface in the discourse of philosophy fifty years later. This belatedness is also symptomatic. Philosophy, too, may be a mode of 'homesickness', but it is, in the words of Novalis (as cited by Lukács), 'the urge to be at home everywhere'.[4] To apply the provisional classification offered by Svetlana Boym, we may describe the nostalgia of traditional philosophy as the 'reconstructive and collective' type, with its emphasis on the *nostos* (home), and its desire to 'return to that mythical place somewhere on the island of Utopia'. It is only in the work of Derrida, Levinas, and Lyotard that philosophy has entered the other phase of nostalgia with its emphasis on the *algia* (longing), and its ultimate acceptance of exile, estrangement, and displacement.[5] It is this exilic mode of being which underlies Conrad's work at the beginning of the century.

But we must not run the risk of turning exile into 'another

---

[3] Michael Seidel, *Exile and the Narrative Imagination* (New Haven and London: Yale University Press, 1986), 1.

[4] Georg Lukàcs, *The Theory of the Novel*, trans. Anna Bostock (first published in 1920; London: Merlin Press, 1971) 29.

[5] 'Estrangement as a Lifestyle: Shklovsky and Brodsky', in *Exile and Creativity: Signposts, Travelers, Outsides, backward Glances*, ed. Susan Rubin Suleiman (Durham, NC, and London: Duke University Press, 1998), 241–62.

euphoric poetic and theoretical trope'.[6] The uncapitalized author is no longer the fatherly sovereign over the text or its 'all-centring premise'; but neither is he a 'vast absence' or a passive junction of discourses.[7] Even when we have discarded the shell/kernel trope of storytelling, we are still not left with a vacuum: the haze/glow metaphor is not a signifier of absence, but a trope of diffusion, of refraction, of less than total visibility. Moral agency, responsibility, and commitment become almost impossible to conceive in the absence of autonomy and sovereignty, but this is precisely when they become all the more pressing and inevitable. It is no longer the question of whether to be or not to be which marks Conrad's presence in his own work. The principle of cohesion which holds together the authorial subject is an unremitting sense of non-cohesion, which serves as a foil—paradoxically perhaps—to the reiterated, thoroughly ethical question of 'how to be'. There is nothing solipsistic about this question.

To end this last brief chapter, a coda rather than a conclusion, I would like to say a few very personal words about my own act of reading, which might serve in lieu of a grander gesture of summation. A pair of binoculars bought as a gift; a parlour game of questions and answers; a letter written to a friend—such traces are hardly the stuff of solid biography which would aspire to contain the authorial presence, to have it 'all there', to comprehend it. But paucity of evidence is not really the issue here. The more serious question is whether subjectivity—fictional, authorial, or readerly—can be comprehended at all within the Eros of knowledge, the desire to systematize, theorize, and neatly package the subject/object of study. What I have tried to offer in this study is related to a different economy.

The 'heterobiographical' perspective which has served as an introductory move in Part I of this study may well be relevant to the question of reading as well: like writing, reading must not rest on the assumption of total readability. It is an 'addressive' act—always unique, singular, and unrepeatable—with a built-in assumption of non-presence. We cannot, and must not, I believe, aspire to a fully noise-free theoretical space which would lay our readerly desire at rest. A good act of reading, like a good act of

[6] Svetlana Boym, 'Estrangement as a Lifestyle', 244.
[7] Sean Burke, *The Death and Return of the Author*, 166.

writing, is a process of defamiliarization, of 'making strange' that which can all too easily become habitual and stale. 'Habitualization,' writes Shklovsky,

devours works, clothes, furniture, one's wife, and the fear of war. . . . And art exists that one may recover the sensation of life; it exists to make one feel things, to make the stone *stony*. . . . The technique of art is to make objects 'unfamiliar', to make forms difficult, to increase the difficulty and length of perception because the process of perception is an aesthetic end in itself and must be prolonged. *Art is a way of experiencing the artfulness of an object; the object is not important.*[8]

The Russian word Shklovsky uses is *ostraneniye*, which literally means 'making strange'.

We might, then, add yet another layer to our palimpsest of strangeness. 'There never has been, never will be, a unique word, a master-name,' writes Derrida, 'and we must think this without nostalgia, that is outside of the myth of a purely maternal or paternal language, a lost naive country of thought.'[9] To 'think this' without nostalgia may well be impossible, and Derrida himself is no exception to this. But it is the *algia* rather than the *nostos* that we have to work with. Reading too should not aspire to a homecoming, to a repossession of meaning, to a full attainment of comprehension. Like writing, it takes place in the arena of subjectivity and is therefore fundamentally heteronomous. It is this recognition of the constitutive strangeness of our being which makes it impossible—*pace* the requirements of academic decorum—to indulge in a sense of closure when we get to the last chapter. Which makes it imperative to move from aesthetics into ethics.

[8] Victor Shklovsky, 'Art as Technique' (1917), reprinted in *Russian Formalist Criticism*, trans. and introd. Lee T. Lemon and Marion J. Reis (Lincoln and London: University of Nebraska Press, 1965), 12. The title of the essay has also been translated as 'Art as a Device'.

[9] 'Qual Quelle', in *Margins of Philosophy*, trans. Alan Bass (Chicago: University of Chicago Press, 1982), 27.

Index of Names